PostgreSQL 9.6 Vol6: Reference - Client/Server

A catalogue record for this book is available from the Hong Kong Public Libraries.

Published in Hong Kong by Samurai Media Limited.

Email: info@samuraimedia.org

ISBN 978-988-8406-73-9

Table of Contents

Preface .... **lxxiii**

    1. What is PostgreSQL? lxxiii

    2. A Brief History of PostgreSQL.. lxxiv

        2.1. The Berkeley POSTGRES Project lxxiv

        2.2. Postgres95... lxxv

        2.3. PostgreSQL.. lxxv

    3. Conventions... lxxvi

    4. Further Information lxxvi

    5. Bug Reporting Guidelines.. lxxvi

        5.1. Identifying Bugs lxxvii

        5.2. What to Report lxxvii

        5.3. Where to Report Bugs lxxix

I. Tutorial **1**

    1. Getting Started 1

        1.1. Installation 1

        1.2. Architectural Fundamentals... 1

        1.3. Creating a Database 2

        1.4. Accessing a Database 3

    2. The SQL Language 6

        2.1. Introduction 6

        2.2. Concepts 6

        2.3. Creating a New Table 6

        2.4. Populating a Table With Rows 7

        2.5. Querying a Table 8

        2.6. Joins Between Tables... 10

        2.7. Aggregate Functions... 12

        2.8. Updates 14

        2.9. Deletions... 14

    3. Advanced Features 16

        3.1. Introduction 16

        3.2. Views 16

        3.3. Foreign Keys 16

        3.4. Transactions.. 17

        3.5. Window Functions.. 19

        3.6. Inheritance 22

        3.7. Conclusion 24

II. The SQL Language..**25**

    4. SQL Syntax 27

        4.1. Lexical Structure.. 27

            4.1.1. Identifiers and Key Words.. 27

            4.1.2. Constants... 29

                4.1.2.1. String Constants 29

                4.1.2.2. String Constants with C-style Escapes.................................. 29

                4.1.2.3. String Constants with Unicode Escapes................................ 31

                4.1.2.4. Dollar-quoted String Constants 32

4.1.2.5. Bit-string Constants 33

4.1.2.6. Numeric Constants 33

4.1.2.7. Constants of Other Types 33

4.1.3. Operators 34

4.1.4. Special Characters 35

4.1.5. Comments 35

4.1.6. Operator Precedence 36

4.2. Value Expressions 37

4.2.1. Column References 38

4.2.2. Positional Parameters 38

4.2.3. Subscripts 39

4.2.4. Field Selection 39

4.2.5. Operator Invocations 40

4.2.6. Function Calls 40

4.2.7. Aggregate Expressions 40

4.2.8. Window Function Calls 43

4.2.9. Type Casts 45

4.2.10. Collation Expressions 45

4.2.11. Scalar Subqueries 46

4.2.12. Array Constructors 47

4.2.13. Row Constructors 48

4.2.14. Expression Evaluation Rules 50

4.3. Calling Functions 51

4.3.1. Using Positional Notation 52

4.3.2. Using Named Notation 52

4.3.3. Using Mixed Notation 53

5. Data Definition 55

5.1. Table Basics 55

5.2. Default Values 56

5.3. Constraints 57

5.3.1. Check Constraints 57

5.3.2. Not-Null Constraints 59

5.3.3. Unique Constraints 60

5.3.4. Primary Keys 61

5.3.5. Foreign Keys 62

5.3.6. Exclusion Constraints 65

5.4. System Columns 65

5.5. Modifying Tables 66

5.5.1. Adding a Column 67

5.5.2. Removing a Column 67

5.5.3. Adding a Constraint 68

5.5.4. Removing a Constraint 68

5.5.5. Changing a Column's Default Value 68

5.5.6. Changing a Column's Data Type 69

5.5.7. Renaming a Column 69

5.5.8. Renaming a Table 69

5.6. Privileges 69

5.7. Row Security Policies 70

5.8. Schemas 75
    5.8.1. Creating a Schema 76
    5.8.2. The Public Schema 77
    5.8.3. The Schema Search Path 77
    5.8.4. Schemas and Privileges 78
    5.8.5. The System Catalog Schema 79
    5.8.6. Usage Patterns 79
    5.8.7. Portability 80
5.9. Inheritance 80
    5.9.1. Caveats 83
5.10. Partitioning 84
    5.10.1. Overview 84
    5.10.2. Implementing Partitioning 85
    5.10.3. Managing Partitions 88
    5.10.4. Partitioning and Constraint Exclusion 88
    5.10.5. Alternative Partitioning Methods 90
    5.10.6. Caveats 90
5.11. Foreign Data 91
5.12. Other Database Objects 92
5.13. Dependency Tracking 92
6. Data Manipulation 94
6.1. Inserting Data 94
6.2. Updating Data 95
6.3. Deleting Data 96
7. Queries 97
7.1. Overview 97
7.2. Table Expressions 97
    7.2.1. The FROM Clause 98
        7.2.1.1. Joined Tables 98
        7.2.1.2. Table and Column Aliases 102
        7.2.1.3. Subqueries 103
        7.2.1.4. Table Functions 104
        7.2.1.5. LATERAL Subqueries 105
    7.2.2. The WHERE Clause 106
    7.2.3. The GROUP BY and HAVING Clauses 107
    7.2.4. GROUPING SETS, CUBE, and ROLLUP 109
    7.2.5. Window Function Processing 112
7.3. Select Lists 112
    7.3.1. Select-List Items 113
    7.3.2. Column Labels 113
    7.3.3. DISTINCT 114
7.4. Combining Queries 114
7.5. Sorting Rows 115
7.6. LIMIT and OFFSET 116
7.7. VALUES Lists 117
7.8. WITH Queries (Common Table Expressions) 118
    7.8.1. SELECT in WITH 118
    7.8.2. Data-Modifying Statements in WITH 121

8. Data Types...124

   8.1. Numeric Types...125

      8.1.1. Integer Types..126

      8.1.2. Arbitrary Precision Numbers..127

      8.1.3. Floating-Point Types..128

      8.1.4. Serial Types..129

   8.2. Monetary Types..130

   8.3. Character Types..131

   8.4. Binary Data Types..133

      8.4.1. `bytea` Hex Format...134

      8.4.2. `bytea` Escape Format..134

   8.5. Date/Time Types..136

      8.5.1. Date/Time Input...137

         8.5.1.1. Dates..138

         8.5.1.2. Times...138

         8.5.1.3. Time Stamps..139

         8.5.1.4. Special Values...140

      8.5.2. Date/Time Output...141

      8.5.3. Time Zones...142

      8.5.4. Interval Input..144

      8.5.5. Interval Output..145

   8.6. Boolean Type...146

   8.7. Enumerated Types..147

      8.7.1. Declaration of Enumerated Types..147

      8.7.2. Ordering...148

      8.7.3. Type Safety...149

      8.7.4. Implementation Details...149

   8.8. Geometric Types..149

      8.8.1. Points..150

      8.8.2. Lines...150

      8.8.3. Line Segments..151

      8.8.4. Boxes..151

      8.8.5. Paths...151

      8.8.6. Polygons...152

      8.8.7. Circles..152

   8.9. Network Address Types..152

      8.9.1. `inet`...153

      8.9.2. `cidr`...153

      8.9.3. `inet` vs. `cidr`...154

      8.9.4. `macaddr`...154

   8.10. Bit String Types...154

   8.11. Text Search Types..155

      8.11.1. `tsvector`...155

      8.11.2. `tsquery`..157

   8.12. UUID Type..158

   8.13. XML Type..159

      8.13.1. Creating XML Values...159

      8.13.2. Encoding Handling...160

8.13.3. Accessing XML Values...161
8.14. JSON Types..161
    8.14.1. JSON Input and Output Syntax...163
    8.14.2. Designing JSON documents effectively 164
    8.14.3. `jsonb` Containment and Existence...164
    8.14.4. `jsonb` Indexing...166
8.15. Arrays..168
    8.15.1. Declaration of Array Types..168
    8.15.2. Array Value Input..169
    8.15.3. Accessing Arrays...170
    8.15.4. Modifying Arrays..173
    8.15.5. Searching in Arrays...176
    8.15.6. Array Input and Output Syntax..177
8.16. Composite Types...178
    8.16.1. Declaration of Composite Types..179
    8.16.2. Composite Value Input...180
    8.16.3. Accessing Composite Types..180
    8.16.4. Modifying Composite Types...181
    8.16.5. Composite Type Input and Output Syntax...182
8.17. Range Types...183
    8.17.1. Built-in Range Types..183
    8.17.2. Examples..183
    8.17.3. Inclusive and Exclusive Bounds 184
    8.17.4. Infinite (Unbounded) Ranges..184
    8.17.5. Range Input/Output...184
    8.17.6. Constructing Ranges..185
    8.17.7. Discrete Range Types...186
    8.17.8. Defining New Range Types...186
    8.17.9. Indexing...187
    8.17.10. Constraints on Ranges..188
8.18. Object Identifier Types 189
8.19. pg_lsn Type...190
8.20. Pseudo-Types...191
9. Functions and Operators 193
9.1. Logical Operators 193
9.2. Comparison Functions and Operators 193
9.3. Mathematical Functions and Operators 196
9.4. String Functions and Operators...200
    9.4.1. `format`...216
9.5. Binary String Functions and Operators 218
9.6. Bit String Functions and Operators 220
9.7. Pattern Matching 221
    9.7.1. `LIKE`..222
    9.7.2. `SIMILAR TO` Regular Expressions..223
    9.7.3. POSIX Regular Expressions 224
        9.7.3.1. Regular Expression Details 227
        9.7.3.2. Bracket Expressions 230
        9.7.3.3. Regular Expression Escapes..231

9.7.3.4. Regular Expression Metasyntax 233
9.7.3.5. Regular Expression Matching Rules 235
9.7.3.6. Limits and Compatibility 236
9.7.3.7. Basic Regular Expressions 237
9.8. Data Type Formatting Functions 237
9.9. Date/Time Functions and Operators 244
9.9.1. EXTRACT, date_part 250
9.9.2. date_trunc 254
9.9.3. AT TIME ZONE 255
9.9.4. Current Date/Time 256
9.9.5. Delaying Execution 257
9.10. Enum Support Functions 258
9.11. Geometric Functions and Operators 259
9.12. Network Address Functions and Operators 263
9.13. Text Search Functions and Operators 266
9.14. XML Functions 271
9.14.1. Producing XML Content 271
9.14.1.1. xmlcomment 271
9.14.1.2. xmlconcat 272
9.14.1.3. xmlelement 272
9.14.1.4. xmlforest 274
9.14.1.5. xmlpi 274
9.14.1.6. xmlroot 275
9.14.1.7. xmlagg 275
9.14.2. XML Predicates 276
9.14.2.1. IS DOCUMENT 276
9.14.2.2. XMLEXISTS 276
9.14.2.3. xml_is_well_formed 277
9.14.3. Processing XML 278
9.14.4. Mapping Tables to XML 279
9.15. JSON Functions and Operators 282
9.16. Sequence Manipulation Functions 291
9.17. Conditional Expressions 294
9.17.1. CASE 294
9.17.2. COALESCE 296
9.17.3. NULLIF 296
9.17.4. GREATEST and LEAST 296
9.18. Array Functions and Operators 297
9.19. Range Functions and Operators 300
9.20. Aggregate Functions 303
9.21. Window Functions 312
9.22. Subquery Expressions 314
9.22.1. EXISTS 314
9.22.2. IN 315
9.22.3. NOT IN 315
9.22.4. ANY/SOME 316
9.22.5. ALL 316
9.22.6. Single-row Comparison 317

9.23. Row and Array Comparisons 317
    9.23.1. IN 317
    9.23.2. NOT IN..318
    9.23.3. ANY/SOME (array) 318
    9.23.4. ALL (array) 318
    9.23.5. Row Constructor Comparison..319
    9.23.6. Composite Type Comparison...320
9.24. Set Returning Functions 320
9.25. System Information Functions 324
9.26. System Administration Functions 340
    9.26.1. Configuration Settings Functions..340
    9.26.2. Server Signaling Functions 341
    9.26.3. Backup Control Functions 342
    9.26.4. Recovery Control Functions 345
    9.26.5. Snapshot Synchronization Functions...347
    9.26.6. Replication Functions 348
    9.26.7. Database Object Management Functions...352
    9.26.8. Index Maintenance Functions 355
    9.26.9. Generic File Access Functions...355
    9.26.10. Advisory Lock Functions..356
9.27. Trigger Functions 358
9.28. Event Trigger Functions 359
    9.28.1. Capturing Changes at Command End..359
    9.28.2. Processing Objects Dropped by a DDL Command 360
    9.28.3. Handling a Table Rewrite Event 362
10. Type Conversion..363
10.1. Overview 363
10.2. Operators 364
10.3. Functions 368
10.4. Value Storage...371
10.5. UNION, CASE, and Related Constructs..372
11. Indexes 374
11.1. Introduction 374
11.2. Index Types..375
11.3. Multicolumn Indexes 377
11.4. Indexes and ORDER BY 378
11.5. Combining Multiple Indexes 379
11.6. Unique Indexes 380
11.7. Indexes on Expressions 381
11.8. Partial Indexes 381
11.9. Operator Classes and Operator Families 384
11.10. Indexes and Collations..386
11.11. Index-Only Scans 386
11.12. Examining Index Usage...388
12. Full Text Search 390
12.1. Introduction 390
    12.1.1. What Is a Document?..391
    12.1.2. Basic Text Matching 392

12.1.3. Configurations 393
12.2. Tables and Indexes 394
12.2.1. Searching a Table 394
12.2.2. Creating Indexes 395
12.3. Controlling Text Search 396
12.3.1. Parsing Documents 396
12.3.2. Parsing Queries 397
12.3.3. Ranking Search Results 399
12.3.4. Highlighting Results 401
12.4. Additional Features 403
12.4.1. Manipulating Documents 403
12.4.2. Manipulating Queries 404
12.4.2.1. Query Rewriting 405
12.4.3. Triggers for Automatic Updates 407
12.4.4. Gathering Document Statistics 408
12.5. Parsers 408
12.6. Dictionaries 410
12.6.1. Stop Words 412
12.6.2. Simple Dictionary 412
12.6.3. Synonym Dictionary 414
12.6.4. Thesaurus Dictionary 415
12.6.4.1. Thesaurus Configuration 416
12.6.4.2. Thesaurus Example 417
12.6.5. Ispell Dictionary 418
12.6.6. Snowball Dictionary 420
12.7. Configuration Example 421
12.8. Testing and Debugging Text Search 422
12.8.1. Configuration Testing 423
12.8.2. Parser Testing 425
12.8.3. Dictionary Testing 426
12.9. GIN and GiST Index Types 427
12.10. psql Support 428
12.11. Limitations 430
12.12. Migration from Pre-8.3 Text Search 431
13. Concurrency Control 432
13.1. Introduction 432
13.2. Transaction Isolation 432
13.2.1. Read Committed Isolation Level 433
13.2.2. Repeatable Read Isolation Level 435
13.2.3. Serializable Isolation Level 436
13.3. Explicit Locking 438
13.3.1. Table-level Locks 439
13.3.2. Row-level Locks 441
13.3.3. Page-level Locks 442
13.3.4. Deadlocks 443
13.3.5. Advisory Locks 444
13.4. Data Consistency Checks at the Application Level...444
13.4.1. Enforcing Consistency With Serializable Transactions 445

13.4.2. Enforcing Consistency With Explicit Blocking Locks 445
13.5. Caveats 446
13.6. Locking and Indexes 447
14. Performance Tips 448
14.1. Using EXPLAIN 448
14.1.1. EXPLAIN Basics 448
14.1.2. EXPLAIN ANALYZE 454
14.1.3. Caveats 458
14.2. Statistics Used by the Planner 459
14.3. Controlling the Planner with Explicit JOIN Clauses 460
14.4. Populating a Database 462
14.4.1. Disable Autocommit 463
14.4.2. Use COPY 463
14.4.3. Remove Indexes 463
14.4.4. Remove Foreign Key Constraints 463
14.4.5. Increase maintenance_work_mem 464
14.4.6. Increase max_wal_size 464
14.4.7. Disable WAL Archival and Streaming Replication 464
14.4.8. Run ANALYZE Afterwards 465
14.4.9. Some Notes About pg_dump 465
14.5. Non-Durable Settings 466
15. Parallel Query 467
15.1. How Parallel Query Works 467
15.2. When Can Parallel Query Be Used? 468
15.3. Parallel Plans 469
15.3.1. Parallel Scans 469
15.3.2. Parallel Joins 469
15.3.3. Parallel Aggregation 469
15.3.4. Parallel Plan Tips 470
15.4. Parallel Safety 470
15.4.1. Parallel Labeling for Functions and Aggregates 471
III. Server Administration **472**
16. Installation from Source Code 474
16.1. Short Version 474
16.2. Requirements 474
16.3. Getting The Source 476
16.4. Installation Procedure 476
16.5. Post-Installation Setup 487
16.5.1. Shared Libraries 487
16.5.2. Environment Variables 487
16.6. Supported Platforms 488
16.7. Platform-specific Notes 489
16.7.1. AIX 489
16.7.1.1. GCC Issues 489
16.7.1.2. Unix-Domain Sockets Broken 490
16.7.1.3. Internet Address Issues 490
16.7.1.4. Memory Management 491

References and Resources 492
16.7.2. Cygwin..492
16.7.3. HP-UX..493
16.7.4. MinGW/Native Windows 494
16.7.4.1. Collecting Crash Dumps on Windows 494
16.7.5. SCO OpenServer and SCO UnixWare....................................494
16.7.5.1. Skunkware...495
16.7.5.2. GNU Make...495
16.7.5.3. Readline...495
16.7.5.4. Using the UDK on OpenServer 495
16.7.5.5. Reading the PostgreSQL Man Pages...................................496
16.7.5.6. C99 Issues with the 7.1.1b Feature Supplement 496
16.7.5.7. Threading on UnixWare 496
16.7.6. Solaris 496
16.7.6.1. Required Tools 496
16.7.6.2. Problems with OpenSSL 496
16.7.6.3. configure Complains About a Failed Test Program 497
16.7.6.4. 64-bit Build Sometimes Crashes 497
16.7.6.5. Compiling for Optimal Performance..................................497
16.7.6.6. Using DTrace for Tracing PostgreSQL 498
17. Installation from Source Code on Windows 499
17.1. Building with Visual C++ or the Microsoft Windows SDK.........499
17.1.1. Requirements 500
17.1.2. Special Considerations for 64-bit Windows 502
17.1.3. Building 502
17.1.4. Cleaning and Installing 502
17.1.5. Running the Regression Tests 503
17.1.6. Building the Documentation 504
17.2. Building libpq with Visual C++ or Borland C++ 504
17.2.1. Generated Files 505
18. Server Setup and Operation 506
18.1. The PostgreSQL User Account 506
18.2. Creating a Database Cluster 506
18.2.1. Use of Secondary File Systems..507
18.2.2. Use of Network File Systems 508
18.3. Starting the Database Server...508
18.3.1. Server Start-up Failures 510
18.3.2. Client Connection Problems 511
18.4. Managing Kernel Resources...511
18.4.1. Shared Memory and Semaphores 511
18.4.2. Resource Limits 517
18.4.3. Linux Memory Overcommit 518
18.4.4. Linux huge pages 519
18.5. Shutting Down the Server...520
18.6. Upgrading a PostgreSQL Cluster 521
18.6.1. Upgrading Data via pg_dumpall..522
18.6.2. Upgrading Data via pg_upgrade 523
18.6.3. Upgrading Data via Replication...523

18.7. Preventing Server Spoofing 524
18.8. Encryption Options 524
18.9. Secure TCP/IP Connections with SSL 526
    18.9.1. Using Client Certificates 526
    18.9.2. SSL Server File Usage 527
    18.9.3. Creating a Self-signed Certificate 527
18.10. Secure TCP/IP Connections with SSH Tunnels 528
18.11. Registering Event Log on Windows 529
19. Server Configuration 530
    19.1. Setting Parameters 530
        19.1.1. Parameter Names and Values 530
        19.1.2. Parameter Interaction via the Configuration File 530
        19.1.3. Parameter Interaction via SQL 531
        19.1.4. Parameter Interaction via the Shell 532
        19.1.5. Managing Configuration File Contents...532
    19.2. File Locations 534
    19.3. Connections and Authentication...535
        19.3.1. Connection Settings 535
        19.3.2. Security and Authentication...537
    19.4. Resource Consumption 540
        19.4.1. Memory..540
        19.4.2. Disk 542
        19.4.3. Kernel Resource Usage 543
        19.4.4. Cost-based Vacuum Delay 543
        19.4.5. Background Writer..544
        19.4.6. Asynchronous Behavior 545
    19.5. Write Ahead Log 547
        19.5.1. Settings..547
        19.5.2. Checkpoints...551
        19.5.3. Archiving 552
    19.6. Replication..553
        19.6.1. Sending Server(s)...553
        19.6.2. Master Server 554
        19.6.3. Standby Servers 556
    19.7. Query Planning..557
        19.7.1. Planner Method Configuration...557
        19.7.2. Planner Cost Constants 558
        19.7.3. Genetic Query Optimizer...560
        19.7.4. Other Planner Options...561
    19.8. Error Reporting and Logging 563
        19.8.1. Where To Log 563
        19.8.2. When To Log 566
        19.8.3. What To Log 568
        19.8.4. Using CSV-Format Log Output 572
        19.8.5. Process Title 573
    19.9. Run-time Statistics...573
        19.9.1. Query and Index Statistics Collector 573
        19.9.2. Statistics Monitoring 574

19.10. Automatic Vacuuming 574
19.11. Client Connection Defaults 576
    19.11.1. Statement Behavior 577
    19.11.2. Locale and Formatting 581
    19.11.3. Shared Library Preloading 582
    19.11.4. Other Defaults 584
19.12. Lock Management 585
19.13. Version and Platform Compatibility 586
    19.13.1. Previous PostgreSQL Versions 586
    19.13.2. Platform and Client Compatibility 588
19.14. Error Handling 588
19.15. Preset Options 588
19.16. Customized Options 590
19.17. Developer Options 590
19.18. Short Options 593
20. Client Authentication 595
20.1. The `pg_hba.conf` File 595
20.2. User Name Maps 602
20.3. Authentication Methods 603
    20.3.1. Trust Authentication 603
    20.3.2. Password Authentication 604
    20.3.3. GSSAPI Authentication 604
    20.3.4. SSPI Authentication 605
    20.3.5. Ident Authentication 606
    20.3.6. Peer Authentication 607
    20.3.7. LDAP Authentication 607
    20.3.8. RADIUS Authentication 610
    20.3.9. Certificate Authentication 610
    20.3.10. PAM Authentication 611
    20.3.11. BSD Authentication 611
20.4. Authentication Problems 612
21. Database Roles 613
21.1. Database Roles 613
21.2. Role Attributes 614
21.3. Role Membership 615
21.4. Dropping Roles 617
21.5. Default Roles 618
21.6. Function and Trigger Security 618
22. Managing Databases 619
22.1. Overview 619
22.2. Creating a Database 619
22.3. Template Databases 620
22.4. Database Configuration 621
22.5. Destroying a Database 622
22.6. Tablespaces 622
23. Localization 625
23.1. Locale Support 625
    23.1.1. Overview 625

23.1.2. Behavior 626
23.1.3. Problems 627
23.2. Collation Support..627
23.2.1. Concepts...628
23.2.2. Managing Collations 629
23.3. Character Set Support..630
23.3.1. Supported Character Sets 631
23.3.2. Setting the Character Set...633
23.3.3. Automatic Character Set Conversion Between Server and Client.................634
23.3.4. Further Reading 637
24. Routine Database Maintenance Tasks..638
24.1. Routine Vacuuming 638
24.1.1. Vacuuming Basics 638
24.1.2. Recovering Disk Space 639
24.1.3. Updating Planner Statistics 640
24.1.4. Updating The Visibility Map 641
24.1.5. Preventing Transaction ID Wraparound Failures...641
24.1.5.1. Multixacts and Wraparound 644
24.1.6. The Autovacuum Daemon 645
24.2. Routine Reindexing 646
24.3. Log File Maintenance..646
25. Backup and Restore 648
25.1. SQL Dump..648
25.1.1. Restoring the Dump 649
25.1.2. Using pg_dumpall 650
25.1.3. Handling Large Databases 650
25.2. File System Level Backup..651
25.3. Continuous Archiving and Point-in-Time Recovery (PITR)..652
25.3.1. Setting Up WAL Archiving..653
25.3.2. Making a Base Backup 655
25.3.3. Making a Base Backup Using the Low Level API 656
25.3.3.1. Making a non-exclusive low level backup 656
25.3.3.2. Making an exclusive low level backup..657
25.3.3.3. Backing up the data directory...658
25.3.4. Recovering Using a Continuous Archive Backup 659
25.3.5. Timelines..661
25.3.6. Tips and Examples 662
25.3.6.1. Standalone Hot Backups 662
25.3.6.2. Compressed Archive Logs 663
25.3.6.3. archive_command Scripts 663
25.3.7. Caveats 663
26. High Availability, Load Balancing, and Replication..665
26.1. Comparison of Different Solutions..665
26.2. Log-Shipping Standby Servers..669
26.2.1. Planning 669
26.2.2. Standby Server Operation 670
26.2.3. Preparing the Master for Standby Servers 670
26.2.4. Setting Up a Standby Server 670

26.2.5. Streaming Replication 671
    26.2.5.1. Authentication 672
    26.2.5.2. Monitoring 673
26.2.6. Replication Slots 673
    26.2.6.1. Querying and manipulating replication slots 673
    26.2.6.2. Configuration Example 673
26.2.7. Cascading Replication 674
26.2.8. Synchronous Replication 674
    26.2.8.1. Basic Configuration 675
    26.2.8.2. Multiple Synchronous Standbys..676
    26.2.8.3. Planning for Performance...676
    26.2.8.4. Planning for High Availability 677
26.2.9. Continuous archiving in standby 677
26.3. Failover 678
26.4. Alternative Method for Log Shipping 679
    26.4.1. Implementation 680
    26.4.2. Record-based Log Shipping...680
26.5. Hot Standby 681
    26.5.1. User's Overview...681
    26.5.2. Handling Query Conflicts 683
    26.5.3. Administrator's Overview 685
    26.5.4. Hot Standby Parameter Reference 687
    26.5.5. Caveats 688
27. Recovery Configuration 689
  27.1. Archive Recovery Settings 689
  27.2. Recovery Target Settings 690
  27.3. Standby Server Settings..691
28. Monitoring Database Activity..694
  28.1. Standard Unix Tools 694
  28.2. The Statistics Collector...695
    28.2.1. Statistics Collection Configuration 695
    28.2.2. Viewing Statistics..696
    28.2.3. Statistics Functions 717
  28.3. Viewing Locks 720
  28.4. Progress Reporting 720
    28.4.1. VACUUM Progress Reporting...720
  28.5. Dynamic Tracing 722
    28.5.1. Compiling for Dynamic Tracing..723
    28.5.2. Built-in Probes 723
    28.5.3. Using Probes 732
    28.5.4. Defining New Probes 733
29. Monitoring Disk Usage..735
  29.1. Determining Disk Usage 735
  29.2. Disk Full Failure...736
30. Reliability and the Write-Ahead Log..737
  30.1. Reliability 737
  30.2. Write-Ahead Logging (WAL) 739
  30.3. Asynchronous Commit 739

30.4. WAL Configuration 741

30.5. WAL Internals 744

31. Regression Tests..746

31.1. Running the Tests 746

31.1.1. Running the Tests Against a Temporary Installation 746

31.1.2. Running the Tests Against an Existing Installation 747

31.1.3. Additional Test Suites 747

31.1.4. Locale and Encoding..748

31.1.5. Extra Tests...748

31.1.6. Testing Hot Standby 748

31.2. Test Evaluation 749

31.2.1. Error Message Differences 750

31.2.2. Locale Differences 750

31.2.3. Date and Time Differences 750

31.2.4. Floating-Point Differences 750

31.2.5. Row Ordering Differences 751

31.2.6. Insufficient Stack Depth 751

31.2.7. The "random" Test 751

31.2.8. Configuration Parameters 752

31.3. Variant Comparison Files 752

31.4. TAP Tests 753

31.5. Test Coverage Examination 753

IV. Client Interfaces **755**

32. libpq - C Library 757

32.1. Database Connection Control Functions 757

32.1.1. Connection Strings...763

32.1.1.1. Keyword/Value Connection Strings 764

32.1.1.2. Connection URIs 764

32.1.2. Parameter Key Words 765

32.2. Connection Status Functions 769

32.3. Command Execution Functions 774

32.3.1. Main Functions 774

32.3.2. Retrieving Query Result Information 782

32.3.3. Retrieving Other Result Information 785

32.3.4. Escaping Strings for Inclusion in SQL Commands 786

32.4. Asynchronous Command Processing 789

32.5. Retrieving Query Results Row-By-Row 793

32.6. Canceling Queries in Progress...794

32.7. The Fast-Path Interface...795

32.8. Asynchronous Notification 796

32.9. Functions Associated with the COPY Command 797

32.9.1. Functions for Sending COPY Data..798

32.9.2. Functions for Receiving COPY Data..799

32.9.3. Obsolete Functions for COPY 799

32.10. Control Functions 801

32.11. Miscellaneous Functions 803

32.12. Notice Processing 805

32.13. Event System 806
    32.13.1. Event Types 807
    32.13.2. Event Callback Procedure 809
    32.13.3. Event Support Functions 809
    32.13.4. Event Example 810
32.14. Environment Variables 813
32.15. The Password File 815
32.16. The Connection Service File 815
32.17. LDAP Lookup of Connection Parameters 816
32.18. SSL Support 817
    32.18.1. Client Verification of Server Certificates 817
    32.18.2. Client Certificates 817
    32.18.3. Protection Provided in Different Modes 818
    32.18.4. SSL Client File Usage 820
    32.18.5. SSL Library Initialization 820
32.19. Behavior in Threaded Programs 821
32.20. Building libpq Programs 822
32.21. Example Programs 823
33. Large Objects 833
33.1. Introduction 833
33.2. Implementation Features 833
33.3. Client Interfaces 833
    33.3.1. Creating a Large Object 834
    33.3.2. Importing a Large Object 834
    33.3.3. Exporting a Large Object 835
    33.3.4. Opening an Existing Large Object 835
    33.3.5. Writing Data to a Large Object 836
    33.3.6. Reading Data from a Large Object 836
    33.3.7. Seeking in a Large Object 836
    33.3.8. Obtaining the Seek Position of a Large Object.......................................837
    33.3.9. Truncating a Large Object 837
    33.3.10. Closing a Large Object Descriptor 837
    33.3.11. Removing a Large Object 838
33.4. Server-side Functions 838
33.5. Example Program 839
34. ECPG - Embedded SQL in C...845
34.1. The Concept...845
34.2. Managing Database Connections 845
    34.2.1. Connecting to the Database Server 845
    34.2.2. Choosing a Connection 847
    34.2.3. Closing a Connection 848
34.3. Running SQL Commands..848
    34.3.1. Executing SQL Statements 848
    34.3.2. Using Cursors..849
    34.3.3. Managing Transactions 850
    34.3.4. Prepared Statements 850
34.4. Using Host Variables 851
    34.4.1. Overview 852

34.4.2. Declare Sections...852
34.4.3. Retrieving Query Results 853
34.4.4. Type Mapping 854
    34.4.4.1. Handling Character Strings 854
    34.4.4.2. Accessing Special Data Types..855
        34.4.4.2.1. timestamp, date 855
        34.4.4.2.2. interval 856
        34.4.4.2.3. numeric, decimal..857
    34.4.4.3. Host Variables with Nonprimitive Types 858
        34.4.4.3.1. Arrays 858
        34.4.4.3.2. Structures 859
        34.4.4.3.3. Typedefs 860
        34.4.4.3.4. Pointers 861
34.4.5. Handling Nonprimitive SQL Data Types..861
    34.4.5.1. Arrays 861
    34.4.5.2. Composite Types 863
    34.4.5.3. User-defined Base Types 865
34.4.6. Indicators..866
34.5. Dynamic SQL...867
34.5.1. Executing Statements without a Result Set 867
34.5.2. Executing a Statement with Input Parameters 867
34.5.3. Executing a Statement with a Result Set 868
34.6. pgtypes Library...869
34.6.1. The numeric Type 869
34.6.2. The date Type...872
34.6.3. The timestamp Type..875
34.6.4. The interval Type 879
34.6.5. The decimal Type..880
34.6.6. errno Values of pgtypeslib 880
34.6.7. Special Constants of pgtypeslib 881
34.7. Using Descriptor Areas 882
34.7.1. Named SQL Descriptor Areas 882
34.7.2. SQLDA Descriptor Areas 884
    34.7.2.1. SQLDA Data Structure..885
        34.7.2.1.1. sqlda_t Structure 885
        34.7.2.1.2. sqlvar_t Structure 886
        34.7.2.1.3. struct sqlname Structure 887
    34.7.2.2. Retrieving a Result Set Using an SQLDA 887
    34.7.2.3. Passing Query Parameters Using an SQLDA...........................889
    34.7.2.4. A Sample Application Using SQLDA 890
34.8. Error Handling..896
34.8.1. Setting Callbacks 896
34.8.2. sqlca 898
34.8.3. SQLSTATE vs. SQLCODE...899
34.9. Preprocessor Directives 903
34.9.1. Including Files 903
34.9.2. The define and undef Directives 904
34.9.3. ifdef, ifndef, else, elif, and endif Directives...905

34.10. Processing Embedded SQL Programs 905

34.11. Library Functions 906

34.12. Large Objects...907

34.13. C++ Applications 909

    34.13.1. Scope for Host Variables...909

    34.13.2. C++ Application Development with External C Module 910

34.14. Embedded SQL Commands 913

    ALLOCATE DESCRIPTOR 913

    CONNECT..915

    DEALLOCATE DESCRIPTOR 918

    DECLARE 919

    DESCRIBE 921

    DISCONNECT 923

    EXECUTE IMMEDIATE..925

    GET DESCRIPTOR 926

    OPEN 929

    PREPARE 931

    SET AUTOCOMMIT 933

    SET CONNECTION 934

    SET DESCRIPTOR 935

    TYPE..937

    VAR...940

    WHENEVER 941

34.15. Informix Compatibility Mode 943

    34.15.1. Additional Types..943

    34.15.2. Additional/Missing Embedded SQL Statements 943

    34.15.3. Informix-compatible SQLDA Descriptor Areas.....................................944

    34.15.4. Additional Functions...947

    34.15.5. Additional Constants...956

34.16. Internals 957

35. The Information Schema...960

35.1. The Schema 960

35.2. Data Types 960

35.3. `information_schema_catalog_name` 961

35.4. `administrable_role_authorizations`...961

35.5. `applicable_roles`..962

35.6. `attributes`...962

35.7. `character_sets` 966

35.8. `check_constraint_routine_usage` 967

35.9. `check_constraints` 968

35.10. `collations`...968

35.11. `collation_character_set_applicability` 969

35.12. `column_domain_usage` 969

35.13. `column_options` 970

35.14. `column_privileges` 970

35.15. `column_udt_usage`...971

35.16. `columns` 972

35.17. `constraint_column_usage` 977

35.18. `constraint_table_usage`..978

35.19. `data_type_privileges`..978

35.20. `domain_constraints`..979

35.21. `domain_udt_usage`..980

35.22. `domains`..980

35.23. `element_types`..984

35.24. `enabled_roles`..987

35.25. `foreign_data_wrapper_options`..987

35.26. `foreign_data_wrappers`..988

35.27. `foreign_server_options`..988

35.28. `foreign_servers`..989

35.29. `foreign_table_options`..989

35.30. `foreign_tables`..990

35.31. `key_column_usage`..990

35.32. `parameters`..991

35.33. `referential_constraints`..994

35.34. `role_column_grants`..995

35.35. `role_routine_grants`..996

35.36. `role_table_grants`..996

35.37. `role_udt_grants`..997

35.38. `role_usage_grants`..998

35.39. `routine_privileges`..999

35.40. `routines`..999

35.41. `schemata`..1005

35.42. `sequences`..1006

35.43. `sql_features`..1007

35.44. `sql_implementation_info`..1008

35.45. `sql_languages`..1009

35.46. `sql_packages`..1009

35.47. `sql_parts`..1010

35.48. `sql_sizing`..1010

35.49. `sql_sizing_profiles`..1011

35.50. `table_constraints`..1011

35.51. `table_privileges`..1012

35.52. `tables`..1013

35.53. `transforms`..1014

35.54. `triggered_update_columns`..1015

35.55. `triggers`..1016

35.56. `udt_privileges`..1017

35.57. `usage_privileges`..1018

35.58. `user_defined_types`..1019

35.59. `user_mapping_options`..1020

35.60. `user_mappings`..1021

35.61. `view_column_usage`..1022

35.62. `view_routine_usage`..1022

35.63. `view_table_usage`..1023

35.64. `views`..1024

V. Server Programming **1026**

  36. Extending SQL...1028

    36.1. How Extensibility Works...1028

    36.2. The PostgreSQL Type System...1028

      36.2.1. Base Types 1028

      36.2.2. Composite Types...1029

      36.2.3. Domains..1029

      36.2.4. Pseudo-Types..1029

      36.2.5. Polymorphic Types 1029

    36.3. User-defined Functions..1030

    36.4. Query Language (SQL) Functions 1031

      36.4.1. Arguments for SQL Functions..1032

      36.4.2. SQL Functions on Base Types...1032

      36.4.3. SQL Functions on Composite Types 1034

      36.4.4. SQL Functions with Output Parameters 1037

      36.4.5. SQL Functions with Variable Numbers of Arguments 1038

      36.4.6. SQL Functions with Default Values for Arguments 1039

      36.4.7. SQL Functions as Table Sources 1040

      36.4.8. SQL Functions Returning Sets 1041

      36.4.9. SQL Functions Returning `TABLE` 1043

      36.4.10. Polymorphic SQL Functions 1044

      36.4.11. SQL Functions with Collations..1045

    36.5. Function Overloading 1046

    36.6. Function Volatility Categories 1047

    36.7. Procedural Language Functions 1049

    36.8. Internal Functions..1049

    36.9. C-Language Functions..1049

      36.9.1. Dynamic Loading..1049

      36.9.2. Base Types in C-Language Functions...1051

      36.9.3. Version 0 Calling Conventions 1053

      36.9.4. Version 1 Calling Conventions 1056

      36.9.5. Writing Code...1059

      36.9.6. Compiling and Linking Dynamically-loaded Functions...............................1059

      36.9.7. Composite-type Arguments 1061

      36.9.8. Returning Rows (Composite Types)..1063

      36.9.9. Returning Sets 1065

      36.9.10. Polymorphic Arguments and Return Types 1070

      36.9.11. Transform Functions 1072

      36.9.12. Shared Memory and LWLocks 1072

      36.9.13. Using C++ for Extensibility..1073

    36.10. User-defined Aggregates 1073

      36.10.1. Moving-Aggregate Mode..1075

      36.10.2. Polymorphic and Variadic Aggregates..1076

      36.10.3. Ordered-Set Aggregates..1078

      36.10.4. Partial Aggregation 1079

      36.10.5. Support Functions for Aggregates 1080

    36.11. User-defined Types 1081

      36.11.1. TOAST Considerations..1084

36.12. User-defined Operators 1085
36.13. Operator Optimization Information 1086
    36.13.1. COMMUTATOR 1087
    36.13.2. NEGATOR 1087
    36.13.3. RESTRICT 1088
    36.13.4. JOIN 1089
    36.13.5. HASHES 1089
    36.13.6. MERGES 1090
36.14. Interfacing Extensions To Indexes 1091
    36.14.1. Index Methods and Operator Classes 1091
    36.14.2. Index Method Strategies 1092
    36.14.3. Index Method Support Routines 1094
    36.14.4. An Example 1097
    36.14.5. Operator Classes and Operator Families..1099
    36.14.6. System Dependencies on Operator Classes 1102
    36.14.7. Ordering Operators 1103
    36.14.8. Special Features of Operator Classes...1103
36.15. Packaging Related Objects into an Extension 1104
    36.15.1. Extension Files..1105
    36.15.2. Extension Relocatability 1107
    36.15.3. Extension Configuration Tables 1108
    36.15.4. Extension Updates 1109
    36.15.5. Extension Example 1110
36.16. Extension Building Infrastructure 1111
37. Triggers 1115
37.1. Overview of Trigger Behavior...1115
37.2. Visibility of Data Changes..1117
37.3. Writing Trigger Functions in C 1118
37.4. A Complete Trigger Example..1121
38. Event Triggers 1125
38.1. Overview of Event Trigger Behavior 1125
38.2. Event Trigger Firing Matrix 1126
38.3. Writing Event Trigger Functions in C 1131
38.4. A Complete Event Trigger Example 1132
38.5. A Table Rewrite Event Trigger Example..1133
39. The Rule System 1135
39.1. The Query Tree...1135
39.2. Views and the Rule System 1137
    39.2.1. How SELECT Rules Work 1137
    39.2.2. View Rules in Non-SELECT Statements 1142
    39.2.3. The Power of Views in PostgreSQL 1143
    39.2.4. Updating a View..1143
39.3. Materialized Views 1144
39.4. Rules on INSERT, UPDATE, and DELETE 1147
    39.4.1. How Update Rules Work 1148
        39.4.1.1. A First Rule Step by Step...1149
    39.4.2. Cooperation with Views...1152
39.5. Rules and Privileges 1158

39.6. Rules and Command Status 1160
39.7. Rules Versus Triggers 1161
40. Procedural Languages 1164
40.1. Installing Procedural Languages 1164
41. PL/pgSQL - SQL Procedural Language 1167
41.1. Overview 1167
41.1.1. Advantages of Using PL/pgSQL 1167
41.1.2. Supported Argument and Result Data Types 1168
41.2. Structure of PL/pgSQL 1168
41.3. Declarations 1170
41.3.1. Declaring Function Parameters 1170
41.3.2. ALIAS 1173
41.3.3. Copying Types 1173
41.3.4. Row Types 1174
41.3.5. Record Types 1174
41.3.6. Collation of PL/pgSQL Variables 1175
41.4. Expressions 1176
41.5. Basic Statements 1176
41.5.1. Assignment 1177
41.5.2. Executing a Command With No Result 1177
41.5.3. Executing a Query with a Single-row Result 1178
41.5.4. Executing Dynamic Commands 1180
41.5.5. Obtaining the Result Status 1183
41.5.6. Doing Nothing At All 1184
41.6. Control Structures 1185
41.6.1. Returning From a Function 1185
41.6.1.1. RETURN 1185
41.6.1.2. RETURN NEXT and RETURN QUERY 1185
41.6.2. Conditionals 1187
41.6.2.1. IF-THEN 1188
41.6.2.2. IF-THEN-ELSE 1188
41.6.2.3. IF-THEN-ELSIF 1188
41.6.2.4. Simple CASE 1189
41.6.2.5. Searched CASE 1190
41.6.3. Simple Loops 1191
41.6.3.1. LOOP 1191
41.6.3.2. EXIT 1191
41.6.3.3. CONTINUE 1192
41.6.3.4. WHILE 1192
41.6.3.5. FOR (Integer Variant) 1193
41.6.4. Looping Through Query Results 1193
41.6.5. Looping Through Arrays 1195
41.6.6. Trapping Errors 1196
41.6.6.1. Obtaining Information About an Error.......................................1198
41.6.7. Obtaining Execution Location Information 1199
41.7. Cursors 1200
41.7.1. Declaring Cursor Variables 1200
41.7.2. Opening Cursors 1201

41.7.2.1. `OPEN FOR` *query* 1201

41.7.2.2. `OPEN FOR EXECUTE` 1201

41.7.2.3. Opening a Bound Cursor...1202

41.7.3. Using Cursors...1203

41.7.3.1. `FETCH` 1203

41.7.3.2. `MOVE` 1203

41.7.3.3. `UPDATE/DELETE WHERE CURRENT OF` 1204

41.7.3.4. `CLOSE` 1204

41.7.3.5. Returning Cursors 1204

41.7.4. Looping Through a Cursor's Result...1206

41.8. Errors and Messages 1206

41.8.1. Reporting Errors and Messages 1207

41.8.2. Checking Assertions 1209

41.9. Trigger Procedures 1209

41.9.1. Triggers on Data Changes 1209

41.9.2. Triggers on Events 1216

41.10. PL/pgSQL Under the Hood 1217

41.10.1. Variable Substitution 1217

41.10.2. Plan Caching 1219

41.11. Tips for Developing in PL/pgSQL..1221

41.11.1. Handling of Quotation Marks 1221

41.11.2. Additional Compile-time Checks 1223

41.12. Porting from Oracle PL/SQL..1224

41.12.1. Porting Examples 1224

41.12.2. Other Things to Watch For...1230

41.12.2.1. Implicit Rollback after Exceptions...1230

41.12.2.2. `EXECUTE` 1231

41.12.2.3. Optimizing PL/pgSQL Functions..1231

41.12.3. Appendix 1231

42. PL/Tcl - Tcl Procedural Language 1234

42.1. Overview 1234

42.2. PL/Tcl Functions and Arguments...1234

42.3. Data Values in PL/Tcl 1236

42.4. Global Data in PL/Tcl 1236

42.5. Database Access from PL/Tcl 1236

42.6. Trigger Procedures in PL/Tcl 1239

42.7. Event Trigger Procedures in PL/Tcl...1240

42.8. Error Handling in PL/Tcl..1241

42.9. Modules and the `unknown` Command..1242

42.10. Tcl Procedure Names 1242

43. PL/Perl - Perl Procedural Language...1243

43.1. PL/Perl Functions and Arguments...1243

43.2. Data Values in PL/Perl...1247

43.3. Built-in Functions 1247

43.3.1. Database Access from PL/Perl...1247

43.3.2. Utility Functions in PL/Perl..1250

43.4. Global Values in PL/Perl 1252

43.5. Trusted and Untrusted PL/Perl 1253

43.6. PL/Perl Triggers 1254

43.7. PL/Perl Event Triggers 1255

43.8. PL/Perl Under the Hood 1256

    43.8.1. Configuration 1256

    43.8.2. Limitations and Missing Features..1257

44. PL/Python - Python Procedural Language 1259

44.1. Python 2 vs. Python 3 1259

44.2. PL/Python Functions 1260

44.3. Data Values 1262

    44.3.1. Data Type Mapping...1262

    44.3.2. Null, None 1263

    44.3.3. Arrays, Lists 1263

    44.3.4. Composite Types..1264

    44.3.5. Set-returning Functions..1266

44.4. Sharing Data 1267

44.5. Anonymous Code Blocks 1267

44.6. Trigger Functions 1268

44.7. Database Access 1268

    44.7.1. Database Access Functions 1269

    44.7.2. Trapping Errors 1271

44.8. Explicit Subtransactions 1272

    44.8.1. Subtransaction Context Managers 1272

    44.8.2. Older Python Versions 1273

44.9. Utility Functions 1274

44.10. Environment Variables 1275

45. Server Programming Interface 1277

45.1. Interface Functions 1277

    SPI_connect 1277

    SPI_finish 1279

    SPI_push 1280

    SPI_pop...1281

    SPI_execute..1282

    SPI_exec..1286

    SPI_execute_with_args 1287

    SPI_prepare...1289

    SPI_prepare_cursor...1291

    SPI_prepare_params 1292

    SPI_getargcount 1293

    SPI_getargtypeid...1294

    SPI_is_cursor_plan 1295

    SPI_execute_plan..1296

    SPI_execute_plan_with_paramlist...1298

    SPI_execp..1299

    SPI_cursor_open 1300

    SPI_cursor_open_with_args 1302

    SPI_cursor_open_with_paramlist..1304

    SPI_cursor_find..1305

    SPI_cursor_fetch..1306

SPI_cursor_move 1307

SPI_scroll_cursor_fetch 1308

SPI_scroll_cursor_move 1309

SPI_cursor_close 1310

SPI_keepplan 1311

SPI_saveplan 1312

45.2. Interface Support Functions 1313

SPI_fname 1313

SPI_fnumber 1314

SPI_getvalue 1315

SPI_getbinval 1316

SPI_gettype 1317

SPI_gettypeid 1318

SPI_getrelname 1319

SPI_getnspname 1320

45.3. Memory Management 1321

SPI_palloc 1321

SPI_repalloc 1323

SPI_pfree 1324

SPI_copytuple 1325

SPI_returntuple 1326

SPI_modifytuple 1327

SPI_freetuple 1329

SPI_freetuptable 1330

SPI_freeplan 1331

45.4. Visibility of Data Changes 1332

45.5. Examples 1332

46. Background Worker Processes 1336

47. Logical Decoding 1340

47.1. Logical Decoding Examples 1340

47.2. Logical Decoding Concepts 1342

47.2.1. Logical Decoding 1342

47.2.2. Replication Slots 1342

47.2.3. Output Plugins 1343

47.2.4. Exported Snapshots 1343

47.3. Streaming Replication Protocol Interface 1343

47.4. Logical Decoding SQL Interface 1344

47.5. System Catalogs Related to Logical Decoding 1344

47.6. Logical Decoding Output Plugins 1344

47.6.1. Initialization Function 1344

47.6.2. Capabilities 1345

47.6.3. Output Modes 1345

47.6.4. Output Plugin Callbacks 1345

47.6.4.1. Startup Callback 1346

47.6.4.2. Shutdown Callback 1346

47.6.4.3. Transaction Begin Callback 1346

47.6.4.4. Transaction End Callback 1347

47.6.4.5. Change Callback 1347

47.6.4.6. Origin Filter Callback..1347

47.6.4.7. Generic Message Callback 1348

47.6.5. Functions for Producing Output..1348

47.7. Logical Decoding Output Writers 1348

47.8. Synchronous Replication Support for Logical Decoding..1349

48. Replication Progress Tracking 1350

VI. Reference..1351

I. SQL Commands..1353

ABORT..1354

ALTER AGGREGATE..1356

ALTER COLLATION 1359

ALTER CONVERSION 1361

ALTER DATABASE 1363

ALTER DEFAULT PRIVILEGES 1366

ALTER DOMAIN 1369

ALTER EVENT TRIGGER 1373

ALTER EXTENSION 1374

ALTER FOREIGN DATA WRAPPER 1378

ALTER FOREIGN TABLE...1380

ALTER FUNCTION 1386

ALTER GROUP 1390

ALTER INDEX 1392

ALTER LANGUAGE...1395

ALTER LARGE OBJECT..1396

ALTER MATERIALIZED VIEW 1397

ALTER OPERATOR 1399

ALTER OPERATOR CLASS...1401

ALTER OPERATOR FAMILY 1403

ALTER POLICY 1407

ALTER ROLE 1409

ALTER RULE 1414

ALTER SCHEMA 1416

ALTER SEQUENCE..1417

ALTER SERVER..1420

ALTER SYSTEM...1422

ALTER TABLE 1424

ALTER TABLESPACE 1437

ALTER TEXT SEARCH CONFIGURATION 1439

ALTER TEXT SEARCH DICTIONARY 1441

ALTER TEXT SEARCH PARSER...1443

ALTER TEXT SEARCH TEMPLATE 1444

ALTER TRIGGER 1445

ALTER TYPE...1447

ALTER USER 1451

ALTER USER MAPPING 1453

ALTER VIEW 1455

ANALYZE..1458

BEGIN..1461

CHECKPOINT...1463

CLOSE 1464

CLUSTER..1466

COMMENT..1469

COMMIT..1474

COMMIT PREPARED...1476

COPY 1478

CREATE ACCESS METHOD...1489

CREATE AGGREGATE 1491

CREATE CAST..1499

CREATE COLLATION...1504

CREATE CONVERSION 1506

CREATE DATABASE..1508

CREATE DOMAIN...1512

CREATE EVENT TRIGGER..1515

CREATE EXTENSION...1517

CREATE FOREIGN DATA WRAPPER...1520

CREATE FOREIGN TABLE 1522

CREATE FUNCTION...1526

CREATE GROUP...1535

CREATE INDEX...1536

CREATE LANGUAGE 1543

CREATE MATERIALIZED VIEW 1547

CREATE OPERATOR 1549

CREATE OPERATOR CLASS 1552

CREATE OPERATOR FAMILY..1556

CREATE POLICY...1558

CREATE ROLE..1562

CREATE RULE..1567

CREATE SCHEMA 1570

CREATE SEQUENCE 1573

CREATE SERVER 1577

CREATE TABLE 1579

CREATE TABLE AS 1595

CREATE TABLESPACE...1598

CREATE TEXT SEARCH CONFIGURATION...1600

CREATE TEXT SEARCH DICTIONARY...1602

CREATE TEXT SEARCH PARSER 1604

CREATE TEXT SEARCH TEMPLATE..1606

CREATE TRANSFORM..1608

CREATE TRIGGER..1611

CREATE TYPE...1617

CREATE USER..1627

CREATE USER MAPPING...1628

CREATE VIEW...1630

DEALLOCATE 1635

DECLARE..1636

DELETE 1640

DISCARD..1643

DO 1645

DROP ACCESS METHOD...1647

DROP AGGREGATE 1649

DROP CAST 1651

DROP COLLATION 1653

DROP CONVERSION...1655

DROP DATABASE 1657

DROP DOMAIN 1658

DROP EVENT TRIGGER 1660

DROP EXTENSION 1662

DROP FOREIGN DATA WRAPPER 1664

DROP FOREIGN TABLE...1666

DROP FUNCTION 1668

DROP GROUP 1670

DROP INDEX 1671

DROP LANGUAGE 1673

DROP MATERIALIZED VIEW 1675

DROP OPERATOR 1677

DROP OPERATOR CLASS..1679

DROP OPERATOR FAMILY 1681

DROP OWNED 1683

DROP POLICY 1685

DROP ROLE 1687

DROP RULE 1689

DROP SCHEMA 1691

DROP SEQUENCE..1693

DROP SERVER..1695

DROP TABLE 1697

DROP TABLESPACE 1699

DROP TEXT SEARCH CONFIGURATION 1701

DROP TEXT SEARCH DICTIONARY 1703

DROP TEXT SEARCH PARSER 1705

DROP TEXT SEARCH TEMPLATE 1707

DROP TRANSFORM 1709

DROP TRIGGER 1711

DROP TYPE..1713

DROP USER 1715

DROP USER MAPPING 1716

DROP VIEW 1718

END..1720

EXECUTE...1722

EXPLAIN 1724

FETCH 1730

GRANT 1734

IMPORT FOREIGN SCHEMA 1742

INSERT 1744

LISTEN 1751
LOAD 1753
LOCK 1754
MOVE 1757
NOTIFY 1759
PREPARE 1762
PREPARE TRANSACTION 1765
REASSIGN OWNED 1767
REFRESH MATERIALIZED VIEW 1769
REINDEX 1771
RELEASE SAVEPOINT 1774
RESET 1776
REVOKE 1778
ROLLBACK 1782
ROLLBACK PREPARED 1784
ROLLBACK TO SAVEPOINT 1786
SAVEPOINT 1788
SECURITY LABEL 1790
SELECT 1793
SELECT INTO 1815
SET 1817
SET CONSTRAINTS 1821
SET ROLE 1823
SET SESSION AUTHORIZATION 1825
SET TRANSACTION 1827
SHOW 1830
START TRANSACTION 1833
TRUNCATE 1834
UNLISTEN 1837
UPDATE 1839
VACUUM 1844
VALUES 1848
II. PostgreSQL Client Applications 1851
clusterdb 1852
createdb 1855
createlang 1859
createuser 1862
dropdb 1867
droplang 1870
dropuser 1873
ecpg 1876
pg_basebackup 1879
pgbench 1886
pg_config 1899
pg_dump 1902
pg_dumpall 1915
pg_isready 1921
pg_receivexlog 1924

pg_recvlogical 1928

pg_restore 1932

psql 1942

reindexdb 1978

vacuumdb 1982

III. PostgreSQL Server Applications 1986

initdb 1987

pg_archivecleanup 1991

pg_controldata 1994

pg_ctl 1995

pg_resetxlog 2001

pg_rewind 2004

pg_test_fsync 2007

pg_test_timing 2009

pg_upgrade 2013

pg_xlogdump 2020

postgres 2023

postmaster 2031

VII. Internals **2032**

49. Overview of PostgreSQL Internals 2034

49.1. The Path of a Query 2034

49.2. How Connections are Established 2034

49.3. The Parser Stage 2035

49.3.1. Parser 2035

49.3.2. Transformation Process 2036

49.4. The PostgreSQL Rule System 2036

49.5. Planner/Optimizer 2037

49.5.1. Generating Possible Plans 2037

49.6. Executor 2038

50. System Catalogs 2040

50.1. Overview 2040

50.2. pg_aggregate 2042

50.3. pg_am 2044

50.4. pg_amop 2045

50.5. pg_amproc 2046

50.6. pg_attrdef 2047

50.7. pg_attribute 2047

50.8. pg_authid 2051

50.9. pg_auth_members 2052

50.10. pg_cast 2052

50.11. pg_class 2054

50.12. pg_collation 2058

50.13. pg_constraint 2059

50.14. pg_conversion 2062

50.15. pg_database 2063

50.16. pg_db_role_setting 2065

50.17. pg_default_acl 2066

50.18. pg_depend..2067

50.19. pg_description...2068

50.20. pg_enum...2069

50.21. pg_event_trigger...2070

50.22. pg_extension..2070

50.23. pg_foreign_data_wrapper 2071

50.24. pg_foreign_server 2072

50.25. pg_foreign_table..2073

50.26. pg_index..2073

50.27. pg_inherits..2076

50.28. pg_init_privs..2077

50.29. pg_language...2078

50.30. pg_largeobject...2079

50.31. pg_largeobject_metadata 2080

50.32. pg_namespace...2080

50.33. pg_opclass...2081

50.34. pg_operator...2082

50.35. pg_opfamily...2083

50.36. pg_pltemplate...2083

50.37. pg_policy..2084

50.38. pg_proc..2085

50.39. pg_range..2090

50.40. pg_replication_origin...2091

50.41. pg_rewrite..2092

50.42. pg_seclabel..2093

50.43. pg_shdepend...2093

50.44. pg_shdescription...2095

50.45. pg_shseclabel..2095

50.46. pg_statistic..2096

50.47. pg_tablespace...2098

50.48. pg_transform...2099

50.49. pg_trigger..2099

50.50. pg_ts_config...2101

50.51. pg_ts_config_map...2102

50.52. pg_ts_dict..2102

50.53. pg_ts_parser...2103

50.54. pg_ts_template...2104

50.55. pg_type..2104

50.56. pg_user_mapping...2113

50.57. System Views 2113

50.58. pg_available_extensions 2114

50.59. pg_available_extension_versions 2115

50.60. pg_config..2115

50.61. pg_cursors..2116

50.62. pg_file_settings...2117

50.63. pg_group..2118

50.64. pg_indexes..2118

50.65. pg_locks..2118

50.66. `pg_matviews` 2122

50.67. `pg_policies` 2123

50.68. `pg_prepared_statements`..2124

50.69. `pg_prepared_xacts` 2125

50.70. `pg_replication_origin_status`..2125

50.71. `pg_replication_slots` 2126

50.72. `pg_roles`...2127

50.73. `pg_rules` 2129

50.74. `pg_seclabels` 2129

50.75. `pg_settings` 2130

50.76. `pg_shadow`...2133

50.77. `pg_stats` 2134

50.78. `pg_tables` 2137

50.79. `pg_timezone_abbrevs` 2138

50.80. `pg_timezone_names` 2138

50.81. `pg_user` 2139

50.82. `pg_user_mappings`..2139

50.83. `pg_views` 2140

51. Frontend/Backend Protocol...2141

51.1. Overview 2141

51.1.1. Messaging Overview...2141

51.1.2. Extended Query Overview 2142

51.1.3. Formats and Format Codes 2142

51.2. Message Flow 2143

51.2.1. Start-up...2143

51.2.2. Simple Query 2145

51.2.3. Extended Query 2146

51.2.4. Function Call..2149

51.2.5. COPY Operations 2150

51.2.6. Asynchronous Operations...2151

51.2.7. Canceling Requests in Progress 2152

51.2.8. Termination..2153

51.2.9. SSL Session Encryption..2153

51.3. Streaming Replication Protocol...2153

51.4. Message Data Types 2160

51.5. Message Formats 2160

51.6. Error and Notice Message Fields 2177

51.7. Summary of Changes since Protocol 2.0...2178

52. PostgreSQL Coding Conventions 2180

52.1. Formatting 2180

52.2. Reporting Errors Within the Server 2181

52.3. Error Message Style Guide...2184

52.3.1. What Goes Where 2184

52.3.2. Formatting..2184

52.3.3. Quotation Marks 2185

52.3.4. Use of Quotes...2185

52.3.5. Grammar and Punctuation 2185

52.3.6. Upper Case vs. Lower Case 2185

52.3.7. Avoid Passive Voice 2186
52.3.8. Present vs. Past Tense 2186
52.3.9. Type of the Object 2186
52.3.10. Brackets..2186
52.3.11. Assembling Error Messages 2187
52.3.12. Reasons for Errors...2187
52.3.13. Function Names 2187
52.3.14. Tricky Words to Avoid 2187
52.3.15. Proper Spelling...2188
52.3.16. Localization..2188
52.4. Miscellaneous Coding Conventions 2188
52.4.1. C Standard...2189
52.4.2. Function-Like Macros and Inline Functions...2189
52.4.3. Writing Signal Handlers 2189
53. Native Language Support 2191
53.1. For the Translator 2191
53.1.1. Requirements 2191
53.1.2. Concepts..2191
53.1.3. Creating and Maintaining Message Catalogs 2192
53.1.4. Editing the PO Files 2193
53.2. For the Programmer...2194
53.2.1. Mechanics 2194
53.2.2. Message-writing Guidelines 2195
54. Writing A Procedural Language Handler 2197
55. Writing A Foreign Data Wrapper 2200
55.1. Foreign Data Wrapper Functions 2200
55.2. Foreign Data Wrapper Callback Routines..2200
55.2.1. FDW Routines For Scanning Foreign Tables 2201
55.2.2. FDW Routines For Scanning Foreign Joins...2203
55.2.3. FDW Routines For Planning Post-Scan/Join Processing...........................2203
55.2.4. FDW Routines For Updating Foreign Tables 2204
55.2.5. FDW Routines For Row Locking 2209
55.2.6. FDW Routines for EXPLAIN...2210
55.2.7. FDW Routines for ANALYZE...2211
55.2.8. FDW Routines For IMPORT FOREIGN SCHEMA.....................................2212
55.2.9. FDW Routines for Parallel Execution...2212
55.3. Foreign Data Wrapper Helper Functions..2213
55.4. Foreign Data Wrapper Query Planning 2214
55.5. Row Locking in Foreign Data Wrappers...2217
56. Writing A Table Sampling Method..2219
56.1. Sampling Method Support Functions 2219
57. Writing A Custom Scan Provider 2223
57.1. Creating Custom Scan Paths 2223
57.1.1. Custom Scan Path Callbacks 2224
57.2. Creating Custom Scan Plans 2224
57.2.1. Custom Scan Plan Callbacks 2225
57.3. Executing Custom Scans 2225
57.3.1. Custom Scan Execution Callbacks 2226

58. Genetic Query Optimizer 2228
    58.1. Query Handling as a Complex Optimization Problem 2228
    58.2. Genetic Algorithms 2228
    58.3. Genetic Query Optimization (GEQO) in PostgreSQL 2229
        58.3.1. Generating Possible Plans with GEQO...2230
        58.3.2. Future Implementation Tasks for PostgreSQL GEQO 2230
    58.4. Further Reading 2231
59. Index Access Method Interface Definition 2232
    59.1. Basic API Structure for Indexes 2232
    59.2. Index Access Method Functions...2234
    59.3. Index Scanning 2239
    59.4. Index Locking Considerations 2241
    59.5. Index Uniqueness Checks 2242
    59.6. Index Cost Estimation Functions..2243
60. Generic WAL Records 2247
61. GiST Indexes..2249
    61.1. Introduction 2249
    61.2. Built-in Operator Classes 2249
    61.3. Extensibility..2250
    61.4. Implementation..2259
        61.4.1. GiST buffering build 2259
    61.5. Examples 2259
62. SP-GiST Indexes..2261
    62.1. Introduction 2261
    62.2. Built-in Operator Classes 2261
    62.3. Extensibility..2262
    62.4. Implementation..2268
        62.4.1. SP-GiST Limits..2269
        62.4.2. SP-GiST Without Node Labels..2269
        62.4.3. "All-the-same" Inner Tuples 2269
    62.5. Examples 2270
63. GIN Indexes 2271
    63.1. Introduction 2271
    63.2. Built-in Operator Classes 2271
    63.3. Extensibility..2272
    63.4. Implementation..2275
        63.4.1. GIN Fast Update Technique...2275
        63.4.2. Partial Match Algorithm 2276
    63.5. GIN Tips and Tricks 2276
    63.6. Limitations..2277
    63.7. Examples 2277
64. BRIN Indexes...2279
    64.1. Introduction 2279
        64.1.1. Index Maintenance...2279
    64.2. Built-in Operator Classes 2279
    64.3. Extensibility..2281
65. Database Physical Storage 2285
    65.1. Database File Layout..2285

65.2. TOAST 2287

    65.2.1. Out-of-line, on-disk TOAST storage 2288

    65.2.2. Out-of-line, in-memory TOAST storage..2290

65.3. Free Space Map 2290

65.4. Visibility Map 2291

65.5. The Initialization Fork 2291

65.6. Database Page Layout 2291

66. BKI Backend Interface 2295

66.1. BKI File Format 2295

66.2. BKI Commands 2295

66.3. Structure of the Bootstrap BKI File...2296

66.4. Example 2297

67. How the Planner Uses Statistics 2298

67.1. Row Estimation Examples..2298

VIII. Appendixes **2304**

A. PostgreSQL Error Codes...2305

B. Date/Time Support 2314

B.1. Date/Time Input Interpretation 2314

B.2. Date/Time Key Words..2315

B.3. Date/Time Configuration Files 2316

B.4. History of Units 2318

C. SQL Key Words..2320

D. SQL Conformance 2345

D.1. Supported Features 2346

D.2. Unsupported Features 2362

E. Release Notes 2378

E.1. Release 9.6 2378

    E.1.1. Overview 2378

    E.1.2. Migration to Version 9.6 2378

    E.1.3. Changes 2380

        E.1.3.1. Server 2380

            E.1.3.1.1. Parallel Queries 2380

            E.1.3.1.2. Indexes...2380

            E.1.3.1.3. Sorting 2381

            E.1.3.1.4. Locking...2381

            E.1.3.1.5. Optimizer Statistics 2381

            E.1.3.1.6. VACUUM...2382

            E.1.3.1.7. General Performance..2382

            E.1.3.1.8. Monitoring..2384

            E.1.3.1.9. Authentication 2384

            E.1.3.1.10. Server Configuration 2385

            E.1.3.1.11. Reliability 2386

         E.1.3.2. Replication and Recovery 2386

        E.1.3.3. Queries 2387

        E.1.3.4. Utility Commands...2388

        E.1.3.5. Permissions Management 2388

        E.1.3.6. Data Types 2389

E.1.3.7. Functions 2390
E.1.3.8. Server-Side Languages 2391
E.1.3.9. Client Interfaces 2391
E.1.3.10. Client Applications 2392
E.1.3.10.1. psql 2392
E.1.3.10.2. pgbench 2393
E.1.3.11. Server Applications 2394
E.1.3.12. Source Code 2394
E.1.3.13. Additional Modules 2396
E.1.3.13.1. postgres_fdw 2397
E.2. Release 9.5.4 2398
E.2.1. Migration to Version 9.5.4 2398
E.2.2. Changes 2398
E.3. Release 9.5.3 2402
E.3.1. Migration to Version 9.5.3 2402
E.3.2. Changes 2403
E.4. Release 9.5.2 2404
E.4.1. Migration to Version 9.5.2 2405
E.4.2. Changes 2405
E.5. Release 9.5.1 2407
E.5.1. Migration to Version 9.5.1 2408
E.5.2. Changes 2408
E.6. Release 9.5 2409
E.6.1. Overview 2409
E.6.2. Migration to Version 9.5 2410
E.6.3. Changes 2411
E.6.3.1. Server 2411
E.6.3.1.1. Indexes 2411
E.6.3.1.2. General Performance 2412
E.6.3.1.3. Monitoring 2412
E.6.3.1.4. SSL 2413
E.6.3.1.5. Server Settings 2413
E.6.3.2. Replication and Recovery 2414
E.6.3.3. Queries 2415
E.6.3.4. Utility Commands 2415
E.6.3.4.1. REINDEX 2415
E.6.3.5. Object Manipulation 2416
E.6.3.5.1. Foreign Tables 2416
E.6.3.5.2. Event Triggers 2417
E.6.3.6. Data Types 2417
E.6.3.6.1. JSON 2417
E.6.3.7. Functions 2418
E.6.3.7.1. System Information Functions and Views.............................2418
E.6.3.7.2. Aggregates 2419
E.6.3.8. Server-Side Languages 2419
E.6.3.8.1. PL/pgSQL Server-Side Language 2419
E.6.3.9. Client Applications 2419
E.6.3.9.1. psql 2420

E.6.3.9.1.1. Backslash Commands 2420
E.6.3.9.2. pg_dump 2421
E.6.3.9.3. pg_ctl 2421
E.6.3.9.4. pg_upgrade 2421
E.6.3.9.5. pgbench 2422
E.6.3.10. Source Code 2422
E.6.3.10.1. MS Windows 2423
E.6.3.11. Additional Modules 2423
E.7. Release 9.4.9 2424
E.7.1. Migration to Version 9.4.9 2424
E.7.2. Changes 2424
E.8. Release 9.4.8 2427
E.8.1. Migration to Version 9.4.8 2428
E.8.2. Changes 2428
E.9. Release 9.4.7 2429
E.9.1. Migration to Version 9.4.7 2430
E.9.2. Changes 2430
E.10. Release 9.4.6 2431
E.10.1. Migration to Version 9.4.6 2432
E.10.2. Changes 2432
E.11. Release 9.4.5 2436
E.11.1. Migration to Version 9.4.5 2436
E.11.2. Changes 2436
E.12. Release 9.4.4 2440
E.12.1. Migration to Version 9.4.4 2441
E.12.2. Changes 2441
E.13. Release 9.4.3 2442
E.13.1. Migration to Version 9.4.3 2442
E.13.2. Changes 2442
E.14. Release 9.4.2 2443
E.14.1. Migration to Version 9.4.2 2443
E.14.2. Changes 2443
E.15. Release 9.4.1 2448
E.15.1. Migration to Version 9.4.1 2448
E.15.2. Changes 2448
E.16. Release 9.4 2451
E.16.1. Overview 2451
E.16.2. Migration to Version 9.4 2452
E.16.3. Changes 2454
E.16.3.1. Server 2454
E.16.3.1.1. Indexes 2454
E.16.3.1.2. General Performance 2455
E.16.3.1.3. Monitoring 2455
E.16.3.1.4. SSL 2456
E.16.3.1.5. Server Settings 2456
E.16.3.2. Replication and Recovery 2457
E.16.3.2.1. Logical Decoding 2458
E.16.3.3. Queries 2458

E.16.3.4. Utility Commands 2458
    E.16.3.4.1. EXPLAIN 2459
    E.16.3.4.2. Views 2459
E.16.3.5. Object Manipulation 2459
E.16.3.6. Data Types 2460
    E.16.3.6.1. JSON 2460
E.16.3.7. Functions..2461
    E.16.3.7.1. System Information Functions 2461
    E.16.3.7.2. Aggregates...2462
E.16.3.8. Server-Side Languages 2462
    E.16.3.8.1. PL/pgSQL Server-Side Language 2462
E.16.3.9. libpq 2462
E.16.3.10. Client Applications 2462
    E.16.3.10.1. psql 2463
        E.16.3.10.1.1. Backslash Commands..2463
    E.16.3.10.2. pg_dump..2464
    E.16.3.10.3. pg_basebackup 2464
E.16.3.11. Source Code 2464
E.16.3.12. Additional Modules 2465
    E.16.3.12.1. pgbench 2466
    E.16.3.12.2. pg_stat_statements 2466
E.17. Release 9.3.14 2467
  E.17.1. Migration to Version 9.3.14...2467
  E.17.2. Changes 2467
E.18. Release 9.3.13 2470
  E.18.1. Migration to Version 9.3.13...2470
  E.18.2. Changes 2471
E.19. Release 9.3.12 2472
  E.19.1. Migration to Version 9.3.12...2472
  E.19.2. Changes 2472
E.20. Release 9.3.11 2473
  E.20.1. Migration to Version 9.3.11...2474
  E.20.2. Changes 2474
E.21. Release 9.3.10 2478
  E.21.1. Migration to Version 9.3.10...2478
  E.21.2. Changes 2478
E.22. Release 9.3.9 2482
  E.22.1. Migration to Version 9.3.9...2482
  E.22.2. Changes 2482
E.23. Release 9.3.8 2483
  E.23.1. Migration to Version 9.3.8...2483
  E.23.2. Changes 2484
E.24. Release 9.3.7 2484
  E.24.1. Migration to Version 9.3.7...2484
  E.24.2. Changes 2484
E.25. Release 9.3.6 2488
  E.25.1. Migration to Version 9.3.6...2489
  E.25.2. Changes 2489

E.26. Release 9.3.5 2496
   E.26.1. Migration to Version 9.3.5..2496
   E.26.2. Changes 2497
E.27. Release 9.3.4 2501
   E.27.1. Migration to Version 9.3.4..2501
   E.27.2. Changes 2501
E.28. Release 9.3.3 2503
   E.28.1. Migration to Version 9.3.3..2503
   E.28.2. Changes 2504
E.29. Release 9.3.2 2509
   E.29.1. Migration to Version 9.3.2..2509
   E.29.2. Changes 2509
E.30. Release 9.3.1 2512
   E.30.1. Migration to Version 9.3.1..2513
   E.30.2. Changes 2513
E.31. Release 9.3 2513
   E.31.1. Overview 2513
   E.31.2. Migration to Version 9.3...2514
      E.31.2.1. Server Settings 2514
      E.31.2.2. Other 2514
   E.31.3. Changes 2515
      E.31.3.1. Server 2515
         E.31.3.1.1. Locking...2515
         E.31.3.1.2. Indexes...2516
         E.31.3.1.3. Optimizer..2516
         E.31.3.1.4. General Performance........................2516
         E.31.3.1.5. Monitoring...2517
         E.31.3.1.6. Authentication 2517
         E.31.3.1.7. Server Settings...................................2517
      E.31.3.2. Replication and Recovery 2518
      E.31.3.3. Queries 2518
      E.31.3.4. Object Manipulation 2519
         E.31.3.4.1. ALTER 2519
         E.31.3.4.2. VIEWs 2519
      E.31.3.5. Data Types 2520
         E.31.3.5.1. JSON 2520
      E.31.3.6. Functions...2520
      E.31.3.7. Server-Side Languages 2521
         E.31.3.7.1. PL/pgSQL Server-Side Language 2521
         E.31.3.7.2. PL/Python Server-Side Language ...2521
      E.31.3.8. Server Programming Interface (SPI) 2521
      E.31.3.9. Client Applications 2522
         E.31.3.9.1. psql 2522
            E.31.3.9.1.1. Backslash Commands...............2522
            E.31.3.9.1.2. Output 2523
         E.31.3.9.2. pg_dump..2523
         E.31.3.9.3. initdb..2523
      E.31.3.10. Source Code 2523

E.31.3.11. Additional Modules 2525
E.31.3.11.1. pg_upgrade 2525
E.31.3.11.2. pgbench 2526
E.31.3.12. Documentation..2526
E.32. Release 9.2.18 2526
E.32.1. Migration to Version 9.2.18..2527
E.32.2. Changes 2527
E.33. Release 9.2.17 2529
E.33.1. Migration to Version 9.2.17..2529
E.33.2. Changes 2529
E.34. Release 9.2.16 2531
E.34.1. Migration to Version 9.2.16..2531
E.34.2. Changes 2531
E.35. Release 9.2.15 2532
E.35.1. Migration to Version 9.2.15..2532
E.35.2. Changes 2532
E.36. Release 9.2.14 2536
E.36.1. Migration to Version 9.2.14..2536
E.36.2. Changes 2536
E.37. Release 9.2.13 2540
E.37.1. Migration to Version 9.2.13..2540
E.37.2. Changes 2540
E.38. Release 9.2.12 2540
E.38.1. Migration to Version 9.2.12..2541
E.38.2. Changes 2541
E.39. Release 9.2.11 2541
E.39.1. Migration to Version 9.2.11..2541
E.39.2. Changes 2542
E.40. Release 9.2.10 2545
E.40.1. Migration to Version 9.2.10..2546
E.40.2. Changes 2546
E.41. Release 9.2.9 2552
E.41.1. Migration to Version 9.2.9..2552
E.41.2. Changes 2553
E.42. Release 9.2.8 2555
E.42.1. Migration to Version 9.2.8..2556
E.42.2. Changes 2556
E.43. Release 9.2.7 2557
E.43.1. Migration to Version 9.2.7..2557
E.43.2. Changes 2557
E.44. Release 9.2.6 2561
E.44.1. Migration to Version 9.2.6..2561
E.44.2. Changes 2561
E.45. Release 9.2.5 2563
E.45.1. Migration to Version 9.2.5..2564
E.45.2. Changes 2564
E.46. Release 9.2.4 2566
E.46.1. Migration to Version 9.2.4..2566

E.46.2. Changes 2566
E.47. Release 9.2.3 2569
    E.47.1. Migration to Version 9.2.3..2569
    E.47.2. Changes 2569
E.48. Release 9.2.2 2572
    E.48.1. Migration to Version 9.2.2..2572
    E.48.2. Changes 2572
E.49. Release 9.2.1 2577
    E.49.1. Migration to Version 9.2.1..2577
    E.49.2. Changes 2577
E.50. Release 9.2 2578
    E.50.1. Overview 2578
    E.50.2. Migration to Version 9.2...2579
        E.50.2.1. System Catalogs..2579
        E.50.2.2. Functions...2579
        E.50.2.3. Object Modification 2580
        E.50.2.4. Command-Line Tools 2580
        E.50.2.5. Server Settings 2580
        E.50.2.6. Monitoring 2581
    E.50.3. Changes 2581
        E.50.3.1. Server 2581
            E.50.3.1.1. Performance 2582
            E.50.3.1.2. Process Management..2583
            E.50.3.1.3. Optimizer..2583
            E.50.3.1.4. Authentication 2584
            E.50.3.1.5. Monitoring..2584
            E.50.3.1.6. Statistical Views 2584
            E.50.3.1.7. Server Settings..2585
                 E.50.3.1.7.1. `postgresql.conf`...2585
        E.50.3.2. Replication and Recovery 2586
        E.50.3.3. Queries...2586
        E.50.3.4. Object Manipulation 2587
            E.50.3.4.1. Constraints..2587
            E.50.3.4.2. `ALTER`...2587
            E.50.3.4.3. `CREATE TABLE` 2588
            E.50.3.4.4. Object Permissions...2588
        E.50.3.5. Utility Operations 2588
        E.50.3.6. Data Types 2589
        E.50.3.7. Functions...2589
        E.50.3.8. Information Schema...2590
        E.50.3.9. Server-Side Languages 2590
            E.50.3.9.1. PL/pgSQL Server-Side Language 2590
            E.50.3.9.2. PL/Python Server-Side Language 2591
            E.50.3.9.3. SQL Server-Side Language..2591
        E.50.3.10. Client Applications 2591
            E.50.3.10.1. psql 2591
            E.50.3.10.2. Informational Commands..2592
            E.50.3.10.3. Tab Completion 2592

E.50.3.10.4. pg_dump 2593
E.50.3.11. libpq 2593
E.50.3.12. Source Code 2594
E.50.3.13. Additional Modules 2594
E.50.3.13.1. pg_upgrade 2595
E.50.3.13.2. pg_stat_statements 2596
E.50.3.13.3. sepgsql 2596
E.50.3.14. Documentation 2596
E.51. Release 9.1.23 2596
E.51.1. Migration to Version 9.1.23 2597
E.51.2. Changes 2597
E.52. Release 9.1.22 2599
E.52.1. Migration to Version 9.1.22 2599
E.52.2. Changes 2599
E.53. Release 9.1.21 2600
E.53.1. Migration to Version 9.1.21 2601
E.53.2. Changes 2601
E.54. Release 9.1.20 2602
E.54.1. Migration to Version 9.1.20 2602
E.54.2. Changes 2602
E.55. Release 9.1.19 2605
E.55.1. Migration to Version 9.1.19 2606
E.55.2. Changes 2606
E.56. Release 9.1.18 2609
E.56.1. Migration to Version 9.1.18 2609
E.56.2. Changes 2610
E.57. Release 9.1.17 2610
E.57.1. Migration to Version 9.1.17 2610
E.57.2. Changes 2610
E.58. Release 9.1.16 2611
E.58.1. Migration to Version 9.1.16 2611
E.58.2. Changes 2611
E.59. Release 9.1.15 2615
E.59.1. Migration to Version 9.1.15 2615
E.59.2. Changes 2615
E.60. Release 9.1.14 2621
E.60.1. Migration to Version 9.1.14 2621
E.60.2. Changes 2621
E.61. Release 9.1.13 2623
E.61.1. Migration to Version 9.1.13 2623
E.61.2. Changes 2624
E.62. Release 9.1.12 2625
E.62.1. Migration to Version 9.1.12 2625
E.62.2. Changes 2625
E.63. Release 9.1.11 2628
E.63.1. Migration to Version 9.1.11 2629
E.63.2. Changes 2629
E.64. Release 9.1.10 2630

E.64.1. Migration to Version 9.1.10...2631
E.64.2. Changes 2631
E.65. Release 9.1.9 2632
E.65.1. Migration to Version 9.1.9...2633
E.65.2. Changes 2633
E.66. Release 9.1.8 2635
E.66.1. Migration to Version 9.1.8...2635
E.66.2. Changes 2635
E.67. Release 9.1.7 2637
E.67.1. Migration to Version 9.1.7...2637
E.67.2. Changes 2637
E.68. Release 9.1.6 2640
E.68.1. Migration to Version 9.1.6...2640
E.68.2. Changes 2640
E.69. Release 9.1.5 2642
E.69.1. Migration to Version 9.1.5...2642
E.69.2. Changes 2642
E.70. Release 9.1.4 2645
E.70.1. Migration to Version 9.1.4...2645
E.70.2. Changes 2645
E.71. Release 9.1.3 2648
E.71.1. Migration to Version 9.1.3...2648
E.71.2. Changes 2648
E.72. Release 9.1.2 2652
E.72.1. Migration to Version 9.1.2...2653
E.72.2. Changes 2653
E.73. Release 9.1.1 2657
E.73.1. Migration to Version 9.1.1...2657
E.73.2. Changes 2657
E.74. Release 9.1 2658
E.74.1. Overview 2658
E.74.2. Migration to Version 9.1...2658
E.74.2.1. Strings 2658
E.74.2.2. Casting 2659
E.74.2.3. Arrays..2659
E.74.2.4. Object Modification 2659
E.74.2.5. Server Settings 2660
E.74.2.6. PL/pgSQL Server-Side Language.......................................2660
E.74.2.7. Contrib 2660
E.74.2.8. Other Incompatibilities 2661
E.74.3. Changes 2661
E.74.3.1. Server 2661
E.74.3.1.1. Performance 2661
E.74.3.1.2. Optimizer..2661
E.74.3.1.3. Authentication 2662
E.74.3.1.4. Monitoring..2662
E.74.3.1.5. Statistical Views 2662
E.74.3.1.6. Server Settings..2663

E.74.3.2. Replication and Recovery 2663
    E.74.3.2.1. Streaming Replication and Continuous Archiving..............2663
    E.74.3.2.2. Replication Monitoring 2664
    E.74.3.2.3. Hot Standby...2664
    E.74.3.2.4. Recovery Control 2664
E.74.3.3. Queries 2665
    E.74.3.3.1. Strings...2666
E.74.3.4. Object Manipulation 2666
    E.74.3.4.1. ALTER Object 2666
    E.74.3.4.2. CREATE/ALTER TABLE 2666
    E.74.3.4.3. Object Permissions...2667
E.74.3.5. Utility Operations 2667
    E.74.3.5.1. COPY 2667
    E.74.3.5.2. EXPLAIN 2667
    E.74.3.5.3. VACUUM 2668
    E.74.3.5.4. CLUSTER 2668
    E.74.3.5.5. Indexes...2668
E.74.3.6. Data Types 2668
    E.74.3.6.1. Casting...2669
    E.74.3.6.2. XML 2669
E.74.3.7. Functions...2669
    E.74.3.7.1. Object Information Functions 2669
    E.74.3.7.2. Function and Trigger Creation 2670
E.74.3.8. Server-Side Languages 2670
    E.74.3.8.1. PL/pgSQL Server-Side Language 2670
    E.74.3.8.2. PL/Perl Server-Side Language 2670
    E.74.3.8.3. PL/Python Server-Side Language 2671
E.74.3.9. Client Applications 2671
    E.74.3.9.1. psql 2671
    E.74.3.9.2. pg_dump..2672
    E.74.3.9.3. pg_ctl 2672
E.74.3.10. Development Tools 2672
    E.74.3.10.1. libpq..2672
    E.74.3.10.2. ECPG..2673
E.74.3.11. Build Options 2673
    E.74.3.11.1. Makefiles 2673
    E.74.3.11.2. Windows 2673
E.74.3.12. Source Code 2673
    E.74.3.12.1. Server Hooks 2674
E.74.3.13. Contrib 2674
    E.74.3.13.1. Security...2675
    E.74.3.13.2. Performance 2675
    E.74.3.13.3. Fsync Testing..2675
E.74.3.14. Documentation...2676
E.75. Release 9.0.23 2676
  E.75.1. Migration to Version 9.0.23...2677
  E.75.2. Changes 2677
E.76. Release 9.0.22 2680

E.76.1. Migration to Version 9.0.22 2680
E.76.2. Changes 2680
E.77. Release 9.0.21 2681
E.77.1. Migration to Version 9.0.21 2681
E.77.2. Changes 2681
E.78. Release 9.0.20 2681
E.78.1. Migration to Version 9.0.20 2682
E.78.2. Changes 2682
E.79. Release 9.0.19 2685
E.79.1. Migration to Version 9.0.19 2685
E.79.2. Changes 2685
E.80. Release 9.0.18 2690
E.80.1. Migration to Version 9.0.18 2690
E.80.2. Changes 2690
E.81. Release 9.0.17 2693
E.81.1. Migration to Version 9.0.17 2693
E.81.2. Changes 2693
E.82. Release 9.0.16 2694
E.82.1. Migration to Version 9.0.16 2694
E.82.2. Changes 2694
E.83. Release 9.0.15 2697
E.83.1. Migration to Version 9.0.15 2698
E.83.2. Changes 2698
E.84. Release 9.0.14 2699
E.84.1. Migration to Version 9.0.14 2699
E.84.2. Changes 2699
E.85. Release 9.0.13 2701
E.85.1. Migration to Version 9.0.13 2701
E.85.2. Changes 2701
E.86. Release 9.0.12 2703
E.86.1. Migration to Version 9.0.12 2703
E.86.2. Changes 2703
E.87. Release 9.0.11 2705
E.87.1. Migration to Version 9.0.11 2705
E.87.2. Changes 2705
E.88. Release 9.0.10 2707
E.88.1. Migration to Version 9.0.10 2708
E.88.2. Changes 2708
E.89. Release 9.0.9 2708
E.89.1. Migration to Version 9.0.9 2709
E.89.2. Changes 2709
E.90. Release 9.0.8 2711
E.90.1. Migration to Version 9.0.8 2711
E.90.2. Changes 2711
E.91. Release 9.0.7 2713
E.91.1. Migration to Version 9.0.7 2713
E.91.2. Changes 2713
E.92. Release 9.0.6 2717

E.92.1. Migration to Version 9.0.6...2717
E.92.2. Changes 2717
E.93. Release 9.0.5 2720
E.93.1. Migration to Version 9.0.5...2720
E.93.2. Changes 2720
E.94. Release 9.0.4 2723
E.94.1. Migration to Version 9.0.4...2724
E.94.2. Changes 2724
E.95. Release 9.0.3 2726
E.95.1. Migration to Version 9.0.3...2726
E.95.2. Changes 2726
E.96. Release 9.0.2 2727
E.96.1. Migration to Version 9.0.2...2727
E.96.2. Changes 2727
E.97. Release 9.0.1 2730
E.97.1. Migration to Version 9.0.1...2730
E.97.2. Changes 2730
E.98. Release 9.0 2731
E.98.1. Overview 2731
E.98.2. Migration to Version 9.0..2732
E.98.2.1. Server Settings 2733
E.98.2.2. Queries 2733
E.98.2.3. Data Types 2733
E.98.2.4. Object Renaming 2734
E.98.2.5. PL/pgSQL 2734
E.98.2.6. Other Incompatibilities 2735
E.98.3. Changes 2735
E.98.3.1. Server 2735
E.98.3.1.1. Continuous Archiving and Streaming Replication..............2735
E.98.3.1.2. Performance 2736
E.98.3.1.3. Optimizer..2736
E.98.3.1.4. GEQO...2736
E.98.3.1.5. Optimizer Statistics 2737
E.98.3.1.6. Authentication 2737
E.98.3.1.7. Monitoring..2737
E.98.3.1.8. Statistics Counters 2737
E.98.3.1.9. Server Settings...2738
E.98.3.2. Queries 2738
E.98.3.2.1. Unicode Strings 2739
E.98.3.3. Object Manipulation 2739
E.98.3.3.1. ALTER TABLE 2739
E.98.3.3.2. CREATE TABLE 2739
E.98.3.3.3. Constraints...2740
E.98.3.3.4. Object Permissions 2740
E.98.3.4. Utility Operations 2741
E.98.3.4.1. COPY 2741
E.98.3.4.2. EXPLAIN..2741
E.98.3.4.3. VACUUM..2741

E.98.3.4.4. Indexes 2742
E.98.3.5. Data Types 2742
E.98.3.5.1. Full Text Search 2743
E.98.3.6. Functions 2743
E.98.3.6.1. Aggregates 2743
E.98.3.6.2. Bit Strings 2744
E.98.3.6.3. Object Information Functions 2744
E.98.3.6.4. Function and Trigger Creation 2744
E.98.3.7. Server-Side Languages 2744
E.98.3.7.1. PL/pgSQL Server-Side Language 2745
E.98.3.7.2. PL/Perl Server-Side Language 2745
E.98.3.7.3. PL/Python Server-Side Language 2746
E.98.3.8. Client Applications 2746
E.98.3.8.1. psql 2746
E.98.3.8.1.1. psql Display 2747
E.98.3.8.1.2. psql \d Commands 2747
E.98.3.8.2. pg_dump 2747
E.98.3.8.3. pg_ctl 2748
E.98.3.9. Development Tools 2748
E.98.3.9.1. libpq 2748
E.98.3.9.2. ecpg 2749
E.98.3.9.2.1. ecpg Cursors 2749
E.98.3.10. Build Options 2749
E.98.3.10.1. Makefiles 2749
E.98.3.10.2. Windows 2750
E.98.3.11. Source Code 2750
E.98.3.11.1. New Build Requirements 2751
E.98.3.11.2. Portability 2751
E.98.3.11.3. Server Programming 2752
E.98.3.11.4. Server Hooks 2752
E.98.3.11.5. Binary Upgrade Support 2752
E.98.3.12. Contrib 2753
E.99. Release 8.4.22 2753
E.99.1. Migration to Version 8.4.22 2754
E.99.2. Changes 2754
E.100. Release 8.4.21 2756
E.100.1. Migration to Version 8.4.21 2756
E.100.2. Changes 2756
E.101. Release 8.4.20 2757
E.101.1. Migration to Version 8.4.20 2757
E.101.2. Changes 2757
E.102. Release 8.4.19 2760
E.102.1. Migration to Version 8.4.19 2760
E.102.2. Changes 2761
E.103. Release 8.4.18 2762
E.103.1. Migration to Version 8.4.18 2762
E.103.2. Changes 2762
E.104. Release 8.4.17 2763

E.104.1. Migration to Version 8.4.17 2763

E.104.2. Changes 2763

E.105. Release 8.4.16 2765

E.105.1. Migration to Version 8.4.16 2765

E.105.2. Changes 2765

E.106. Release 8.4.15 2766

E.106.1. Migration to Version 8.4.15 2766

E.106.2. Changes 2766

E.107. Release 8.4.14 2768

E.107.1. Migration to Version 8.4.14 2768

E.107.2. Changes 2768

E.108. Release 8.4.13 2769

E.108.1. Migration to Version 8.4.13 2769

E.108.2. Changes 2769

E.109. Release 8.4.12 2771

E.109.1. Migration to Version 8.4.12 2771

E.109.2. Changes 2771

E.110. Release 8.4.11 2773

E.110.1. Migration to Version 8.4.11 2773

E.110.2. Changes 2773

E.111. Release 8.4.10 2776

E.111.1. Migration to Version 8.4.10 2776

E.111.2. Changes 2776

E.112. Release 8.4.9 2778

E.112.1. Migration to Version 8.4.9 2778

E.112.2. Changes 2779

E.113. Release 8.4.8 2781

E.113.1. Migration to Version 8.4.8 2782

E.113.2. Changes 2782

E.114. Release 8.4.7 2783

E.114.1. Migration to Version 8.4.7 2783

E.114.2. Changes 2783

E.115. Release 8.4.6 2784

E.115.1. Migration to Version 8.4.6 2784

E.115.2. Changes 2785

E.116. Release 8.4.5 2786

E.116.1. Migration to Version 8.4.5 2787

E.116.2. Changes 2787

E.117. Release 8.4.4 2790

E.117.1. Migration to Version 8.4.4 2790

E.117.2. Changes 2790

E.118. Release 8.4.3 2792

E.118.1. Migration to Version 8.4.3 2792

E.118.2. Changes 2792

E.119. Release 8.4.2 2795

E.119.1. Migration to Version 8.4.2 2795

E.119.2. Changes 2795

E.120. Release 8.4.1 2799

E.120.1. Migration to Version 8.4.1 2799
E.120.2. Changes 2799
E.121. Release 8.4 2801
E.121.1. Overview 2801
E.121.2. Migration to Version 8.4 2801
E.121.2.1. General 2802
E.121.2.2. Server Settings 2802
E.121.2.3. Queries 2802
E.121.2.4. Functions and Operators 2803
E.121.2.4.1. Temporal Functions and Operators 2804
E.121.3. Changes 2804
E.121.3.1. Performance 2804
E.121.3.2. Server 2805
E.121.3.2.1. Settings 2805
E.121.3.2.2. Authentication and security...2805
E.121.3.2.3. pg_hba.conf 2806
E.121.3.2.4. Continuous Archiving 2807
E.121.3.2.5. Monitoring 2807
E.121.3.3. Queries 2808
E.121.3.3.1. TRUNCATE 2808
E.121.3.3.2. EXPLAIN 2809
E.121.3.3.3. LIMIT/OFFSET 2809
E.121.3.4. Object Manipulation 2809
E.121.3.4.1. ALTER 2810
E.121.3.4.2. Database Manipulation...2810
E.121.3.5. Utility Operations 2810
E.121.3.5.1. Indexes...2811
E.121.3.5.2. Full Text Indexes 2811
E.121.3.5.3. VACUUM 2811
E.121.3.6. Data Types 2812
E.121.3.6.1. Temporal Data Types..2812
E.121.3.6.2. Arrays 2813
E.121.3.6.3. Wide-Value Storage (TOAST) 2813
E.121.3.7. Functions..2813
E.121.3.7.1. Object Information Functions 2814
E.121.3.7.2. Function Creation...2814
E.121.3.7.3. PL/pgSQL Server-Side Language 2815
E.121.3.8. Client Applications 2815
E.121.3.8.1. psql 2816
E.121.3.8.2. psql \d* commands...2816
E.121.3.8.3. pg_dump...2817
E.121.3.9. Programming Tools..2817
E.121.3.9.1. libpq..2818
E.121.3.9.2. libpq SSL (Secure Sockets Layer) support 2818
E.121.3.9.3. ecpg 2818
E.121.3.9.4. Server Programming Interface (SPI)..2819
E.121.3.10. Build Options 2819
E.121.3.11. Source Code 2820

E.121.3.12. Contrib 2821
E.122. Release 8.3.23 2822
    E.122.1. Migration to Version 8.3.23 2822
    E.122.2. Changes 2822
E.123. Release 8.3.22 2823
    E.123.1. Migration to Version 8.3.22 2823
    E.123.2. Changes 2823
E.124. Release 8.3.21 2825
    E.124.1. Migration to Version 8.3.21 2825
    E.124.2. Changes 2826
E.125. Release 8.3.20 2826
    E.125.1. Migration to Version 8.3.20 2826
    E.125.2. Changes 2826
E.126. Release 8.3.19 2828
    E.126.1. Migration to Version 8.3.19 2828
    E.126.2. Changes 2828
E.127. Release 8.3.18 2830
    E.127.1. Migration to Version 8.3.18 2830
    E.127.2. Changes 2830
E.128. Release 8.3.17 2832
    E.128.1. Migration to Version 8.3.17 2832
    E.128.2. Changes 2832
E.129. Release 8.3.16 2834
    E.129.1. Migration to Version 8.3.16 2834
    E.129.2. Changes 2834
E.130. Release 8.3.15 2836
    E.130.1. Migration to Version 8.3.15 2836
    E.130.2. Changes 2837
E.131. Release 8.3.14 2837
    E.131.1. Migration to Version 8.3.14 2838
    E.131.2. Changes 2838
E.132. Release 8.3.13 2839
    E.132.1. Migration to Version 8.3.13 2839
    E.132.2. Changes 2839
E.133. Release 8.3.12 2840
    E.133.1. Migration to Version 8.3.12 2841
    E.133.2. Changes 2841
E.134. Release 8.3.11 2843
    E.134.1. Migration to Version 8.3.11 2843
    E.134.2. Changes 2843
E.135. Release 8.3.10 2845
    E.135.1. Migration to Version 8.3.10 2845
    E.135.2. Changes 2845
E.136. Release 8.3.9 2847
    E.136.1. Migration to Version 8.3.9...2847
    E.136.2. Changes 2847
E.137. Release 8.3.8 2849
    E.137.1. Migration to Version 8.3.8...2850

E.137.2. Changes 2850
E.138. Release 8.3.7 2851
    E.138.1. Migration to Version 8.3.7..2852
    E.138.2. Changes 2852
E.139. Release 8.3.6 2853
    E.139.1. Migration to Version 8.3.6..2853
    E.139.2. Changes 2854
E.140. Release 8.3.5 2855
    E.140.1. Migration to Version 8.3.5..2855
    E.140.2. Changes 2856
E.141. Release 8.3.4 2857
    E.141.1. Migration to Version 8.3.4..2857
    E.141.2. Changes 2857
E.142. Release 8.3.3 2859
    E.142.1. Migration to Version 8.3.3..2860
    E.142.2. Changes 2860
E.143. Release 8.3.2 2860
    E.143.1. Migration to Version 8.3.2..2860
    E.143.2. Changes 2860
E.144. Release 8.3.1 2863
    E.144.1. Migration to Version 8.3.1..2863
    E.144.2. Changes 2863
E.145. Release 8.3 2865
    E.145.1. Overview 2865
    E.145.2. Migration to Version 8.3..2866
        E.145.2.1. General..2866
        E.145.2.2. Configuration Parameters...2868
        E.145.2.3. Character Encodings 2868
    E.145.3. Changes 2869
        E.145.3.1. Performance 2869
        E.145.3.2. Server 2870
        E.145.3.3. Monitoring 2871
        E.145.3.4. Authentication..2872
        E.145.3.5. Write-Ahead Log (WAL) and Continuous Archiving 2873
        E.145.3.6. Queries..2873
        E.145.3.7. Object Manipulation 2874
        E.145.3.8. Utility Commands...2875
        E.145.3.9. Data Types 2875
        E.145.3.10. Functions...2876
        E.145.3.11. PL/pgSQL Server-Side Language...............................2877
        E.145.3.12. Other Server-Side Languages 2877
        E.145.3.13. psql..2878
        E.145.3.14. pg_dump 2878
        E.145.3.15. Other Client Applications 2878
        E.145.3.16. libpq 2879
        E.145.3.17. ecpg...2879
        E.145.3.18. Windows Port...2879
        E.145.3.19. Server Programming Interface (SPI) 2880

E.145.3.20. Build Options 2880
E.145.3.21. Source Code 2880
E.145.3.22. Contrib 2881
E.146. Release 8.2.23 2882
E.146.1. Migration to Version 8.2.23 2882
E.146.2. Changes 2882
E.147. Release 8.2.22 2883
E.147.1. Migration to Version 8.2.22 2884
E.147.2. Changes 2884
E.148. Release 8.2.21 2885
E.148.1. Migration to Version 8.2.21 2886
E.148.2. Changes 2886
E.149. Release 8.2.20 2886
E.149.1. Migration to Version 8.2.20 2887
E.149.2. Changes 2887
E.150. Release 8.2.19 2888
E.150.1. Migration to Version 8.2.19 2888
E.150.2. Changes 2888
E.151. Release 8.2.18 2889
E.151.1. Migration to Version 8.2.18 2889
E.151.2. Changes 2890
E.152. Release 8.2.17 2891
E.152.1. Migration to Version 8.2.17 2892
E.152.2. Changes 2892
E.153. Release 8.2.16 2893
E.153.1. Migration to Version 8.2.16 2893
E.153.2. Changes 2893
E.154. Release 8.2.15 2895
E.154.1. Migration to Version 8.2.15 2895
E.154.2. Changes 2895
E.155. Release 8.2.14 2897
E.155.1. Migration to Version 8.2.14 2897
E.155.2. Changes 2897
E.156. Release 8.2.13 2898
E.156.1. Migration to Version 8.2.13 2898
E.156.2. Changes 2899
E.157. Release 8.2.12 2900
E.157.1. Migration to Version 8.2.12 2900
E.157.2. Changes 2900
E.158. Release 8.2.11 2901
E.158.1. Migration to Version 8.2.11 2901
E.158.2. Changes 2901
E.159. Release 8.2.10 2902
E.159.1. Migration to Version 8.2.10 2903
E.159.2. Changes 2903
E.160. Release 8.2.9 2904
E.160.1. Migration to Version 8.2.9 2904
E.160.2. Changes 2904

E.161. Release 8.2.8 2905
    E.161.1. Migration to Version 8.2.8 2905
    E.161.2. Changes 2905
E.162. Release 8.2.7 2906
    E.162.1. Migration to Version 8.2.7 2906
    E.162.2. Changes 2906
E.163. Release 8.2.6 2908
    E.163.1. Migration to Version 8.2.6 2908
    E.163.2. Changes 2908
E.164. Release 8.2.5 2910
    E.164.1. Migration to Version 8.2.5 2910
    E.164.2. Changes 2910
E.165. Release 8.2.4 2911
    E.165.1. Migration to Version 8.2.4 2912
    E.165.2. Changes 2912
E.166. Release 8.2.3 2912
    E.166.1. Migration to Version 8.2.3 2913
    E.166.2. Changes 2913
E.167. Release 8.2.2 2913
    E.167.1. Migration to Version 8.2.2 2913
    E.167.2. Changes 2913
E.168. Release 8.2.1 2914
    E.168.1. Migration to Version 8.2.1 2914
    E.168.2. Changes 2914
E.169. Release 8.2 2915
    E.169.1. Overview 2915
    E.169.2. Migration to Version 8.2 2916
    E.169.3. Changes 2918
        E.169.3.1. Performance Improvements 2918
        E.169.3.2. Server Changes 2919
        E.169.3.3. Query Changes..2920
        E.169.3.4. Object Manipulation Changes 2922
        E.169.3.5. Utility Command Changes..2923
        E.169.3.6. Date/Time Changes...2923
        E.169.3.7. Other Data Type and Function Changes 2924
        E.169.3.8. PL/pgSQL Server-Side Language Changes...................................2925
        E.169.3.9. PL/Perl Server-Side Language Changes 2925
        E.169.3.10. PL/Python Server-Side Language Changes 2925
        E.169.3.11. psql Changes 2925
        E.169.3.12. pg_dump Changes...2926
        E.169.3.13. libpq Changes 2926
        E.169.3.14. ecpg Changes 2927
        E.169.3.15. Windows Port...2927
        E.169.3.16. Source Code Changes 2927
        E.169.3.17. Contrib Changes 2928
E.170. Release 8.1.23 2930
    E.170.1. Migration to Version 8.1.23..2930
    E.170.2. Changes 2930

E.171. Release 8.1.22 2931
    E.171.1. Migration to Version 8.1.22...2931
    E.171.2. Changes 2932
E.172. Release 8.1.21 2933
    E.172.1. Migration to Version 8.1.21...2933
    E.172.2. Changes 2933
E.173. Release 8.1.20 2934
    E.173.1. Migration to Version 8.1.20...2934
    E.173.2. Changes 2935
E.174. Release 8.1.19 2936
    E.174.1. Migration to Version 8.1.19...2936
    E.174.2. Changes 2936
E.175. Release 8.1.18 2937
    E.175.1. Migration to Version 8.1.18...2937
    E.175.2. Changes 2937
E.176. Release 8.1.17 2938
    E.176.1. Migration to Version 8.1.17...2938
    E.176.2. Changes 2939
E.177. Release 8.1.16 2939
    E.177.1. Migration to Version 8.1.16...2940
    E.177.2. Changes 2940
E.178. Release 8.1.15 2940
    E.178.1. Migration to Version 8.1.15...2941
    E.178.2. Changes 2941
E.179. Release 8.1.14 2942
    E.179.1. Migration to Version 8.1.14...2942
    E.179.2. Changes 2942
E.180. Release 8.1.13 2943
    E.180.1. Migration to Version 8.1.13...2943
    E.180.2. Changes 2943
E.181. Release 8.1.12 2944
    E.181.1. Migration to Version 8.1.12...2944
    E.181.2. Changes 2944
E.182. Release 8.1.11 2945
    E.182.1. Migration to Version 8.1.11...2946
    E.182.2. Changes 2946
E.183. Release 8.1.10 2947
    E.183.1. Migration to Version 8.1.10...2948
    E.183.2. Changes 2948
E.184. Release 8.1.9 2948
    E.184.1. Migration to Version 8.1.9...2948
    E.184.2. Changes 2949
E.185. Release 8.1.8 2949
    E.185.1. Migration to Version 8.1.8...2949
    E.185.2. Changes 2949
E.186. Release 8.1.7 2949
    E.186.1. Migration to Version 8.1.7...2950
    E.186.2. Changes 2950

E.187. Release 8.1.6 2950
    E.187.1. Migration to Version 8.1.6...2950
    E.187.2. Changes 2951
E.188. Release 8.1.5 2951
    E.188.1. Migration to Version 8.1.5...2951
    E.188.2. Changes 2952
E.189. Release 8.1.4 2952
    E.189.1. Migration to Version 8.1.4...2953
    E.189.2. Changes 2953
E.190. Release 8.1.3 2954
    E.190.1. Migration to Version 8.1.3...2954
    E.190.2. Changes 2955
E.191. Release 8.1.2 2956
    E.191.1. Migration to Version 8.1.2...2956
    E.191.2. Changes 2956
E.192. Release 8.1.1 2957
    E.192.1. Migration to Version 8.1.1...2957
    E.192.2. Changes 2957
E.193. Release 8.1 2958
    E.193.1. Overview 2958
    E.193.2. Migration to Version 8.1...2960
    E.193.3. Additional Changes 2962
        E.193.3.1. Performance Improvements 2962
        E.193.3.2. Server Changes 2963
        E.193.3.3. Query Changes 2964
        E.193.3.4. Object Manipulation Changes 2965
        E.193.3.5. Utility Command Changes...2965
        E.193.3.6. Data Type and Function Changes 2966
        E.193.3.7. Encoding and Locale Changes 2968
        E.193.3.8. General Server-Side Language Changes...2968
        E.193.3.9. PL/pgSQL Server-Side Language Changes...................................2969
        E.193.3.10. PL/Perl Server-Side Language Changes 2969
        E.193.3.11. psql Changes 2970
        E.193.3.12. pg_dump Changes..2971
        E.193.3.13. libpq Changes 2971
        E.193.3.14. Source Code Changes 2971
        E.193.3.15. Contrib Changes 2972
E.194. Release 8.0.26 2973
    E.194.1. Migration to Version 8.0.26...2973
    E.194.2. Changes 2973
E.195. Release 8.0.25 2974
    E.195.1. Migration to Version 8.0.25...2975
    E.195.2. Changes 2975
E.196. Release 8.0.24 2976
    E.196.1. Migration to Version 8.0.24...2976
    E.196.2. Changes 2976
E.197. Release 8.0.23 2977
    E.197.1. Migration to Version 8.0.23...2977

E.197.2. Changes 2977
E.198. Release 8.0.22 2978
    E.198.1. Migration to Version 8.0.22 2979
    E.198.2. Changes 2979
E.199. Release 8.0.21 2980
    E.199.1. Migration to Version 8.0.21 2980
    E.199.2. Changes 2980
E.200. Release 8.0.20 2980
    E.200.1. Migration to Version 8.0.20 2981
    E.200.2. Changes 2981
E.201. Release 8.0.19 2981
    E.201.1. Migration to Version 8.0.19 2981
    E.201.2. Changes 2981
E.202. Release 8.0.18 2982
    E.202.1. Migration to Version 8.0.18 2982
    E.202.2. Changes 2982
E.203. Release 8.0.17 2983
    E.203.1. Migration to Version 8.0.17 2983
    E.203.2. Changes 2984
E.204. Release 8.0.16 2984
    E.204.1. Migration to Version 8.0.16 2984
    E.204.2. Changes 2984
E.205. Release 8.0.15 2985
    E.205.1. Migration to Version 8.0.15 2986
    E.205.2. Changes 2986
E.206. Release 8.0.14 2987
    E.206.1. Migration to Version 8.0.14 2987
    E.206.2. Changes 2987
E.207. Release 8.0.13 2988
    E.207.1. Migration to Version 8.0.13 2988
    E.207.2. Changes 2988
E.208. Release 8.0.12 2989
    E.208.1. Migration to Version 8.0.12 2989
    E.208.2. Changes 2989
E.209. Release 8.0.11 2989
    E.209.1. Migration to Version 8.0.11 2989
    E.209.2. Changes 2989
E.210. Release 8.0.10 2990
    E.210.1. Migration to Version 8.0.10 2990
    E.210.2. Changes 2990
E.211. Release 8.0.9 2991
    E.211.1. Migration to Version 8.0.9 2991
    E.211.2. Changes 2991
E.212. Release 8.0.8 2991
    E.212.1. Migration to Version 8.0.8 2992
    E.212.2. Changes 2992
E.213. Release 8.0.7 2993
    E.213.1. Migration to Version 8.0.7 2993

E.213.2. Changes 2993

E.214. Release 8.0.6 2994
    E.214.1. Migration to Version 8.0.6...2994
    E.214.2. Changes 2994

E.215. Release 8.0.5 2995
    E.215.1. Migration to Version 8.0.5...2995
    E.215.2. Changes 2995

E.216. Release 8.0.4 2996
    E.216.1. Migration to Version 8.0.4...2996
    E.216.2. Changes 2996

E.217. Release 8.0.3 2998
    E.217.1. Migration to Version 8.0.3...2998
    E.217.2. Changes 2998

E.218. Release 8.0.2 2999
    E.218.1. Migration to Version 8.0.2...2999
    E.218.2. Changes 3000

E.219. Release 8.0.1 3001
    E.219.1. Migration to Version 8.0.1...3001
    E.219.2. Changes 3002

E.220. Release 8.0 3002
    E.220.1. Overview 3002
    E.220.2. Migration to Version 8.0..3003
    E.220.3. Deprecated Features 3005
    E.220.4. Changes 3005
        E.220.4.1. Performance Improvements 3006
        E.220.4.2. Server Changes 3007
        E.220.4.3. Query Changes..3009
        E.220.4.4. Object Manipulation Changes 3010
        E.220.4.5. Utility Command Changes...3011
        E.220.4.6. Data Type and Function Changes 3012
        E.220.4.7. Server-Side Language Changes 3013
        E.220.4.8. psql Changes 3014
        E.220.4.9. pg_dump Changes..3015
        E.220.4.10. libpq Changes 3015
        E.220.4.11. Source Code Changes 3016
        E.220.4.12. Contrib Changes 3017

E.221. Release 7.4.30 3017
    E.221.1. Migration to Version 7.4.30...3018
    E.221.2. Changes 3018

E.222. Release 7.4.29 3019
    E.222.1. Migration to Version 7.4.29...3019
    E.222.2. Changes 3019

E.223. Release 7.4.28 3020
    E.223.1. Migration to Version 7.4.28...3020
    E.223.2. Changes 3020

E.224. Release 7.4.27 3021
    E.224.1. Migration to Version 7.4.27...3021
    E.224.2. Changes 3021

E.225. Release 7.4.26 3022
    E.225.1. Migration to Version 7.4.26..3022
    E.225.2. Changes 3022
E.226. Release 7.4.25 3023
    E.226.1. Migration to Version 7.4.25..3023
    E.226.2. Changes 3023
E.227. Release 7.4.24 3024
    E.227.1. Migration to Version 7.4.24..3024
    E.227.2. Changes 3024
E.228. Release 7.4.23 3024
    E.228.1. Migration to Version 7.4.23..3025
    E.228.2. Changes 3025
E.229. Release 7.4.22 3025
    E.229.1. Migration to Version 7.4.22..3025
    E.229.2. Changes 3026
E.230. Release 7.4.21 3026
    E.230.1. Migration to Version 7.4.21..3026
    E.230.2. Changes 3026
E.231. Release 7.4.20 3027
    E.231.1. Migration to Version 7.4.20..3027
    E.231.2. Changes 3027
E.232. Release 7.4.19 3028
    E.232.1. Migration to Version 7.4.19..3028
    E.232.2. Changes 3028
E.233. Release 7.4.18 3029
    E.233.1. Migration to Version 7.4.18..3029
    E.233.2. Changes 3029
E.234. Release 7.4.17 3030
    E.234.1. Migration to Version 7.4.17..3030
    E.234.2. Changes 3030
E.235. Release 7.4.16 3030
    E.235.1. Migration to Version 7.4.16..3031
    E.235.2. Changes 3031
E.236. Release 7.4.15 3031
    E.236.1. Migration to Version 7.4.15..3031
    E.236.2. Changes 3031
E.237. Release 7.4.14 3032
    E.237.1. Migration to Version 7.4.14..3032
    E.237.2. Changes 3032
E.238. Release 7.4.13 3032
    E.238.1. Migration to Version 7.4.13..3033
    E.238.2. Changes 3033
E.239. Release 7.4.12 3034
    E.239.1. Migration to Version 7.4.12..3034
    E.239.2. Changes 3034
E.240. Release 7.4.11 3035
    E.240.1. Migration to Version 7.4.11..3035
    E.240.2. Changes 3035

E.241. Release 7.4.10 3035
    E.241.1. Migration to Version 7.4.10...3036
    E.241.2. Changes 3036
E.242. Release 7.4.9 3036
    E.242.1. Migration to Version 7.4.9...3036
    E.242.2. Changes 3036
E.243. Release 7.4.8 3037
    E.243.1. Migration to Version 7.4.8...3037
    E.243.2. Changes 3039
E.244. Release 7.4.7 3040
    E.244.1. Migration to Version 7.4.7...3040
    E.244.2. Changes 3040
E.245. Release 7.4.6 3041
    E.245.1. Migration to Version 7.4.6...3041
    E.245.2. Changes 3041
E.246. Release 7.4.5 3042
    E.246.1. Migration to Version 7.4.5...3042
    E.246.2. Changes 3042
E.247. Release 7.4.4 3042
    E.247.1. Migration to Version 7.4.4...3042
    E.247.2. Changes 3042
E.248. Release 7.4.3 3043
    E.248.1. Migration to Version 7.4.3...3043
    E.248.2. Changes 3043
E.249. Release 7.4.2 3044
    E.249.1. Migration to Version 7.4.2...3044
    E.249.2. Changes 3045
E.250. Release 7.4.1 3046
    E.250.1. Migration to Version 7.4.1...3046
    E.250.2. Changes 3047
E.251. Release 7.4 3048
    E.251.1. Overview 3048
    E.251.2. Migration to Version 7.4..3050
    E.251.3. Changes 3051
        E.251.3.1. Server Operation Changes 3051
        E.251.3.2. Performance Improvements 3052
        E.251.3.3. Server Configuration Changes 3053
        E.251.3.4. Query Changes...3054
        E.251.3.5. Object Manipulation Changes 3055
        E.251.3.6. Utility Command Changes...3056
        E.251.3.7. Data Type and Function Changes 3057
        E.251.3.8. Server-Side Language Changes 3059
        E.251.3.9. psql Changes 3059
        E.251.3.10. pg_dump Changes..3060
        E.251.3.11. libpq Changes 3060
        E.251.3.12. JDBC Changes...3061
        E.251.3.13. Miscellaneous Interface Changes 3061
        E.251.3.14. Source Code Changes 3062

E.251.3.15. Contrib Changes 3062
E.252. Release 7.3.21 3063
    E.252.1. Migration to Version 7.3.21 3063
    E.252.2. Changes 3064
E.253. Release 7.3.20 3064
    E.253.1. Migration to Version 7.3.20 3064
    E.253.2. Changes 3065
E.254. Release 7.3.19 3065
    E.254.1. Migration to Version 7.3.19 3065
    E.254.2. Changes 3065
E.255. Release 7.3.18 3065
    E.255.1. Migration to Version 7.3.18 3066
    E.255.2. Changes 3066
E.256. Release 7.3.17 3066
    E.256.1. Migration to Version 7.3.17 3066
    E.256.2. Changes 3066
E.257. Release 7.3.16 3067
    E.257.1. Migration to Version 7.3.16 3067
    E.257.2. Changes 3067
E.258. Release 7.3.15 3067
    E.258.1. Migration to Version 7.3.15 3067
    E.258.2. Changes 3068
E.259. Release 7.3.14 3068
    E.259.1. Migration to Version 7.3.14 3069
    E.259.2. Changes 3069
E.260. Release 7.3.13 3069
    E.260.1. Migration to Version 7.3.13 3069
    E.260.2. Changes 3069
E.261. Release 7.3.12 3070
    E.261.1. Migration to Version 7.3.12 3070
    E.261.2. Changes 3070
E.262. Release 7.3.11 3071
    E.262.1. Migration to Version 7.3.11 3071
    E.262.2. Changes 3071
E.263. Release 7.3.10 3071
    E.263.1. Migration to Version 7.3.10 3072
    E.263.2. Changes 3072
E.264. Release 7.3.9 3073
    E.264.1. Migration to Version 7.3.9 3073
    E.264.2. Changes 3073
E.265. Release 7.3.8 3074
    E.265.1. Migration to Version 7.3.8 3074
    E.265.2. Changes 3074
E.266. Release 7.3.7 3075
    E.266.1. Migration to Version 7.3.7 3075
    E.266.2. Changes 3075
E.267. Release 7.3.6 3075
    E.267.1. Migration to Version 7.3.6 3075

E.267.2. Changes 3076
E.268. Release 7.3.5 3076
    E.268.1. Migration to Version 7.3.5..3076
    E.268.2. Changes 3076
E.269. Release 7.3.4 3077
    E.269.1. Migration to Version 7.3.4..3077
    E.269.2. Changes 3077
E.270. Release 7.3.3 3078
    E.270.1. Migration to Version 7.3.3..3078
    E.270.2. Changes 3078
E.271. Release 7.3.2 3080
    E.271.1. Migration to Version 7.3.2..3080
    E.271.2. Changes 3081
E.272. Release 7.3.1 3082
    E.272.1. Migration to Version 7.3.1..3082
    E.272.2. Changes 3082
E.273. Release 7.3 3082
    E.273.1. Overview 3083
    E.273.2. Migration to Version 7.3..3083
    E.273.3. Changes 3084
        E.273.3.1. Server Operation 3084
        E.273.3.2. Performance 3084
        E.273.3.3. Privileges..3085
        E.273.3.4. Server Configuration 3085
        E.273.3.5. Queries 3086
        E.273.3.6. Object Manipulation 3087
        E.273.3.7. Utility Commands..3088
        E.273.3.8. Data Types and Functions 3089
        E.273.3.9. Internationalization 3090
        E.273.3.10. Server-side Languages 3090
        E.273.3.11. psql...3091
        E.273.3.12. libpq 3091
        E.273.3.13. JDBC...3091
        E.273.3.14. Miscellaneous Interfaces..3092
        E.273.3.15. Source Code 3092
        E.273.3.16. Contrib 3094
E.274. Release 7.2.8 3094
    E.274.1. Migration to Version 7.2.8..3095
    E.274.2. Changes 3095
E.275. Release 7.2.7 3095
    E.275.1. Migration to Version 7.2.7..3095
    E.275.2. Changes 3095
E.276. Release 7.2.6 3096
    E.276.1. Migration to Version 7.2.6..3096
    E.276.2. Changes 3096
E.277. Release 7.2.5 3097
    E.277.1. Migration to Version 7.2.5..3097
    E.277.2. Changes 3097

E.278. Release 7.2.4 3097

    E.278.1. Migration to Version 7.2.4...3097

    E.278.2. Changes 3098

E.279. Release 7.2.3 3098

    E.279.1. Migration to Version 7.2.3...3098

    E.279.2. Changes 3098

E.280. Release 7.2.2 3098

    E.280.1. Migration to Version 7.2.2...3099

    E.280.2. Changes 3099

E.281. Release 7.2.1 3099

    E.281.1. Migration to Version 7.2.1...3099

    E.281.2. Changes 3100

E.282. Release 7.2 3100

    E.282.1. Overview 3100

    E.282.2. Migration to Version 7.2...3101

    E.282.3. Changes 3102

        E.282.3.1. Server Operation 3102

        E.282.3.2. Performance 3102

        E.282.3.3. Privileges..3103

        E.282.3.4. Client Authentication 3103

        E.282.3.5. Server Configuration 3103

        E.282.3.6. Queries 3103

        E.282.3.7. Schema Manipulation 3104

        E.282.3.8. Utility Commands...3104

        E.282.3.9. Data Types and Functions 3105

        E.282.3.10. Internationalization 3106

        E.282.3.11. PL/pgSQL 3106

        E.282.3.12. PL/Perl 3107

        E.282.3.13. PL/Tcl 3107

        E.282.3.14. PL/Python 3107

        E.282.3.15. psql...3107

        E.282.3.16. libpq 3107

        E.282.3.17. JDBC...3108

        E.282.3.18. ODBC 3109

        E.282.3.19. ECPG 3109

        E.282.3.20. Misc. Interfaces..3109

        E.282.3.21. Build and Install...3110

        E.282.3.22. Source Code 3110

        E.282.3.23. Contrib 3110

E.283. Release 7.1.3 3111

    E.283.1. Migration to Version 7.1.3...3111

    E.283.2. Changes 3111

E.284. Release 7.1.2 3111

    E.284.1. Migration to Version 7.1.2...3112

    E.284.2. Changes 3112

E.285. Release 7.1.1 3112

    E.285.1. Migration to Version 7.1.1...3112

    E.285.2. Changes 3112

E.286. Release 7.1 3113
    E.286.1. Migration to Version 7.1...3113
    E.286.2. Changes 3113
E.287. Release 7.0.3 3117
    E.287.1. Migration to Version 7.0.3..3117
    E.287.2. Changes 3117
E.288. Release 7.0.2 3118
    E.288.1. Migration to Version 7.0.2..3119
    E.288.2. Changes 3119
E.289. Release 7.0.1 3119
    E.289.1. Migration to Version 7.0.1..3119
    E.289.2. Changes 3119
E.290. Release 7.0 3120
    E.290.1. Migration to Version 7.0...3120
    E.290.2. Changes 3121
E.291. Release 6.5.3 3127
    E.291.1. Migration to Version 6.5.3..3127
    E.291.2. Changes 3127
E.292. Release 6.5.2 3127
    E.292.1. Migration to Version 6.5.2..3128
    E.292.2. Changes 3128
E.293. Release 6.5.1 3128
    E.293.1. Migration to Version 6.5.1..3129
    E.293.2. Changes 3129
E.294. Release 6.5 3129
    E.294.1. Migration to Version 6.5...3130
        E.294.1.1. Multiversion Concurrency Control 3131
    E.294.2. Changes 3131
E.295. Release 6.4.2 3134
    E.295.1. Migration to Version 6.4.2..3135
    E.295.2. Changes 3135
E.296. Release 6.4.1 3135
    E.296.1. Migration to Version 6.4.1..3135
    E.296.2. Changes 3135
E.297. Release 6.4 3136
    E.297.1. Migration to Version 6.4...3137
    E.297.2. Changes 3137
E.298. Release 6.3.2 3141
    E.298.1. Changes 3141
E.299. Release 6.3.1 3142
    E.299.1. Changes 3142
E.300. Release 6.3 3143
    E.300.1. Migration to Version 6.3...3144
    E.300.2. Changes 3144
E.301. Release 6.2.1 3147
    E.301.1. Migration from version 6.2 to version 6.2.1 3148
    E.301.2. Changes 3148
E.302. Release 6.2 3149

E.302.1. Migration from version 6.1 to version 6.2...3149

E.302.2. Migration from version 1.x to version 6.2 3149

E.302.3. Changes 3149

E.303. Release 6.1.1 3151

E.303.1. Migration from version 6.1 to version 6.1.1...3151

E.303.2. Changes 3151

E.304. Release 6.1 3152

E.304.1. Migration to Version 6.1 3152

E.304.2. Changes 3153

E.305. Release 6.0 3155

E.305.1. Migration from version 1.09 to version 6.0...3155

E.305.2. Migration from pre-1.09 to version 6.0 3155

E.305.3. Changes 3155

E.306. Release 1.09 3157

E.307. Release 1.02 3157

E.307.1. Migration from version 1.02 to version 1.02.1.......................................3157

E.307.2. Dump/Reload Procedure 3158

E.307.3. Changes 3158

E.308. Release 1.01 3159

E.308.1. Migration from version 1.0 to version 1.01 3159

E.308.2. Changes 3161

E.309. Release 1.0 3162

E.309.1. Changes 3162

E.310. Postgres95 Release 0.03 3163

E.310.1. Changes 3163

E.311. Postgres95 Release 0.02 3165

E.311.1. Changes 3165

E.312. Postgres95 Release 0.01 3166

F. Additional Supplied Modules 3167

F.1. adminpack...3168

F.2. auth_delay...3169

F.2.1. Configuration Parameters...3169

F.2.2. Author 3169

F.3. auto_explain..3169

F.3.1. Configuration Parameters...3170

F.3.2. Example 3171

F.3.3. Author 3172

F.4. bloom 3172

F.4.1. Parameters 3172

F.4.2. Examples 3173

F.4.3. Operator Class Interface 3175

F.4.4. Limitations 3175

F.4.5. Authors 3175

F.5. btree_gin 3175

F.5.1. Example Usage 3176

F.5.2. Authors 3176

F.6. btree_gist 3176

F.6.1. Example Usage 3176

F.6.2. Authors 3177
F.7. chkpass 3177
F.7.1. Author 3178
F.8. citext 3178
F.8.1. Rationale 3178
F.8.2. How to Use It 3179
F.8.3. String Comparison Behavior 3179
F.8.4. Limitations 3180
F.8.5. Author 3181
F.9. cube 3181
F.9.1. Syntax 3181
F.9.2. Precision 3181
F.9.3. Usage 3182
F.9.4. Defaults 3186
F.9.5. Notes 3187
F.9.6. Credits 3187
F.10. dblink 3187
dblink_connect 3188
dblink_connect_u 3191
dblink_disconnect 3192
dblink 3193
dblink_exec 3196
dblink_open 3198
dblink_fetch 3200
dblink_close 3202
dblink_get_connections 3204
dblink_error_message 3205
dblink_send_query 3206
dblink_is_busy 3207
dblink_get_notify 3208
dblink_get_result 3210
dblink_cancel_query 3213
dblink_get_pkey 3214
dblink_build_sql_insert 3216
dblink_build_sql_delete 3218
dblink_build_sql_update 3220
F.11. dict_int 3222
F.11.1. Configuration 3222
F.11.2. Usage 3222
F.12. dict_xsyn 3222
F.12.1. Configuration 3223
F.12.2. Usage 3223
F.13. earthdistance 3224
F.13.1. Cube-based Earth Distances 3224
F.13.2. Point-based Earth Distances 3226
F.14. file_fdw 3226
F.15. fuzzystrmatch 3228
F.15.1. Soundex 3229

F.15.2. Levenshtein 3229
F.15.3. Metaphone 3230
F.15.4. Double Metaphone 3231
F.16. hstore 3231
F.16.1. hstore External Representation 3231
F.16.2. hstore Operators and Functions 3232
F.16.3. Indexes 3236
F.16.4. Examples 3236
F.16.5. Statistics 3237
F.16.6. Compatibility 3238
F.16.7. Transforms 3238
F.16.8. Authors 3239
F.17. intagg 3239
F.17.1. Functions 3239
F.17.2. Sample Uses 3239
F.18. intarray 3240
F.18.1. intarray Functions and Operators 3240
F.18.2. Index Support 3242
F.18.3. Example 3242
F.18.4. Benchmark 3243
F.18.5. Authors 3243
F.19. isn 3243
F.19.1. Data Types 3243
F.19.2. Casts 3244
F.19.3. Functions and Operators 3245
F.19.4. Examples 3246
F.19.5. Bibliography 3247
F.19.6. Author 3247
F.20. lo 3247
F.20.1. Rationale 3247
F.20.2. How to Use It 3248
F.20.3. Limitations 3248
F.20.4. Author 3248
F.21. ltree 3249
F.21.1. Definitions 3249
F.21.2. Operators and Functions 3250
F.21.3. Indexes 3253
F.21.4. Example 3253
F.21.5. Transforms 3255
F.21.6. Authors 3256
F.22. pageinspect 3256
F.22.1. Functions 3256
F.23. passwordcheck 3260
F.24. pg_buffercache 3260
F.24.1. The pg_buffercache View 3261
F.24.2. Sample Output 3262
F.24.3. Authors 3262
F.25. pgcrypto 3262

F.25.1. General Hashing Functions 3262
    F.25.1.1. `digest()` 3262
    F.25.1.2. `hmac()` 3263
F.25.2. Password Hashing Functions 3263
    F.25.2.1. `crypt()` 3264
    F.25.2.2. `gen_salt()` 3264
F.25.3. PGP Encryption Functions..3265
    F.25.3.1. `pgp_sym_encrypt()` 3266
    F.25.3.2. `pgp_sym_decrypt()` 3266
    F.25.3.3. `pgp_pub_encrypt()` 3267
    F.25.3.4. `pgp_pub_decrypt()` 3267
    F.25.3.5. `pgp_key_id()` 3267
    F.25.3.6. `armor()`, `dearmor()` 3267
    F.25.3.7. `pgp_armor_headers` 3268
    F.25.3.8. Options for PGP Functions..3268
        F.25.3.8.1. cipher-algo 3268
        F.25.3.8.2. compress-algo 3268
        F.25.3.8.3. compress-level 3269
        F.25.3.8.4. convert-crlf 3269
        F.25.3.8.5. disable-mdc 3269
        F.25.3.8.6. sess-key 3269
        F.25.3.8.7. s2k-mode 3269
        F.25.3.8.8. s2k-count 3270
        F.25.3.8.9. s2k-digest-algo 3270
        F.25.3.8.10. s2k-cipher-algo 3270
        F.25.3.8.11. unicode-mode...3270
    F.25.3.9. Generating PGP Keys with GnuPG................................3270
    F.25.3.10. Limitations of PGP Code 3271
F.25.4. Raw Encryption Functions...3271
F.25.5. Random-Data Functions 3272
F.25.6. Notes 3273
    F.25.6.1. Configuration..3273
    F.25.6.2. NULL Handling 3273
    F.25.6.3. Security Limitations 3274
    F.25.6.4. Useful Reading 3274
    F.25.6.5. Technical References...3274
F.25.7. Author 3275
F.26. pg_freespacemap 3275
F.26.1. Functions...3275
F.26.2. Sample Output 3276
F.26.3. Author 3276
F.27. pg_prewarm 3277
F.27.1. Functions...3277
F.27.2. Author 3277
F.28. pgrowlocks...3277
F.28.1. Overview..3277
F.28.2. Sample Output 3278
F.28.3. Author 3279

F.29. pg_stat_statements 3279
    F.29.1. The `pg_stat_statements` View 3279
    F.29.2. Functions 3282
    F.29.3. Configuration Parameters...3282
    F.29.4. Sample Output 3283
    F.29.5. Authors 3284
F.30. pgstattuple..3284
    F.30.1. Functions 3284
    F.30.2. Authors 3288
F.31. pg_trgm 3288
    F.31.1. Trigram (or Trigraph) Concepts 3288
    F.31.2. Functions and Operators 3288
    F.31.3. GUC Parameters 3290
    F.31.4. Index Support...3290
    F.31.5. Text Search Integration 3292
    F.31.6. References 3292
    F.31.7. Authors 3293
F.32. pg_visibility 3293
    F.32.1. Functions 3293
    F.32.2. Author 3294
F.33. postgres_fdw 3294
    F.33.1. FDW Options of postgres_fdw 3295
        F.33.1.1. Connection Options..3295
        F.33.1.2. Object Name Options 3296
        F.33.1.3. Cost Estimation Options...3296
        F.33.1.4. Remote Execution Options...3297
        F.33.1.5. Updatability Options 3297
        F.33.1.6. Importing Options 3297
    F.33.2. Connection Management 3298
    F.33.3. Transaction Management 3298
    F.33.4. Remote Query Optimization 3299
    F.33.5. Remote Query Execution Environment 3299
    F.33.6. Cross-Version Compatibility..3300
    F.33.7. Examples 3300
    F.33.8. Author 3301
F.34. seg...3301
    F.34.1. Rationale 3301
    F.34.2. Syntax 3302
    F.34.3. Precision...3303
    F.34.4. Usage..3303
    F.34.5. Notes 3304
    F.34.6. Credits 3304
F.35. sepgsql 3304
    F.35.1. Overview 3305
    F.35.2. Installation..3305
    F.35.3. Regression Tests..3306
    F.35.4. GUC Parameters 3307
    F.35.5. Features 3307

F.35.5.1. Controlled Object Classes 3308
F.35.5.2. DML Permissions...3308
F.35.5.3. DDL Permissions 3309
F.35.5.4. Trusted Procedures 3309
F.35.5.5. Dynamic Domain Transitions...3310
F.35.5.6. Miscellaneous 3311
F.35.6. Sepgsql Functions 3311
F.35.7. Limitations 3312
F.35.8. External Resources...3312
F.35.9. Author 3313
F.36. spi...3313
F.36.1. refint — Functions for Implementing Referential Integrity......................3313
F.36.2. timetravel — Functions for Implementing Time Travel 3313
F.36.3. autoinc — Functions for Autoincrementing Fields 3314
F.36.4. insert_username — Functions for Tracking Who Changed a Table 3315
F.36.5. moddatetime — Functions for Tracking Last Modification Time 3315
F.37. sslinfo...3315
F.37.1. Functions Provided 3315
F.37.2. Author 3317
F.38. tablefunc 3317
F.38.1. Functions Provided 3317
F.38.1.1. normal_rand 3318
F.38.1.2. crosstab(text) 3319
F.38.1.3. crosstabN(text) 3321
F.38.1.4. crosstab(text, text) 3322
F.38.1.5. connectby...3325
F.38.2. Author 3327
F.39. tcn 3328
F.40. test_decoding 3328
F.41. tsearch2 3329
F.41.1. Portability Issues...3329
F.41.2. Converting a pre-8.3 Installation..3330
F.41.3. References..3330
F.42. tsm_system_rows 3331
F.42.1. Examples 3331
F.43. tsm_system_time 3331
F.43.1. Examples 3332
F.44. unaccent 3332
F.44.1. Configuration 3332
F.44.2. Usage...3333
F.44.3. Functions 3334
F.45. uuid-ossp..3334
F.45.1. uuid-ossp Functions 3334
F.45.2. Building uuid-ossp 3336
F.45.3. Author 3336
F.46. xml2...3336
F.46.1. Deprecation Notice 3336
F.46.2. Description of Functions...3337

F.46.3. `xpath_table` 3338

    F.46.3.1. Multivalued Results 3339

F.46.4. XSLT Functions 3340

    F.46.4.1. `xslt_process` 3341

F.46.5. Author 3341

G. Additional Supplied Programs 3342

  G.1. Client Applications 3342

    oid2name 3342

    vacuumlo 3347

  G.2. Server Applications 3349

    pg_standby 3349

H. External Projects 3353

  H.1. Client Interfaces 3353

  H.2. Administration Tools 3353

  H.3. Procedural Languages 3354

  H.4. Extensions 3354

I. The Source Code Repository 3355

  I.1. Getting The Source via Git 3355

J. Documentation 3356

  J.1. DocBook 3356

  J.2. Tool Sets 3356

    J.2.1. Installation on Fedora, RHEL, and Derivatives....................................3357

    J.2.2. Installation on FreeBSD 3358

    J.2.3. Debian Packages..3358

    J.2.4. OS X 3358

    J.2.5. Manual Installation from Source 3358

      J.2.5.1. Installing OpenJade 3359

      J.2.5.2. Installing the DocBook DTD Kit..3359

      J.2.5.3. Installing the DocBook DSSSL Style Sheets 3360

      J.2.5.4. Installing JadeTeX 3360

    J.2.6. Detection by `configure` 3361

  J.3. Building The Documentation..3361

    J.3.1. HTML..3361

    J.3.2. Manpages..3362

    J.3.3. Print Output via JadeTeX 3362

    J.3.4. Overflow Text 3363

    J.3.5. Print Output via RTF 3363

    J.3.6. Plain Text Files 3365

    J.3.7. Syntax Check..3365

  J.4. Documentation Authoring 3365

    J.4.1. Emacs/PSGML..3365

    J.4.2. Other Emacs Modes 3366

  J.5. Style Guide..3366

    J.5.1. Reference Pages 3367

K. Acronyms 3369

Bibliography **3375**

Index..**3377**

II. PostgreSQL Client Applications

This part contains reference information for PostgreSQL client applications and utilities. Not all of these commands are of general utility; some might require special privileges. The common feature of these applications is that they can be run on any host, independent of where the database server resides.

When specified on the command line, user and database names have their case preserved — the presence of spaces or special characters might require quoting. Table names and other identifiers do not have their case preserved, except where documented, and might require quoting.

clusterdb

Name

clusterdb — cluster a PostgreSQL database

Synopsis

clusterdb [*connection-option*...] [--verbose | -v] [--table | -t *table*] ... [*dbname*]

clusterdb [*connection-option*...] [--verbose | -v] --all | -a

Description

clusterdb is a utility for reclustering tables in a PostgreSQL database. It finds tables that have previously been clustered, and clusters them again on the same index that was last used. Tables that have never been clustered are not affected.

clusterdb is a wrapper around the SQL command CLUSTER. There is no effective difference between clustering databases via this utility and via other methods for accessing the server.

Options

clusterdb accepts the following command-line arguments:

-a
--all

> Cluster all databases.

[-d] *dbname*
[--dbname=]*dbname*

> Specifies the name of the database to be clustered. If this is not specified and -a (or --all) is not used, the database name is read from the environment variable PGDATABASE. If that is not set, the user name specified for the connection is used.

-e
--echo

> Echo the commands that clusterdb generates and sends to the server.

`-q`
`--quiet`

Do not display progress messages.

`-t` *table*
`--table=`*table*

Cluster *table* only. Multiple tables can be clustered by writing multiple `-t` switches.

`-v`
`--verbose`

Print detailed information during processing.

`-V`
`--version`

Print the clusterdb version and exit.

`-?`
`--help`

Show help about clusterdb command line arguments, and exit.

clusterdb also accepts the following command-line arguments for connection parameters:

`-h` *host*
`--host=`*host*

Specifies the host name of the machine on which the server is running. If the value begins with a slash, it is used as the directory for the Unix domain socket.

`-p` *port*
`--port=`*port*

Specifies the TCP port or local Unix domain socket file extension on which the server is listening for connections.

`-U` *username*
`--username=`*username*

User name to connect as.

`-w`
`--no-password`

Never issue a password prompt. If the server requires password authentication and a password is not available by other means such as a `.pgpass` file, the connection attempt will fail. This option can be useful in batch jobs and scripts where no user is present to enter a password.

`-W`
`--password`

Force clusterdb to prompt for a password before connecting to a database.

This option is never essential, since clusterdb will automatically prompt for a password if the server demands password authentication. However, clusterdb will waste a connection attempt finding out that the server wants a password. In some cases it is worth typing `-W` to avoid the extra connection attempt.

`--maintenance-db=`*dbname*

> Specifies the name of the database to connect to discover what other databases should be clustered. If not specified, the `postgres` database will be used, and if that does not exist, `template1` will be used.

Environment

`PGDATABASE`
`PGHOST`
`PGPORT`
`PGUSER`

> Default connection parameters

This utility, like most other PostgreSQL utilities, also uses the environment variables supported by libpq (see Section 32.14).

Diagnostics

In case of difficulty, see CLUSTER and psql for discussions of potential problems and error messages. The database server must be running at the targeted host. Also, any default connection settings and environment variables used by the libpq front-end library will apply.

Examples

To cluster the database `test`:

```
$ clusterdb test
```

To cluster a single table `foo` in a database named `xyzzy`:

```
$ clusterdb --table foo xyzzy
```

See Also

CLUSTER

createdb

Name

createdb — create a new PostgreSQL database

Synopsis

createdb [*connection-option*...] [*option*...] [*dbname* [*description*]]

Description

createdb creates a new PostgreSQL database.

Normally, the database user who executes this command becomes the owner of the new database. However, a different owner can be specified via the -o option, if the executing user has appropriate privileges.

createdb is a wrapper around the SQL command CREATE DATABASE. There is no effective difference between creating databases via this utility and via other methods for accessing the server.

Options

createdb accepts the following command-line arguments:

dbname

Specifies the name of the database to be created. The name must be unique among all PostgreSQL databases in this cluster. The default is to create a database with the same name as the current system user.

description

Specifies a comment to be associated with the newly created database.

-D *tablespace*
--tablespace=*tablespace*

Specifies the default tablespace for the database. (This name is processed as a double-quoted identifier.)

-e
--echo

Echo the commands that createdb generates and sends to the server.

-E *encoding*
--encoding=*encoding*

Specifies the character encoding scheme to be used in this database. The character sets supported by the PostgreSQL server are described in Section 23.3.1.

```
-l locale
--locale=locale
```

Specifies the locale to be used in this database. This is equivalent to specifying both `--lc-collate` and `--lc-ctype`.

```
--lc-collate=locale
```

Specifies the LC_COLLATE setting to be used in this database.

```
--lc-ctype=locale
```

Specifies the LC_CTYPE setting to be used in this database.

```
-O owner
--owner=owner
```

Specifies the database user who will own the new database. (This name is processed as a double-quoted identifier.)

```
-T template
--template=template
```

Specifies the template database from which to build this database. (This name is processed as a double-quoted identifier.)

```
-V
--version
```

Print the createdb version and exit.

```
-?
--help
```

Show help about createdb command line arguments, and exit.

The options `-D`, `-l`, `-E`, `-O`, and `-T` correspond to options of the underlying SQL command CREATE DATABASE; see there for more information about them.

createdb also accepts the following command-line arguments for connection parameters:

```
-h host
--host=host
```

Specifies the host name of the machine on which the server is running. If the value begins with a slash, it is used as the directory for the Unix domain socket.

```
-p port
--port=port
```

Specifies the TCP port or the local Unix domain socket file extension on which the server is listening for connections.

```
-U username
--username=username
```

User name to connect as.

-w

--no-password

> Never issue a password prompt. If the server requires password authentication and a password is not available by other means such as a .pgpass file, the connection attempt will fail. This option can be useful in batch jobs and scripts where no user is present to enter a password.

-W

--password

> Force createdb to prompt for a password before connecting to a database.

> This option is never essential, since createdb will automatically prompt for a password if the server demands password authentication. However, createdb will waste a connection attempt finding out that the server wants a password. In some cases it is worth typing -W to avoid the extra connection attempt.

--maintenance-db=*dbname*

> Specifies the name of the database to connect to when creating the new database. If not specified, the postgres database will be used; if that does not exist (or if it is the name of the new database being created), template1 will be used.

Environment

PGDATABASE

> If set, the name of the database to create, unless overridden on the command line.

PGHOST
PGPORT
PGUSER

> Default connection parameters. PGUSER also determines the name of the database to create, if it is not specified on the command line or by PGDATABASE.

This utility, like most other PostgreSQL utilities, also uses the environment variables supported by libpq (see Section 32.14).

Diagnostics

In case of difficulty, see CREATE DATABASE and psql for discussions of potential problems and error messages. The database server must be running at the targeted host. Also, any default connection settings and environment variables used by the libpq front-end library will apply.

Examples

To create the database demo using the default database server:

```
$ createdb demo
```

To create the database demo using the server on host eden, port 5000, using the LATIN1 encoding scheme with a look at the underlying command:

```
$ createdb -p 5000 -h eden -E LATIN1 -e demo
CREATE DATABASE demo ENCODING 'LATIN1';
```

See Also

dropdb, CREATE DATABASE

createlang

Name

`createlang` — install a PostgreSQL procedural language

Synopsis

`createlang` [`connection-option`...] `langname` [`dbname`]

`createlang` [`connection-option`...] `--list` | `-l` [`dbname`]

Description

createlang is a utility for adding a procedural language to a PostgreSQL database.

createlang is just a wrapper around the CREATE EXTENSION SQL command.

> ### Caution
>
> createlang is deprecated and may be removed in a future PostgreSQL release. Direct use of the `CREATE EXTENSION` command is recommended instead.

Options

createlang accepts the following command-line arguments:

`langname`

> Specifies the name of the procedural language to be installed. (This name is lower-cased.)

[`-d`] `dbname`
[`--dbname=`] `dbname`

> Specifies the database to which the language should be added. The default is to use the database with the same name as the current system user.

`-e`
`--echo`

> Display SQL commands as they are executed.

`-l`
`--list`

> Show a list of already installed languages in the target database.

```
-V
--version
```

Print the createlang version and exit.

```
-?
--help
```

Show help about createlang command line arguments, and exit.

createlang also accepts the following command-line arguments for connection parameters:

```
-h host
--host=host
```

Specifies the host name of the machine on which the server is running. If the value begins with a slash, it is used as the directory for the Unix domain socket.

```
-p port
--port=port
```

Specifies the TCP port or local Unix domain socket file extension on which the server is listening for connections.

```
-U username
--username=username
```

User name to connect as.

```
-w
--no-password
```

Never issue a password prompt. If the server requires password authentication and a password is not available by other means such as a .pgpass file, the connection attempt will fail. This option can be useful in batch jobs and scripts where no user is present to enter a password.

```
-W
--password
```

Force createlang to prompt for a password before connecting to a database.

This option is never essential, since createlang will automatically prompt for a password if the server demands password authentication. However, createlang will waste a connection attempt finding out that the server wants a password. In some cases it is worth typing -W to avoid the extra connection attempt.

Environment

PGDATABASE
PGHOST
PGPORT
PGUSER

Default connection parameters

This utility, like most other PostgreSQL utilities, also uses the environment variables supported by libpq (see Section 32.14).

Diagnostics

Most error messages are self-explanatory. If not, run createlang with the --echo option and see the respective SQL command for details. Also, any default connection settings and environment variables used by the libpq front-end library will apply.

Notes

Use droplang to remove a language.

Examples

To install the language pltcl into the database template1:

```
$ createlang pltcl template1
```

Note that installing the language into template1 will cause it to be automatically installed into subsequently-created databases as well.

See Also

droplang, CREATE EXTENSION, CREATE LANGUAGE

createuser

Name

createuser — define a new PostgreSQL user account

Synopsis

createuser [*connection-option*...] [*option*...] [*username*]

Description

createuser creates a new PostgreSQL user (or more precisely, a role). Only superusers and users with CREATEROLE privilege can create new users, so createuser must be invoked by someone who can connect as a superuser or a user with CREATEROLE privilege.

If you wish to create a new superuser, you must connect as a superuser, not merely with CREATEROLE privilege. Being a superuser implies the ability to bypass all access permission checks within the database, so superuserdom should not be granted lightly.

createuser is a wrapper around the SQL command CREATE ROLE. There is no effective difference between creating users via this utility and via other methods for accessing the server.

Options

createuser accepts the following command-line arguments:

username

> Specifies the name of the PostgreSQL user to be created. This name must be different from all existing roles in this PostgreSQL installation.

-c *number*
--connection-limit=*number*

> Set a maximum number of connections for the new user. The default is to set no limit.

-d
--createdb

> The new user will be allowed to create databases.

-D
--no-createdb

> The new user will not be allowed to create databases. This is the default.

`-e`
`--echo`

> Echo the commands that createuser generates and sends to the server.

`-E`
`--encrypted`

> Encrypts the user's password stored in the database. If not specified, the default password behavior is used.

`-g` *role*
`--role=`*role*

> Indicates role to which this role will be added immediately as a new member. Multiple roles to which this role will be added as a member can be specified by writing multiple `-g` switches.

`-i`
`--inherit`

> The new role will automatically inherit privileges of roles it is a member of. This is the default.

`-I`
`--no-inherit`

> The new role will not automatically inherit privileges of roles it is a member of.

`--interactive`

> Prompt for the user name if none is specified on the command line, and also prompt for whichever of the options `-d`/`-D`, `-r`/`-R`, `-s`/`-S` is not specified on the command line. (This was the default behavior up to PostgreSQL 9.1.)

`-l`
`--login`

> The new user will be allowed to log in (that is, the user name can be used as the initial session user identifier). This is the default.

`-L`
`--no-login`

> The new user will not be allowed to log in. (A role without login privilege is still useful as a means of managing database permissions.)

`-N`
`--unencrypted`

> Does not encrypt the user's password stored in the database. If not specified, the default password behavior is used.

`-P`
`--pwprompt`

> If given, createuser will issue a prompt for the password of the new user. This is not necessary if you do not plan on using password authentication.

`-r`
`--createrole`

> The new user will be allowed to create new roles (that is, this user will have CREATEROLE privilege).

```
-R
--no-createrole
```

The new user will not be allowed to create new roles. This is the default.

```
-s
--superuser
```

The new user will be a superuser.

```
-S
--no-superuser
```

The new user will not be a superuser. This is the default.

```
-V
--version
```

Print the createuser version and exit.

```
--replication
```

The new user will have the REPLICATION privilege, which is described more fully in the documentation for CREATE ROLE.

```
--no-replication
```

The new user will not have the REPLICATION privilege, which is described more fully in the documentation for CREATE ROLE.

```
-?
--help
```

Show help about createuser command line arguments, and exit.

createuser also accepts the following command-line arguments for connection parameters:

```
-h host
--host=host
```

Specifies the host name of the machine on which the server is running. If the value begins with a slash, it is used as the directory for the Unix domain socket.

```
-p port
--port=port
```

Specifies the TCP port or local Unix domain socket file extension on which the server is listening for connections.

```
-U username
--username=username
```

User name to connect as (not the user name to create).

```
-w
--no-password
```

Never issue a password prompt. If the server requires password authentication and a password is not available by other means such as a .pgpass file, the connection attempt will fail. This option can be useful in batch jobs and scripts where no user is present to enter a password.

```
-W
--password
```

> Force createuser to prompt for a password (for connecting to the server, not for the password of the new user).
>
> This option is never essential, since createuser will automatically prompt for a password if the server demands password authentication. However, createuser will waste a connection attempt finding out that the server wants a password. In some cases it is worth typing -W to avoid the extra connection attempt.

Environment

```
PGHOST
PGPORT
PGUSER
```

> Default connection parameters

This utility, like most other PostgreSQL utilities, also uses the environment variables supported by libpq (see Section 32.14).

Diagnostics

In case of difficulty, see CREATE ROLE and psql for discussions of potential problems and error messages. The database server must be running at the targeted host. Also, any default connection settings and environment variables used by the libpq front-end library will apply.

Examples

To create a user joe on the default database server:

```
$ createuser joe
```

To create a user joe on the default database server with prompting for some additional attributes:

```
$ createuser --interactive joe
Shall the new role be a superuser? (y/n) n
Shall the new role be allowed to create databases? (y/n) n
Shall the new role be allowed to create more new roles? (y/n) n
```

To create the same user joe using the server on host eden, port 5000, with attributes explicitly specified, taking a look at the underlying command:

```
$ createuser -h eden -p 5000 -S -D -R -e joe
CREATE ROLE joe NOSUPERUSER NOCREATEDB NOCREATEROLE INHERIT LOGIN;
```

To create the user `joe` as a superuser, and assign a password immediately:

```
$ createuser -P -s -e joe
Enter password for new role: xyzzy
Enter it again: xyzzy
CREATE ROLE joe PASSWORD 'md5b5f5ba1a423792b526f799ae4eb3d59e' SUPERUSER CREATEDB CREATEROLE ]
```

In the above example, the new password isn't actually echoed when typed, but we show what was typed for clarity. As you see, the password is encrypted before it is sent to the client. If the option `--unencrypted` is used, the password *will* appear in the echoed command (and possibly also in the server log and elsewhere), so you don't want to use `-e` in that case, if anyone else can see your screen.

See Also

dropuser, CREATE ROLE

dropdb

Name

dropdb — remove a PostgreSQL database

Synopsis

dropdb [*connection-option*...] [*option*...] *dbname*

Description

dropdb destroys an existing PostgreSQL database. The user who executes this command must be a database superuser or the owner of the database.

dropdb is a wrapper around the SQL command DROP DATABASE. There is no effective difference between dropping databases via this utility and via other methods for accessing the server.

Options

dropdb accepts the following command-line arguments:

dbname

> Specifies the name of the database to be removed.

-e
--echo

> Echo the commands that dropdb generates and sends to the server.

-i
--interactive

> Issues a verification prompt before doing anything destructive.

-V
--version

> Print the dropdb version and exit.

--if-exists

> Do not throw an error if the database does not exist. A notice is issued in this case.

-?
--help

> Show help about dropdb command line arguments, and exit.

dropdb also accepts the following command-line arguments for connection parameters:

-h *host*

--host=*host*

> Specifies the host name of the machine on which the server is running. If the value begins with a slash, it is used as the directory for the Unix domain socket.

-p *port*

--port=*port*

> Specifies the TCP port or local Unix domain socket file extension on which the server is listening for connections.

-U *username*

--username=*username*

> User name to connect as.

-w

--no-password

> Never issue a password prompt. If the server requires password authentication and a password is not available by other means such as a .pgpass file, the connection attempt will fail. This option can be useful in batch jobs and scripts where no user is present to enter a password.

-W

--password

> Force dropdb to prompt for a password before connecting to a database.

> This option is never essential, since dropdb will automatically prompt for a password if the server demands password authentication. However, dropdb will waste a connection attempt finding out that the server wants a password. In some cases it is worth typing -W to avoid the extra connection attempt.

--maintenance-db=*dbname*

> Specifies the name of the database to connect to in order to drop the target database. If not specified, the postgres database will be used; if that does not exist (or is the database being dropped), template1 will be used.

Environment

PGHOST

PGPORT

PGUSER

> Default connection parameters

This utility, like most other PostgreSQL utilities, also uses the environment variables supported by libpq (see Section 32.14).

Diagnostics

In case of difficulty, see DROP DATABASE and psql for discussions of potential problems and error messages. The database server must be running at the targeted host. Also, any default connection settings and environment variables used by the libpq front-end library will apply.

Examples

To destroy the database demo on the default database server:

```
$ dropdb demo
```

To destroy the database demo using the server on host eden, port 5000, with verification and a peek at the underlying command:

```
$ dropdb -p 5000 -h eden -i -e demo
Database "demo" will be permanently deleted.
Are you sure? (y/n) y
DROP DATABASE demo;
```

See Also

createdb, DROP DATABASE

droplang

Name

droplang — remove a PostgreSQL procedural language

Synopsis

droplang [*connection-option*...] *langname* [*dbname*]

droplang [*connection-option*...] --list | -l [*dbname*]

Description

droplang is a utility for removing an existing procedural language from a PostgreSQL database. droplang is just a wrapper around the DROP EXTENSION SQL command.

Caution

droplang is deprecated and may be removed in a future PostgreSQL release. Direct use of the DROP EXTENSION command is recommended instead.

Options

droplang accepts the following command line arguments:

langname

Specifies the name of the procedural language to be removed. (This name is lower-cased.)

[-d] *dbname*
[--dbname=]*dbname*

Specifies from which database the language should be removed. The default is to use the database with the same name as the current system user.

-e
--echo

Display SQL commands as they are executed.

-l
--list

Show a list of already installed languages in the target database.

```
-V
--version
```

Print the droplang version and exit.

```
-?
--help
```

Show help about droplang command line arguments, and exit.

droplang also accepts the following command line arguments for connection parameters:

```
-h host
--host=host
```

Specifies the host name of the machine on which the server is running. If host begins with a slash, it is used as the directory for the Unix domain socket.

```
-p port
--port=port
```

Specifies the Internet TCP/IP port or local Unix domain socket file extension on which the server is listening for connections.

```
-U username
--username=username
```

User name to connect as.

```
-w
--no-password
```

Never issue a password prompt. If the server requires password authentication and a password is not available by other means such as a `.pgpass` file, the connection attempt will fail. This option can be useful in batch jobs and scripts where no user is present to enter a password.

```
-W
--password
```

Force droplang to prompt for a password before connecting to a database.

This option is never essential, since droplang will automatically prompt for a password if the server demands password authentication. However, droplang will waste a connection attempt finding out that the server wants a password. In some cases it is worth typing -W to avoid the extra connection attempt.

Environment

```
PGDATABASE
PGHOST
PGPORT
PGUSER
```

> Default connection parameters

This utility, like most other PostgreSQL utilities, also uses the environment variables supported by libpq (see Section 32.14).

Diagnostics

Most error messages are self-explanatory. If not, run droplang with the `--echo` option and see under the respective SQL command for details. Also, any default connection settings and environment variables used by the libpq front-end library will apply.

Notes

Use createlang to add a language.

Examples

To remove the language `pltcl`:

```
$ droplang pltcl dbname
```

See Also

createlang, DROP EXTENSION, DROP LANGUAGE

dropuser

Name

dropuser — remove a PostgreSQL user account

Synopsis

dropuser [*connection-option*...] [*option*...] [*username*]

Description

dropuser removes an existing PostgreSQL user. Only superusers and users with the CREATEROLE privilege can remove PostgreSQL users. (To remove a superuser, you must yourself be a superuser.)

dropuser is a wrapper around the SQL command DROP ROLE. There is no effective difference between dropping users via this utility and via other methods for accessing the server.

Options

dropuser accepts the following command-line arguments:

username

> Specifies the name of the PostgreSQL user to be removed. You will be prompted for a name if none is specified on the command line and the -i/--interactive option is used.

-e

--echo

> Echo the commands that dropuser generates and sends to the server.

-i

--interactive

> Prompt for confirmation before actually removing the user, and prompt for the user name if none is specified on the command line.

-V

--version

> Print the dropuser version and exit.

--if-exists

> Do not throw an error if the user does not exist. A notice is issued in this case.

-?
--help

> Show help about dropuser command line arguments, and exit.

dropuser also accepts the following command-line arguments for connection parameters:

-h *host*
--host=*host*

> Specifies the host name of the machine on which the server is running. If the value begins with a slash, it is used as the directory for the Unix domain socket.

-p *port*
--port=*port*

> Specifies the TCP port or local Unix domain socket file extension on which the server is listening for connections.

-U *username*
--username=*username*

> User name to connect as (not the user name to drop).

-w
--no-password

> Never issue a password prompt. If the server requires password authentication and a password is not available by other means such as a .pgpass file, the connection attempt will fail. This option can be useful in batch jobs and scripts where no user is present to enter a password.

-W
--password

> Force dropuser to prompt for a password before connecting to a database.

> This option is never essential, since dropuser will automatically prompt for a password if the server demands password authentication. However, dropuser will waste a connection attempt finding out that the server wants a password. In some cases it is worth typing -W to avoid the extra connection attempt.

Environment

PGHOST
PGPORT
PGUSER

> Default connection parameters

This utility, like most other PostgreSQL utilities, also uses the environment variables supported by libpq (see Section 32.14).

Diagnostics

In case of difficulty, see DROP ROLE and psql for discussions of potential problems and error messages. The database server must be running at the targeted host. Also, any default connection settings and environment variables used by the libpq front-end library will apply.

Examples

To remove user joe from the default database server:

```
$ dropuser joe
```

To remove user joe using the server on host eden, port 5000, with verification and a peek at the underlying command:

```
$ dropuser -p 5000 -h eden -i -e joe
Role "joe" will be permanently removed.
Are you sure? (y/n) y
DROP ROLE joe;
```

See Also

createuser, DROP ROLE

ecpg

Name

ecpg — embedded SQL C preprocessor

Synopsis

ecpg [*option*...] *file*...

Description

ecpg is the embedded SQL preprocessor for C programs. It converts C programs with embedded SQL statements to normal C code by replacing the SQL invocations with special function calls. The output files can then be processed with any C compiler tool chain.

ecpg will convert each input file given on the command line to the corresponding C output file. Input files preferably have the extension .pgc, in which case the extension will be replaced by .c to determine the output file name. If the extension of the input file is not .pgc, then the output file name is computed by appending .c to the full file name. The output file name can also be overridden using the -o option.

This reference page does not describe the embedded SQL language. See Chapter 34 for more information on that topic.

Options

ecpg accepts the following command-line arguments:

-c

Automatically generate certain C code from SQL code. Currently, this works for EXEC SQL TYPE.

-C *mode*

Set a compatibility mode. *mode* can be INFORMIX or INFORMIX_SE.

-D *symbol*

Define a C preprocessor symbol.

-i

Parse system include files as well.

-I *directory*

Specify an additional include path, used to find files included via EXEC SQL INCLUDE. Defaults are . (current directory), /usr/local/include, the PostgreSQL include directory which is defined at compile time (default: /usr/local/pgsql/include), and /usr/include, in that order.

-o *filename*

> Specifies that ecpg should write all its output to the given *filename*.

-r *option*

> Selects run-time behavior. *Option* can be one of the following:

> no_indicator

> > Do not use indicators but instead use special values to represent null values. Historically there have been databases using this approach.

> prepare

> > Prepare all statements before using them. Libecpg will keep a cache of prepared statements and reuse a statement if it gets executed again. If the cache runs full, libecpg will free the least used statement.

> questionmarks

> > Allow question mark as placeholder for compatibility reasons. This used to be the default long ago.

-t

> Turn on autocommit of transactions. In this mode, each SQL command is automatically committed unless it is inside an explicit transaction block. In the default mode, commands are committed only when EXEC SQL COMMIT is issued.

-v

> Print additional information including the version and the "include" path.

--version

> Print the ecpg version and exit.

-?
--help

> Show help about ecpg command line arguments, and exit.

Notes

When compiling the preprocessed C code files, the compiler needs to be able to find the ECPG header files in the PostgreSQL include directory. Therefore, you might have to use the -I option when invoking the compiler (e.g., -I/usr/local/pgsql/include).

Programs using C code with embedded SQL have to be linked against the libecpg library, for example using the linker options -L/usr/local/pgsql/lib -lecpg.

The value of either of these directories that is appropriate for the installation can be found out using pg_config.

Examples

If you have an embedded SQL C source file named `prog1.pgc`, you can create an executable program using the following sequence of commands:

```
ecpg prog1.pgc
cc -I/usr/local/pgsql/include -c prog1.c
cc -o prog1 prog1.o -L/usr/local/pgsql/lib -lecpg
```

pg_basebackup

Name

pg_basebackup — take a base backup of a PostgreSQL cluster

Synopsis

pg_basebackup [option...]

Description

pg_basebackup is used to take base backups of a running PostgreSQL database cluster. These are taken without affecting other clients to the database, and can be used both for point-in-time recovery (see Section 25.3) and as the starting point for a log shipping or streaming replication standby servers (see Section 26.2).

pg_basebackup makes a binary copy of the database cluster files, while making sure the system is put in and out of backup mode automatically. Backups are always taken of the entire database cluster; it is not possible to back up individual databases or database objects. For individual database backups, a tool such as pg_dump must be used.

The backup is made over a regular PostgreSQL connection, and uses the replication protocol. The connection must be made with a superuser or a user having REPLICATION permissions (see Section 21.2), and pg_hba.conf must explicitly permit the replication connection. The server must also be configured with max_wal_senders set high enough to leave at least one session available for the backup.

There can be multiple pg_basebackups running at the same time, but it is better from a performance point of view to take only one backup, and copy the result.

pg_basebackup can make a base backup from not only the master but also the standby. To take a backup from the standby, set up the standby so that it can accept replication connections (that is, set max_wal_senders and hot_standby, and configure host-based authentication). You will also need to enable full_page_writes on the master.

Note that there are some limitations in an online backup from the standby:

- The backup history file is not created in the database cluster backed up.

- There is no guarantee that all WAL files required for the backup are archived at the end of backup. If you are planning to use the backup for an archive recovery and want to ensure that all required files are available at that moment, you need to include them into the backup by using -x option.

- If the standby is promoted to the master during online backup, the backup fails.

- All WAL records required for the backup must contain sufficient full-page writes, which requires you to enable full_page_writes on the master and not to use a tool like pg_compresslog as archive_command to remove full-page writes from WAL files.

Options

The following command-line options control the location and format of the output.

`-D directory`
`--pgdata=directory`

> Directory to write the output to. pg_basebackup will create the directory and any parent directories if necessary. The directory may already exist, but it is an error if the directory already exists and is not empty.
>
> When the backup is in tar mode, and the directory is specified as – (dash), the tar file will be written to `stdout`.
>
> This option is required.

`-F format`
`--format=format`

> Selects the format for the output. `format` can be one of the following:
>
> `p`
> `plain`
>
> > Write the output as plain files, with the same layout as the current data directory and tablespaces. When the cluster has no additional tablespaces, the whole database will be placed in the target directory. If the cluster contains additional tablespaces, the main data directory will be placed in the target directory, but all other tablespaces will be placed in the same absolute path as they have on the server.
> >
> > This is the default format.
>
> `t`
> `tar`
>
> > Write the output as tar files in the target directory. The main data directory will be written to a file named `base.tar`, and all other tablespaces will be named after the tablespace OID.
> >
> > If the value – (dash) is specified as target directory, the tar contents will be written to standard output, suitable for piping to for example gzip. This is only possible if the cluster has no additional tablespaces.

`-r rate`
`--max-rate=rate`

> The maximum transfer rate of data transferred from the server. Values are in kilobytes per second. Use a suffix of `M` to indicate megabytes per second. A suffix of `k` is also accepted, and has no effect. Valid values are between 32 kilobytes per second and 1024 megabytes per second.
>
> The purpose is to limit the impact of pg_basebackup on the running server.
>
> This option always affects transfer of the data directory. Transfer of WAL files is only affected if the collection method is `fetch`.

`-R`

`--write-recovery-conf`

> Write a minimal `recovery.conf` in the output directory (or into the base archive file when using tar format) to ease setting up a standby server. The `recovery.conf` file will record the connection settings and, if specified, the replication slot that pg_basebackup is using, so that the streaming replication will use the same settings later on.

`-S` *slotname*

`--slot=`*slotname*

> This option can only be used together with `-X stream`. It causes the WAL streaming to use the specified replication slot. If the base backup is intended to be used as a streaming replication standby using replication slots, it should then use the same replication slot name in `recovery.conf`. That way, it is ensured that the server does not remove any necessary WAL data in the time between the end of the base backup and the start of streaming replication.

`-T` *olddir*=*newdir*

`--tablespace-mapping=`*olddir*=*newdir*

> Relocate the tablespace in directory *olddir* to *newdir* during the backup. To be effective, *olddir* must exactly match the path specification of the tablespace as it is currently defined. (But it is not an error if there is no tablespace in *olddir* contained in the backup.) Both *olddir* and *newdir* must be absolute paths. If a path happens to contain a = sign, escape it with a backslash. This option can be specified multiple times for multiple tablespaces. See examples below.

> If a tablespace is relocated in this way, the symbolic links inside the main data directory are updated to point to the new location. So the new data directory is ready to be used for a new server instance with all tablespaces in the updated locations.

`--xlogdir=`*xlogdir*

> Specifies the location for the transaction log directory. *xlogdir* must be an absolute path. The transaction log directory can only be specified when the backup is in plain mode.

`-x`

`--xlog`

> Using this option is equivalent of using `-X` with method `fetch`.

`-X` *method*

`--xlog-method=`*method*

> Includes the required transaction log files (WAL files) in the backup. This will include all transaction logs generated during the backup. If this option is specified, it is possible to start a postmaster directly in the extracted directory without the need to consult the log archive, thus making this a completely standalone backup.

> The following methods for collecting the transaction logs are supported:

> `f`

> `fetch`

>> The transaction log files are collected at the end of the backup. Therefore, it is necessary for the wal_keep_segments parameter to be set high enough that the log is not removed before the end of the backup. If the log has been rotated when it's time to transfer it, the backup will fail and be unusable.

```
s
stream
```

> Stream the transaction log while the backup is created. This will open a second connection to the server and start streaming the transaction log in parallel while running the backup. Therefore, it will use up two connections configured by the max_wal_senders parameter. As long as the client can keep up with transaction log received, using this mode requires no extra transaction logs to be saved on the master.

```
-z
--gzip
```

> Enables gzip compression of tar file output, with the default compression level. Compression is only available when using the tar format.

```
-Z level
--compress=level
```

> Enables gzip compression of tar file output, and specifies the compression level (0 through 9, 0 being no compression and 9 being best compression). Compression is only available when using the tar format.

The following command-line options control the generation of the backup and the running of the program.

```
-c fast|spread
--checkpoint=fast|spread
```

> Sets checkpoint mode to fast or spread (default) (see Section 25.3.3).

```
-l label
--label=label
```

> Sets the label for the backup. If none is specified, a default value of "pg_basebackup base backup" will be used.

```
-P
--progress
```

> Enables progress reporting. Turning this on will deliver an approximate progress report during the backup. Since the database may change during the backup, this is only an approximation and may not end at exactly 100%. In particular, when WAL log is included in the backup, the total amount of data cannot be estimated in advance, and in this case the estimated target size will increase once it passes the total estimate without WAL.

> When this is enabled, the backup will start by enumerating the size of the entire database, and then go back and send the actual contents. This may make the backup take slightly longer, and in particular it will take longer before the first data is sent.

```
-v
--verbose
```

> Enables verbose mode. Will output some extra steps during startup and shutdown, as well as show the exact file name that is currently being processed if progress reporting is also enabled.

The following command-line options control the database connection parameters.

`-d connstr`

`--dbname=connstr`

> Specifies parameters used to connect to the server, as a connection string. See Section 32.1.1 for more information.
>
> The option is called `--dbname` for consistency with other client applications, but because pg_basebackup doesn't connect to any particular database in the cluster, database name in the connection string will be ignored.

`-h host`

`--host=host`

> Specifies the host name of the machine on which the server is running. If the value begins with a slash, it is used as the directory for the Unix domain socket. The default is taken from the `PGHOST` environment variable, if set, else a Unix domain socket connection is attempted.

`-p port`

`--port=port`

> Specifies the TCP port or local Unix domain socket file extension on which the server is listening for connections. Defaults to the `PGPORT` environment variable, if set, or a compiled-in default.

`-s interval`

`--status-interval=interval`

> Specifies the number of seconds between status packets sent back to the server. This allows for easier monitoring of the progress from server. A value of zero disables the periodic status updates completely, although an update will still be sent when requested by the server, to avoid timeout disconnect. The default value is 10 seconds.

`-U username`

`--username=username`

> User name to connect as.

`-w`

`--no-password`

> Never issue a password prompt. If the server requires password authentication and a password is not available by other means such as a `.pgpass` file, the connection attempt will fail. This option can be useful in batch jobs and scripts where no user is present to enter a password.

`-W`

`--password`

> Force pg_basebackup to prompt for a password before connecting to a database.
>
> This option is never essential, since pg_basebackup will automatically prompt for a password if the server demands password authentication. However, pg_basebackup will waste a connection attempt finding out that the server wants a password. In some cases it is worth typing `-W` to avoid the extra connection attempt.

Other options are also available:

```
-V
--version
```

Print the pg_basebackup version and exit.

```
-?
--help
```

Show help about pg_basebackup command line arguments, and exit.

Environment

This utility, like most other PostgreSQL utilities, uses the environment variables supported by libpq (see Section 32.14).

Notes

The backup will include all files in the data directory and tablespaces, including the configuration files and any additional files placed in the directory by third parties. But only regular files and directories are copied. Symbolic links (other than those used for tablespaces) and special device files are skipped. (See Section 51.3 for the precise details.)

Tablespaces will in plain format by default be backed up to the same path they have on the server, unless the option `--tablespace-mapping` is used. Without this option, running a plain format base backup on the same host as the server will not work if tablespaces are in use, because the backup would have to be written to the same directory locations as the original tablespaces.

When tar format mode is used, it is the user's responsibility to unpack each tar file before starting the PostgreSQL server. If there are additional tablespaces, the tar files for them need to be unpacked in the correct locations. In this case the symbolic links for those tablespaces will be created by the server according to the contents of the `tablespace_map` file that is included in the `base.tar` file.

pg_basebackup works with servers of the same or an older major version, down to 9.1. However, WAL streaming mode (`-X stream`) only works with server version 9.3 and later, and tar format mode (`--format=tar`) of the current version only works with server version 9.5 or later.

Examples

To create a base backup of the server at `mydbserver` and store it in the local directory `/usr/local/pgsql/data`:

```
$ pg_basebackup -h mydbserver -D /usr/local/pgsql/data
```

To create a backup of the local server with one compressed tar file for each tablespace, and store it in the directory `backup`, showing a progress report while running:

```
$ pg_basebackup -D backup -Ft -z -P
```

To create a backup of a single-tablespace local database and compress this with bzip2:

```
$ pg_basebackup -D - -Ft | bzip2 > backup.tar.bz2
```

(This command will fail if there are multiple tablespaces in the database.)

To create a backup of a local database where the tablespace in /opt/ts is relocated to ./backup/ts:

```
$ pg_basebackup -D backup/data -T /opt/ts=$(pwd)/backup/ts
```

See Also

pg_dump

pgbench

Name

pgbench — run a benchmark test on PostgreSQL

Synopsis

pgbench -i [*option*...] [*dbname*]

pgbench [*option*...] [*dbname*]

Description

pgbench is a simple program for running benchmark tests on PostgreSQL. It runs the same sequence of SQL commands over and over, possibly in multiple concurrent database sessions, and then calculates the average transaction rate (transactions per second). By default, pgbench tests a scenario that is loosely based on TPC-B, involving five SELECT, UPDATE, and INSERT commands per transaction. However, it is easy to test other cases by writing your own transaction script files.

Typical output from pgbench looks like:

```
transaction type: <builtin: TPC-B (sort of)>
scaling factor: 10
query mode: simple
number of clients: 10
number of threads: 1
number of transactions per client: 1000
number of transactions actually processed: 10000/10000
tps = 85.184871 (including connections establishing)
tps = 85.296346 (excluding connections establishing)
```

The first six lines report some of the most important parameter settings. The next line reports the number of transactions completed and intended (the latter being just the product of number of clients and number of transactions per client); these will be equal unless the run failed before completion. (In -T mode, only the actual number of transactions is printed.) The last two lines report the number of transactions per second, figured with and without counting the time to start database sessions.

The default TPC-B-like transaction test requires specific tables to be set up beforehand. pgbench should be invoked with the -i (initialize) option to create and populate these tables. (When you are testing a custom script, you don't need this step, but will instead need to do whatever setup your test needs.) Initialization looks like:

```
pgbench -i [ other-options ] dbname
```

where *dbname* is the name of the already-created database to test in. (You may also need -h, -p, and/or -U options to specify how to connect to the database server.)

> # **Caution**
>
> `pgbench -i` creates four tables `pgbench_accounts`, `pgbench_branches`, `pgbench_history`, and `pgbench_tellers`, destroying any existing tables of these names. Be very careful to use another database if you have tables having these names!

At the default "scale factor" of 1, the tables initially contain this many rows:

```
table                    # of rows
---------------------------------
pgbench_branches         1
pgbench_tellers          10
pgbench_accounts         100000
pgbench_history          0
```

You can (and, for most purposes, probably should) increase the number of rows by using the `-s` (scale factor) option. The `-F` (fillfactor) option might also be used at this point.

Once you have done the necessary setup, you can run your benchmark with a command that doesn't include `-i`, that is

```
pgbench [ options ] dbname
```

In nearly all cases, you'll need some options to make a useful test. The most important options are `-c` (number of clients), `-t` (number of transactions), `-T` (time limit), and `-f` (specify a custom script file). See below for a full list.

Options

The following is divided into three subsections: Different options are used during database initialization and while running benchmarks, some options are useful in both cases.

Initialization Options

pgbench accepts the following command-line initialization arguments:

`-i`
`--initialize`

> Required to invoke initialization mode.

`-F fillfactor`
`--fillfactor=fillfactor`

> Create the `pgbench_accounts`, `pgbench_tellers` and `pgbench_branches` tables with the given fillfactor. Default is 100.

`-n`
`--no-vacuum`

> Perform no vacuuming after initialization.

```
-q
--quiet
```

Switch logging to quiet mode, producing only one progress message per 5 seconds. The default logging prints one message each 100000 rows, which often outputs many lines per second (especially on good hardware).

```
-s scale_factor
--scale=scale_factor
```

Multiply the number of rows generated by the scale factor. For example, -s 100 will create 10,000,000 rows in the pgbench_accounts table. Default is 1. When the scale is 20,000 or larger, the columns used to hold account identifiers (aid columns) will switch to using larger integers (bigint), in order to be big enough to hold the range of account identifiers.

```
--foreign-keys
```

Create foreign key constraints between the standard tables.

```
--index-tablespace=index_tablespace
```

Create indexes in the specified tablespace, rather than the default tablespace.

```
--tablespace=tablespace
```

Create tables in the specified tablespace, rather than the default tablespace.

```
--unlogged-tables
```

Create all tables as unlogged tables, rather than permanent tables.

Benchmarking Options

pgbench accepts the following command-line benchmarking arguments:

```
-b scriptname[@weight]
--builtin=scriptname[@weight]
```

Add the specified built-in script to the list of executed scripts. An optional integer weight after @ allows to adjust the probability of drawing the script. If not specified, it is set to 1. Available built-in scripts are: tpcb-like, simple-update and select-only. Unambiguous prefixes of built-in names are accepted. With special name list, show the list of built-in scripts and exit immediately.

```
-c clients
--client=clients
```

Number of clients simulated, that is, number of concurrent database sessions. Default is 1.

```
-C
--connect
```

Establish a new connection for each transaction, rather than doing it just once per client session. This is useful to measure the connection overhead.

```
-d
--debug
```

> Print debugging output.

```
-D varname=value
--define=varname=value
```

> Define a variable for use by a custom script (see below). Multiple -D options are allowed.

```
-f filename[@weight]
--file=filename[@weight]
```

> Add a transaction script read from `filename` to the list of executed scripts. An optional integer weight after @ allows to adjust the probability of drawing the test. See below for details.

```
-j threads
--jobs=threads
```

> Number of worker threads within pgbench. Using more than one thread can be helpful on multi-CPU machines. Clients are distributed as evenly as possible among available threads. Default is 1.

```
-l
--log
```

> Write the time taken by each transaction to a log file. See below for details.

```
-L limit
--latency-limit=limit
```

> Transaction which last more than `limit` milliseconds are counted and reported separately, as *late*.

> When throttling is used (--rate=...), transactions that lag behind schedule by more than `limit` ms, and thus have no hope of meeting the latency limit, are not sent to the server at all. They are counted and reported separately as *skipped*.

```
-M querymode
--protocol=querymode
```

> Protocol to use for submitting queries to the server:

> - `simple`: use simple query protocol.

> - `extended`: use extended query protocol.

> - `prepared`: use extended query protocol with prepared statements.

> The default is simple query protocol. (See Chapter 51 for more information.)

```
-n
--no-vacuum
```

> Perform no vacuuming before running the test. This option is *necessary* if you are running a custom test scenario that does not include the standard tables `pgbench_accounts`, `pgbench_branches`, `pgbench_history`, and `pgbench_tellers`.

```
-N
--skip-some-updates
```

> Run built-in simple-update script. Shorthand for -b simple-update.

-P *sec*

--progress=*sec*

> Show progress report every *sec* seconds. The report includes the time since the beginning of the run, the tps since the last report, and the transaction latency average and standard deviation since the last report. Under throttling (-R), the latency is computed with respect to the transaction scheduled start time, not the actual transaction beginning time, thus it also includes the average schedule lag time.

-r

--report-latencies

> Report the average per-statement latency (execution time from the perspective of the client) of each command after the benchmark finishes. See below for details.

-R *rate*

--rate=*rate*

> Execute transactions targeting the specified rate instead of running as fast as possible (the default). The rate is given in transactions per second. If the targeted rate is above the maximum possible rate, the rate limit won't impact the results.

> The rate is targeted by starting transactions along a Poisson-distributed schedule time line. The expected start time schedule moves forward based on when the client first started, not when the previous transaction ended. That approach means that when transactions go past their original scheduled end time, it is possible for later ones to catch up again.

> When throttling is active, the transaction latency reported at the end of the run is calculated from the scheduled start times, so it includes the time each transaction had to wait for the previous transaction to finish. The wait time is called the schedule lag time, and its average and maximum are also reported separately. The transaction latency with respect to the actual transaction start time, i.e. the time spent executing the transaction in the database, can be computed by subtracting the schedule lag time from the reported latency.

> If --latency-limit is used together with --rate, a transaction can lag behind so much that it is already over the latency limit when the previous transaction ends, because the latency is calculated from the scheduled start time. Such transactions are not sent to the server, but are skipped altogether and counted separately.

> A high schedule lag time is an indication that the system cannot process transactions at the specified rate, with the chosen number of clients and threads. When the average transaction execution time is longer than the scheduled interval between each transaction, each successive transaction will fall further behind, and the schedule lag time will keep increasing the longer the test run is. When that happens, you will have to reduce the specified transaction rate.

-s *scale_factor*

--scale=*scale_factor*

> Report the specified scale factor in pgbench's output. With the built-in tests, this is not necessary; the correct scale factor will be detected by counting the number of rows in the pgbench_branches table. However, when testing only custom benchmarks (-f option), the scale factor will be reported as 1 unless this option is used.

-S

--select-only

> Run built-in select-only script. Shorthand for -b select-only.

```
-t transactions
--transactions=transactions
```

Number of transactions each client runs. Default is 10.

```
-T seconds
--time=seconds
```

Run the test for this many seconds, rather than a fixed number of transactions per client. `-t` and `-T` are mutually exclusive.

```
-v
--vacuum-all
```

Vacuum all four standard tables before running the test. With neither `-n` nor `-v`, pgbench will vacuum the `pgbench_tellers` and `pgbench_branches` tables, and will truncate `pgbench_history`.

```
--aggregate-interval=seconds
```

Length of aggregation interval (in seconds). May be used only together with -l - with this option, the log contains per-interval summary (number of transactions, min/max latency and two additional fields useful for variance estimation).

This option is not currently supported on Windows.

```
--progress-timestamp
```

When showing progress (option `-P`), use a timestamp (Unix epoch) instead of the number of seconds since the beginning of the run. The unit is in seconds, with millisecond precision after the dot. This helps compare logs generated by various tools.

```
--sampling-rate=rate
```

Sampling rate, used when writing data into the log, to reduce the amount of log generated. If this option is given, only the specified fraction of transactions are logged. 1.0 means all transactions will be logged, 0.05 means only 5% of the transactions will be logged.

Remember to take the sampling rate into account when processing the log file. For example, when computing tps values, you need to multiply the numbers accordingly (e.g. with 0.01 sample rate, you'll only get 1/100 of the actual tps).

Common Options

pgbench accepts the following command-line common arguments:

```
-h hostname
--host=hostname
```

The database server's host name

```
-p port
--port=port
```

The database server's port number

```
-U login
--username=login
```

    The user name to connect as

```
-V
--version
```

    Print the pgbench version and exit.

```
-?
--help
```

    Show help about pgbench command line arguments, and exit.

Notes

What is the "Transaction" Actually Performed in pgbench?

pgbench executes test scripts chosen randomly from a specified list. They include built-in scripts with `-b` and user-provided custom scripts with `-f`. Each script may be given a relative weight specified after a `@` so as to change its drawing probability. The default weight is `1`. Scripts with a weight of `0` are ignored.

The default built-in transaction script (also invoked with `-b tpcb-like`) issues seven commands per transaction over randomly chosen `aid`, `tid`, `bid` and `balance`. The scenario is inspired by the TPC-B benchmark, but is not actually TPC-B, hence the name.

1. `BEGIN;`

2. `UPDATE pgbench_accounts SET abalance = abalance + :delta WHERE aid = :aid;`

3. `SELECT abalance FROM pgbench_accounts WHERE aid = :aid;`

4. `UPDATE pgbench_tellers SET tbalance = tbalance + :delta WHERE tid = :tid;`

5. `UPDATE pgbench_branches SET bbalance = bbalance + :delta WHERE bid = :bid;`

6. `INSERT INTO pgbench_history (tid, bid, aid, delta, mtime) VALUES (:tid, :bid, :aid, :delta, CURRENT_TIMESTAMP);`

7. `END;`

If you select the `simple-update` built-in (also `-N`), steps 4 and 5 aren't included in the transaction. This will avoid update contention on these tables, but it makes the test case even less like TPC-B.

If you select the `select-only` built-in (also `-S`), only the `SELECT` is issued.

Custom Scripts

pgbench has support for running custom benchmark scenarios by replacing the default transaction script (described above) with a transaction script read from a file (`-f` option). In this case a "transaction" counts as one execution of a script file.

A script file contains one or more SQL commands terminated by semicolons. Empty lines and lines beginning with -- are ignored. Script files can also contain "meta commands", which are interpreted by pgbench itself, as described below.

> **Note:** Before PostgreSQL 9.6, SQL commands in script files were terminated by newlines, and so they could not be continued across lines. Now a semicolon is *required* to separate consecutive SQL commands (though a SQL command does not need one if it is followed by a meta command). If you need to create a script file that works with both old and new versions of pgbench, be sure to write each SQL command on a single line ending with a semicolon.

There is a simple variable-substitution facility for script files. Variables can be set by the command-line -D option, explained above, or by the meta commands explained below. In addition to any variables preset by -D command-line options, there are a few variables that are preset automatically, listed in Table 1. A value specified for these variables using -D takes precedence over the automatic presets. Once set, a variable's value can be inserted into a SQL command by writing :*variablename*. When running more than one client session, each session has its own set of variables.

Table 1. Automatic Variables

Variable	Description
scale	current scale factor
client_id	unique number identifying the client session (starts from zero)

Script file meta commands begin with a backslash (\) and extend to the end of the line. Arguments to a meta command are separated by white space. These meta commands are supported:

\set *varname expression*

Sets variable *varname* to a value calculated from *expression*. The expression may contain integer constants such as 5432, double constants such as 3.14159, references to variables :*variablename*, unary operators (+, -) and binary operators (+, -, *, /, %) with their usual precedence and associativity, function calls, and parentheses.

Examples:

```
\set ntellers 10 * :scale
\set aid (1021 * random(1, 100000 * :scale)) % (100000 * :scale) + 1
```

\sleep *number* [us | ms | s]

Causes script execution to sleep for the specified duration in microseconds (us), milliseconds (ms) or seconds (s). If the unit is omitted then seconds are the default. *number* can be either an integer constant or a :*variablename* reference to a variable having an integer value.

Example:

```
\sleep 10 ms
```

\setshell *varname command* [*argument* ...]

Sets variable *varname* to the result of the shell command *command* with the given *argument*(s). The command must return an integer value through its standard output.

command and each *argument* can be either a text constant or a :*variablename* reference to a variable. If you want to use an *argument* starting with a colon, write an additional colon at the beginning of *argument*.

Example:

```
\setshell variable_to_be_assigned command literal_argument :variable ::literal_st
```

```
\shell command [ argument ... ]
```

Same as \setshell, but the result of the command is discarded.

Example:

```
\shell command literal_argument :variable ::literal_starting_with_colon
```

Built-In Functions

The functions listed in Table 2 are built into pgbench and may be used in expressions appearing in \set.

Table 2. pgbench Functions

Function	Return Type	Description	Example	Result
abs(a)	same as a	absolute value	abs(-17)	17
debug(a)	same as a	print a to stderr, and return a	debug(5432.1)	5432.1
double(i)	double	cast to double	double(5432)	5432.0
greatest(a [, ...])	double if any a is double, else integer	largest value among arguments	greatest(5, 4, 3, 2)	5
int(x)	integer	cast to int	int(5.4 + 3.8)	9
least(a [, ...])	double if any a is double, else integer	smallest value among arguments	least(5, 4, 3, 2.1)	2.1
pi()	double	value of the constant PI	pi()	3.14159265358979 32384
random(lb, ub)	integer	uniformly-distributed random integer in [lb, ub]	random(1, 10)	an integer between 1 and 10
random_exponential(lb, ub, parameter)	integer	exponentially-distributed random integer in [lb, ub], see below	random_exponential(1, 10, 3.0)	an integer between 1 and 10
random_gaussian(lb, ub, parameter)	integer	Gaussian-distributed random integer in [lb, ub], see below	random_gaussian(1, 10, 2.5)	an integer between 1 and 10
sqrt(x)	double	square root	sqrt(2.0)	1.414213562

The `random` function generates values using a uniform distribution, that is all the values are drawn within the specified range with equal probability. The `random_exponential` and `random_gaussian` functions require an additional double parameter which determines the precise shape of the distribution.

- For an exponential distribution, *parameter* controls the distribution by truncating a quickly-decreasing exponential distribution at *parameter*, and then projecting onto integers between the bounds. To be precise, with

  f(x) = exp(-parameter * (x - min) / (max - min + 1)) / (1 - exp(-parameter))

  Then value *i* between *min* and *max* inclusive is drawn with probability: `f(x) - f(x + 1)`.

  Intuitively, the larger the *parameter*, the more frequently values close to *min* are accessed, and the less frequently values close to *max* are accessed. The closer to 0 *parameter* is, the flatter (more uniform) the access distribution. A crude approximation of the distribution is that the most frequent 1% values in the range, close to *min*, are drawn *parameter*% of the time. The *parameter* value must be strictly positive.

- For a Gaussian distribution, the interval is mapped onto a standard normal distribution (the classical bell-shaped Gaussian curve) truncated at `-parameter` on the left and `+parameter` on the right. Values in the middle of the interval are more likely to be drawn. To be precise, if `PHI(x)` is the cumulative distribution function of the standard normal distribution, with mean `mu` defined as `(max + min) / 2.0`, with

  f(x) = PHI(2.0 * parameter * (x - mu) / (max - min + 1)) /
      (2.0 * PHI(parameter) - 1)

  then value *i* between *min* and *max* inclusive is drawn with probability: `f(i + 0.5) - f(i - 0.5)`. Intuitively, the larger the *parameter*, the more frequently values close to the middle of the interval are drawn, and the less frequently values close to the *min* and *max* bounds. About 67% of values are drawn from the middle `1.0 / parameter`, that is a relative `0.5 / parameter` around the mean, and 95% in the middle `2.0 / parameter`, that is a relative `1.0 / parameter` around the mean; for instance, if *parameter* is 4.0, 67% of values are drawn from the middle quarter (1.0 / 4.0) of the interval (i.e. from `3.0 / 8.0` to `5.0 / 8.0`) and 95% from the middle half (`2.0 / 4.0`) of the interval (second and third quartiles). The minimum *parameter* is 2.0 for performance of the Box-Muller transform.

As an example, the full definition of the built-in TPC-B-like transaction is:

```
\set aid random(1, 100000 * :scale)
\set bid random(1, 1 * :scale)
\set tid random(1, 10 * :scale)
\set delta random(-5000, 5000)
BEGIN;
UPDATE pgbench_accounts SET abalance = abalance + :delta WHERE aid = :aid;
SELECT abalance FROM pgbench_accounts WHERE aid = :aid;
UPDATE pgbench_tellers SET tbalance = tbalance + :delta WHERE tid = :tid;
UPDATE pgbench_branches SET bbalance = bbalance + :delta WHERE bid = :bid;
INSERT INTO pgbench_history (tid, bid, aid, delta, mtime) VALUES (:tid, :bid, :aid,
END;
```

This script allows each iteration of the transaction to reference different, randomly-chosen rows. (This example also shows why it's important for each client session to have its own variables — otherwise they'd not be independently touching different rows.)

Per-Transaction Logging

With the -l option but without the --aggregate-interval, pgbench writes the time taken by each transaction to a log file. The log file will be named pgbench_log.*nnn*, where *nnn* is the PID of the pgbench process. If the -j option is 2 or higher, creating multiple worker threads, each will have its own log file. The first worker will use the same name for its log file as in the standard single worker case. The additional log files for the other workers will be named pgbench_log.*nnn*.*mmm*, where *mmm* is a sequential number for each worker starting with 1.

The format of the log is:

client_id transaction_no time script_no time_epoch time_us [schedule_lag]

where *time* is the total elapsed transaction time in microseconds, *script_no* identifies which script file was used (useful when multiple scripts were specified with -f or -b), and *time_epoch/time_us* are a Unix epoch format time stamp and an offset in microseconds (suitable for creating an ISO 8601 time stamp with fractional seconds) showing when the transaction completed. Field *schedule_lag* is the difference between the transaction's scheduled start time, and the time it actually started, in microseconds. It is only present when the --rate option is used. When both --rate and --latency-limit are used, the *time* for a skipped transaction will be reported as skipped.

Here is a snippet of the log file generated:

```
0 199 2241 0 1175850568 995598
0 200 2465 0 1175850568 998079
0 201 2513 0 1175850569 608
0 202 2038 0 1175850569 2663
```

Another example with --rate=100 and --latency-limit=5 (note the additional *schedule_lag* column):

```
0 81 4621 0 1412881037 912698 3005
0 82 6173 0 1412881037 914578 4304
0 83 skipped 0 1412881037 914578 5217
0 83 skipped 0 1412881037 914578 5099
0 83 4722 0 1412881037 916203 3108
0 84 4142 0 1412881037 918023 2333
0 85 2465 0 1412881037 919759 740
```

In this example, transaction 82 was late, because its latency (6.173 ms) was over the 5 ms limit. The next two transactions were skipped, because they were already late before they were even started.

When running a long test on hardware that can handle a lot of transactions, the log files can become very large. The --sampling-rate option can be used to log only a random sample of transactions.

Aggregated Logging

With the --aggregate-interval option, the logs use a bit different format:

interval_start num_of_transactions latency_sum latency_2_sum min_latency max_latency [lag_sum

where *interval_start* is the start of the interval (Unix epoch format time stamp), *num_of_transactions* is the number of transactions within the interval, *latency_sum* is a sum of latencies (so you can compute average latency easily). The following two fields are useful for variance estimation - `latency_sum` is a sum of latencies and `latency_2_sum` is a sum of 2nd powers of latencies. The next two fields are `min_latency` - a minimum latency within the interval, and `max_latency` - maximum latency within the interval. A transaction is counted into the interval when it was committed. The fields in the end, `lag_sum`, `lag_2_sum`, `min_lag`, and `max_lag`, are only present if the `--rate` option is used. The very last one, `skipped_transactions`, is only present if the option `--latency-limit` is present, too. They are calculated from the time each transaction had to wait for the previous one to finish, i.e. the difference between each transaction's scheduled start time and the time it actually started.

Here is example output:

```
1345828501 5601 1542744 483552416 61 2573
1345828503 7884 1979812 565806736 60 1479
1345828505 7208 1979422 567277552 59 1391
1345828507 7685 1980268 569784714 60 1398
1345828509 7073 1979779 573489941 236 1411
```

Notice that while the plain (unaggregated) log file contains a reference to the custom script files, the aggregated log does not. Therefore if you need per script data, you need to aggregate the data on your own.

Per-Statement Latencies

With the `-r` option, pgbench collects the elapsed transaction time of each statement executed by every client. It then reports an average of those values, referred to as the latency for each statement, after the benchmark has finished.

For the default script, the output will look similar to this:

```
starting vacuum...end.
transaction type: <builtin: TPC-B (sort of)>
scaling factor: 1
query mode: simple
number of clients: 10
number of threads: 1
number of transactions per client: 1000
number of transactions actually processed: 10000/10000
latency average = 15.844 ms
latency stddev = 2.715 ms
tps = 618.764555 (including connections establishing)
tps = 622.977698 (excluding connections establishing)
script statistics:
 - statement latencies in milliseconds:
         0.002  \set aid random(1, 100000 * :scale)
         0.005  \set bid random(1, 1 * :scale)
         0.002  \set tid random(1, 10 * :scale)
         0.001  \set delta random(-5000, 5000)
         0.326  BEGIN;
         0.603  UPDATE pgbench_accounts SET abalance = abalance + :delta WHERE aid =
         0.454  SELECT abalance FROM pgbench_accounts WHERE aid = :aid;
```

```
5.528  UPDATE pgbench_tellers SET tbalance = tbalance + :delta WHERE tid = :
7.335  UPDATE pgbench_branches SET bbalance = bbalance + :delta WHERE bid =
0.371  INSERT INTO pgbench_history (tid, bid, aid, delta, mtime) VALUES (:ti
1.212  END;
```

If multiple script files are specified, the averages are reported separately for each script file.

Note that collecting the additional timing information needed for per-statement latency computation adds some overhead. This will slow average execution speed and lower the computed TPS. The amount of slowdown varies significantly depending on platform and hardware. Comparing average TPS values with and without latency reporting enabled is a good way to measure if the timing overhead is significant.

Good Practices

It is very easy to use pgbench to produce completely meaningless numbers. Here are some guidelines to help you get useful results.

In the first place, *never* believe any test that runs for only a few seconds. Use the -t or -T option to make the run last at least a few minutes, so as to average out noise. In some cases you could need hours to get numbers that are reproducible. It's a good idea to try the test run a few times, to find out if your numbers are reproducible or not.

For the default TPC-B-like test scenario, the initialization scale factor (-s) should be at least as large as the largest number of clients you intend to test (-c); else you'll mostly be measuring update contention. There are only -s rows in the pgbench_branches table, and every transaction wants to update one of them, so -c values in excess of -s will undoubtedly result in lots of transactions blocked waiting for other transactions.

The default test scenario is also quite sensitive to how long it's been since the tables were initialized: accumulation of dead rows and dead space in the tables changes the results. To understand the results you must keep track of the total number of updates and when vacuuming happens. If autovacuum is enabled it can result in unpredictable changes in measured performance.

A limitation of pgbench is that it can itself become the bottleneck when trying to test a large number of client sessions. This can be alleviated by running pgbench on a different machine from the database server, although low network latency will be essential. It might even be useful to run several pgbench instances concurrently, on several client machines, against the same database server.

pg_config

Name

pg_config — retrieve information about the installed version of PostgreSQL

Synopsis

pg_config [*option*...]

Description

The pg_config utility prints configuration parameters of the currently installed version of PostgreSQL. It is intended, for example, to be used by software packages that want to interface to PostgreSQL to facilitate finding the required header files and libraries.

Options

To use pg_config, supply one or more of the following options:

--bindir

> Print the location of user executables. Use this, for example, to find the psql program. This is normally also the location where the pg_config program resides.

--docdir

> Print the location of documentation files.

--htmldir

> Print the location of HTML documentation files.

--includedir

> Print the location of C header files of the client interfaces.

--pkgincludedir

> Print the location of other C header files.

--includedir-server

> Print the location of C header files for server programming.

--libdir

> Print the location of object code libraries.

`--pkglibdir`

Print the location of dynamically loadable modules, or where the server would search for them. (Other architecture-dependent data files might also be installed in this directory.)

`--localedir`

Print the location of locale support files. (This will be an empty string if locale support was not configured when PostgreSQL was built.)

`--mandir`

Print the location of manual pages.

`--sharedir`

Print the location of architecture-independent support files.

`--sysconfdir`

Print the location of system-wide configuration files.

`--pgxs`

Print the location of extension makefiles.

`--configure`

Print the options that were given to the `configure` script when PostgreSQL was configured for building. This can be used to reproduce the identical configuration, or to find out with what options a binary package was built. (Note however that binary packages often contain vendor-specific custom patches.) See also the examples below.

`--cc`

Print the value of the `CC` variable that was used for building PostgreSQL. This shows the C compiler used.

`--cppflags`

Print the value of the `CPPFLAGS` variable that was used for building PostgreSQL. This shows C compiler switches needed at preprocessing time (typically, `-I` switches).

`--cflags`

Print the value of the `CFLAGS` variable that was used for building PostgreSQL. This shows C compiler switches.

`--cflags_sl`

Print the value of the `CFLAGS_SL` variable that was used for building PostgreSQL. This shows extra C compiler switches used for building shared libraries.

`--ldflags`

Print the value of the `LDFLAGS` variable that was used for building PostgreSQL. This shows linker switches.

`--ldflags_ex`

Print the value of the `LDFLAGS_EX` variable that was used for building PostgreSQL. This shows linker switches used for building executables only.

```
--ldflags_sl
```

Print the value of the LDFLAGS_SL variable that was used for building PostgreSQL. This shows linker switches used for building shared libraries only.

```
--libs
```

Print the value of the LIBS variable that was used for building PostgreSQL. This normally contains -1 switches for external libraries linked into PostgreSQL.

```
--version
```

Print the version of PostgreSQL.

```
-?
--help
```

Show help about pg_config command line arguments, and exit.

If more than one option is given, the information is printed in that order, one item per line. If no options are given, all available information is printed, with labels.

Notes

The options --docdir, --pkgincludedir, --localedir, --mandir, --sharedir, --sysconfdir, --cc, --cppflags, --cflags, --cflags_sl, --ldflags, --ldflags_sl, and --libs were added in PostgreSQL 8.1. The option --htmldir was added in PostgreSQL 8.4. The option --ldflags_ex was added in PostgreSQL 9.0.

Example

To reproduce the build configuration of the current PostgreSQL installation, run the following command:

```
eval ./configure `pg_config --configure`
```

The output of pg_config --configure contains shell quotation marks so arguments with spaces are represented correctly. Therefore, using eval is required for proper results.

pg_dump

Name

pg_dump — extract a PostgreSQL database into a script file or other archive file

Synopsis

pg_dump [*connection-option*...] [*option*...] [*dbname*]

Description

pg_dump is a utility for backing up a PostgreSQL database. It makes consistent backups even if the database is being used concurrently. pg_dump does not block other users accessing the database (readers or writers).

pg_dump only dumps a single database. To backup global objects that are common to all databases in a cluster, such as roles and tablespaces, use pg_dumpall.

Dumps can be output in script or archive file formats. Script dumps are plain-text files containing the SQL commands required to reconstruct the database to the state it was in at the time it was saved. To restore from such a script, feed it to psql. Script files can be used to reconstruct the database even on other machines and other architectures; with some modifications, even on other SQL database products.

The alternative archive file formats must be used with pg_restore to rebuild the database. They allow pg_restore to be selective about what is restored, or even to reorder the items prior to being restored. The archive file formats are designed to be portable across architectures.

When used with one of the archive file formats and combined with pg_restore, pg_dump provides a flexible archival and transfer mechanism. pg_dump can be used to backup an entire database, then pg_restore can be used to examine the archive and/or select which parts of the database are to be restored. The most flexible output file formats are the "custom" format (-Fc) and the "directory" format(-Fd). They allow for selection and reordering of all archived items, support parallel restoration, and are compressed by default. The "directory" format is the only format that supports parallel dumps.

While running pg_dump, one should examine the output for any warnings (printed on standard error), especially in light of the limitations listed below.

Options

The following command-line options control the content and format of the output.

dbname

> Specifies the name of the database to be dumped. If this is not specified, the environment variable PGDATABASE is used. If that is not set, the user name specified for the connection is used.

```
-a
--data-only
```

Dump only the data, not the schema (data definitions). Table data, large objects, and sequence values are dumped.

This option is similar to, but for historical reasons not identical to, specifying `--section=data`.

```
-b
--blobs
```

Include large objects in the dump. This is the default behavior except when `--schema`, `--table`, or `--schema-only` is specified, so the `-b` switch is only useful to add large objects to selective dumps.

```
-c
--clean
```

Output commands to clean (drop) database objects prior to outputting the commands for creating them. (Unless `--if-exists` is also specified, restore might generate some harmless error messages, if any objects were not present in the destination database.)

This option is only meaningful for the plain-text format. For the archive formats, you can specify the option when you call `pg_restore`.

```
-C
--create
```

Begin the output with a command to create the database itself and reconnect to the created database. (With a script of this form, it doesn't matter which database in the destination installation you connect to before running the script.) If `--clean` is also specified, the script drops and recreates the target database before reconnecting to it.

This option is only meaningful for the plain-text format. For the archive formats, you can specify the option when you call `pg_restore`.

```
-E encoding
--encoding=encoding
```

Create the dump in the specified character set encoding. By default, the dump is created in the database encoding. (Another way to get the same result is to set the `PGCLIENTENCODING` environment variable to the desired dump encoding.)

```
-f file
--file=file
```

Send output to the specified file. This parameter can be omitted for file based output formats, in which case the standard output is used. It must be given for the directory output format however, where it specifies the target directory instead of a file. In this case the directory is created by `pg_dump` and must not exist before.

```
-F format
--format=format
```

Selects the format of the output. `format` can be one of the following:

```
p
plain
```

Output a plain-text SQL script file (the default).

```
c
custom
```

Output a custom-format archive suitable for input into pg_restore. Together with the directory output format, this is the most flexible output format in that it allows manual selection and reordering of archived items during restore. This format is also compressed by default.

```
d
directory
```

Output a directory-format archive suitable for input into pg_restore. This will create a directory with one file for each table and blob being dumped, plus a so-called Table of Contents file describing the dumped objects in a machine-readable format that pg_restore can read. A directory format archive can be manipulated with standard Unix tools; for example, files in an uncompressed archive can be compressed with the gzip tool. This format is compressed by default and also supports parallel dumps.

```
t
tar
```

Output a `tar`-format archive suitable for input into pg_restore. The tar format is compatible with the directory format: extracting a tar-format archive produces a valid directory-format archive. However, the tar format does not support compression. Also, when using tar format the relative order of table data items cannot be changed during restore.

```
-j njobs
--jobs=njobs
```

Run the dump in parallel by dumping `njobs` tables simultaneously. This option reduces the time of the dump but it also increases the load on the database server. You can only use this option with the directory output format because this is the only output format where multiple processes can write their data at the same time.

pg_dump will open `njobs` + 1 connections to the database, so make sure your max_connections setting is high enough to accommodate all connections.

Requesting exclusive locks on database objects while running a parallel dump could cause the dump to fail. The reason is that the pg_dump master process requests shared locks on the objects that the worker processes are going to dump later in order to make sure that nobody deletes them and makes them go away while the dump is running. If another client then requests an exclusive lock on a table, that lock will not be granted but will be queued waiting for the shared lock of the master process to be released. Consequently any other access to the table will not be granted either and will queue after the exclusive lock request. This includes the worker process trying to dump the table. Without any precautions this would be a classic deadlock situation. To detect this conflict, the pg_dump worker process requests another shared lock using the NOWAIT option. If the worker process is not granted this shared lock, somebody else must have requested an exclusive lock in the meantime and there is no way to continue with the dump, so pg_dump has no choice but to abort the dump.

For a consistent backup, the database server needs to support synchronized snapshots, a feature that was introduced in PostgreSQL 9.2. With this feature, database clients can ensure they see the same data set even though they use different connections. `pg_dump -j` uses multiple database connections; it connects to the database once with the master process and once again for each worker job. Without the synchronized snapshot feature, the different worker jobs wouldn't be guaranteed to see the same data in each connection, which could lead to an inconsistent backup.

If you want to run a parallel dump of a pre-9.2 server, you need to make sure that the database content doesn't change from between the time the master connects to the database until the last worker job has connected to the database. The easiest way to do this is to halt any data modifying processes (DDL and DML) accessing the database before starting the backup. You also need to specify the `--no-synchronized-snapshots` parameter when running `pg_dump -j` against a pre-9.2 PostgreSQL server.

`-n` *schema*

`--schema=`*schema*

Dump only schemas matching *schema*; this selects both the schema itself, and all its contained objects. When this option is not specified, all non-system schemas in the target database will be dumped. Multiple schemas can be selected by writing multiple -n switches. Also, the *schema* parameter is interpreted as a pattern according to the same rules used by psql's \d commands (see *Patterns*), so multiple schemas can also be selected by writing wildcard characters in the pattern. When using wildcards, be careful to quote the pattern if needed to prevent the shell from expanding the wildcards; see *Examples*.

> **Note:** When -n is specified, pg_dump makes no attempt to dump any other database objects that the selected schema(s) might depend upon. Therefore, there is no guarantee that the results of a specific-schema dump can be successfully restored by themselves into a clean database.

> **Note:** Non-schema objects such as blobs are not dumped when -n is specified. You can add blobs back to the dump with the --blobs switch.

`-N` *schema*

`--exclude-schema=`*schema*

Do not dump any schemas matching the *schema* pattern. The pattern is interpreted according to the same rules as for -n. -N can be given more than once to exclude schemas matching any of several patterns.

When both -n and -N are given, the behavior is to dump just the schemas that match at least one -n switch but no -N switches. If -N appears without -n, then schemas matching -N are excluded from what is otherwise a normal dump.

```
-o
--oids
```

Dump object identifiers (OIDs) as part of the data for every table. Use this option if your application references the OID columns in some way (e.g., in a foreign key constraint). Otherwise, this option should not be used.

```
-O
--no-owner
```

Do not output commands to set ownership of objects to match the original database. By default, pg_dump issues ALTER OWNER or SET SESSION AUTHORIZATION statements to set ownership of created database objects. These statements will fail when the script is run unless it is started by a superuser (or the same user that owns all of the objects in the script). To make a script that can be restored by any user, but will give that user ownership of all the objects, specify -O.

This option is only meaningful for the plain-text format. For the archive formats, you can specify the option when you call pg_restore.

```
-R
--no-reconnect
```

This option is obsolete but still accepted for backwards compatibility.

```
-s
--schema-only
```

Dump only the object definitions (schema), not data.

This option is the inverse of --data-only. It is similar to, but for historical reasons not identical to, specifying --section=pre-data --section=post-data.

(Do not confuse this with the --schema option, which uses the word "schema" in a different meaning.)

To exclude table data for only a subset of tables in the database, see --exclude-table-data.

```
-S username
--superuser=username
```

Specify the superuser user name to use when disabling triggers. This is relevant only if --disable-triggers is used. (Usually, it's better to leave this out, and instead start the resulting script as superuser.)

```
-t table
--table=table
```

Dump only tables with names matching *table*. For this purpose, "table" includes views, materialized views, sequences, and foreign tables. Multiple tables can be selected by writing multiple -t switches. Also, the *table* parameter is interpreted as a pattern according to the same rules used by psql's \d commands (see *Patterns*), so multiple tables can also be selected by writing wildcard characters in the pattern. When using wildcards, be careful to quote the pattern if needed to prevent the shell from expanding the wildcards; see *Examples*.

The -n and -N switches have no effect when -t is used, because tables selected by -t will be dumped regardless of those switches, and non-table objects will not be dumped.

Note: When `-t` is specified, pg_dump makes no attempt to dump any other database objects that the selected table(s) might depend upon. Therefore, there is no guarantee that the results of a specific-table dump can be successfully restored by themselves into a clean database.

Note: The behavior of the `-t` switch is not entirely upward compatible with pre-8.2 PostgreSQL versions. Formerly, writing `-t tab` would dump all tables named `tab`, but now it just dumps whichever one is visible in your default search path. To get the old behavior you can write `-t '*.tab'`. Also, you must write something like `-t sch.tab` to select a table in a particular schema, rather than the old locution of `-n sch -t tab`.

`-T` *table*

`--exclude-table=`*table*

> Do not dump any tables matching the *table* pattern. The pattern is interpreted according to the same rules as for `-t`. `-T` can be given more than once to exclude tables matching any of several patterns.
>
> When both `-t` and `-T` are given, the behavior is to dump just the tables that match at least one `-t` switch but no `-T` switches. If `-T` appears without `-t`, then tables matching `-T` are excluded from what is otherwise a normal dump.

`-v`

`--verbose`

> Specifies verbose mode. This will cause pg_dump to output detailed object comments and start/stop times to the dump file, and progress messages to standard error.

`-V`

`--version`

> Print the pg_dump version and exit.

`-x`

`--no-privileges`

`--no-acl`

> Prevent dumping of access privileges (grant/revoke commands).

`-Z` *0..9*

`--compress=`*0..9*

> Specify the compression level to use. Zero means no compression. For the custom archive format, this specifies compression of individual table-data segments, and the default is to compress at a moderate level. For plain text output, setting a nonzero compression level causes the entire output file to be compressed, as though it had been fed through gzip; but the default is not to compress. The tar archive format currently does not support compression at all.

`--binary-upgrade`

> This option is for use by in-place upgrade utilities. Its use for other purposes is not recommended or supported. The behavior of the option may change in future releases without notice.

`--column-inserts`
`--attribute-inserts`

> Dump data as INSERT commands with explicit column names (INSERT INTO *table* (*column*, ...) VALUES ...). This will make restoration very slow; it is mainly useful for making dumps that can be loaded into non-PostgreSQL databases. However, since this option generates a separate command for each row, an error in reloading a row causes only that row to be lost rather than the entire table contents.

`--disable-dollar-quoting`

> This option disables the use of dollar quoting for function bodies, and forces them to be quoted using SQL standard string syntax.

`--disable-triggers`

> This option is relevant only when creating a data-only dump. It instructs pg_dump to include commands to temporarily disable triggers on the target tables while the data is reloaded. Use this if you have referential integrity checks or other triggers on the tables that you do not want to invoke during data reload.

> Presently, the commands emitted for `--disable-triggers` must be done as superuser. So, you should also specify a superuser name with `-S`, or preferably be careful to start the resulting script as a superuser.

> This option is only meaningful for the plain-text format. For the archive formats, you can specify the option when you call `pg_restore`.

`--enable-row-security`

> This option is relevant only when dumping the contents of a table which has row security. By default, pg_dump will set row_security to off, to ensure that all data is dumped from the table. If the user does not have sufficient privileges to bypass row security, then an error is thrown. This parameter instructs pg_dump to set row_security to on instead, allowing the user to dump the parts of the contents of the table that they have access to.

`--exclude-table-data=`*table*

> Do not dump data for any tables matching the *table* pattern. The pattern is interpreted according to the same rules as for `-t`. `--exclude-table-data` can be given more than once to exclude tables matching any of several patterns. This option is useful when you need the definition of a particular table even though you do not need the data in it.

> To exclude data for all tables in the database, see `--schema-only`.

`--if-exists`

> Use conditional commands (i.e. add an IF EXISTS clause) when cleaning database objects. This option is not valid unless `--clean` is also specified.

`--inserts`

> Dump data as INSERT commands (rather than COPY). This will make restoration very slow; it is mainly useful for making dumps that can be loaded into non-PostgreSQL databases. However, since this option generates a separate command for each row, an error in reloading a row causes only that row to be lost rather than the entire table contents. Note that the restore might fail altogether if you have rearranged column order. The `--column-inserts` option is safe against column order changes, though even slower.

`--lock-wait-timeout=`*timeout*

> Do not wait forever to acquire shared table locks at the beginning of the dump. Instead fail if unable to lock a table within the specified *timeout*. The timeout may be specified in any of the formats accepted by SET statement_timeout. (Allowed values vary depending on the server version you are dumping from, but an integer number of milliseconds is accepted by all versions since 7.3. This option is ignored when dumping from a pre-7.3 server.)

`--no-security-labels`

> Do not dump security labels.

`--no-synchronized-snapshots`

> This option allows running pg_dump -j against a pre-9.2 server, see the documentation of the -j parameter for more details.

`--no-tablespaces`

> Do not output commands to select tablespaces. With this option, all objects will be created in whichever tablespace is the default during restore.
>
> This option is only meaningful for the plain-text format. For the archive formats, you can specify the option when you call pg_restore.

`--no-unlogged-table-data`

> Do not dump the contents of unlogged tables. This option has no effect on whether or not the table definitions (schema) are dumped; it only suppresses dumping the table data. Data in unlogged tables is always excluded when dumping from a standby server.

`--quote-all-identifiers`

> Force quoting of all identifiers. This option is recommended when dumping a database from a server whose PostgreSQL major version is different from pg_dump's, or when the output is intended to be loaded into a server of a different major version. By default, pg_dump quotes only identifiers that are reserved words in its own major version. This sometimes results in compatibility issues when dealing with servers of other versions that may have slightly different sets of reserved words. Using --quote-all-identifiers prevents such issues, at the price of a harder-to-read dump script.

`--section=`*sectionname*

> Only dump the named section. The section name can be pre-data, data, or post-data. This option can be specified more than once to select multiple sections. The default is to dump all sections.
>
> The data section contains actual table data, large-object contents, and sequence values. Post-data items include definitions of indexes, triggers, rules, and constraints other than validated check constraints. Pre-data items include all other data definition items.

`--serializable-deferrable`

> Use a serializable transaction for the dump, to ensure that the snapshot used is consistent with later database states; but do this by waiting for a point in the transaction stream at which no anomalies can be present, so that there isn't a risk of the dump failing or causing other transactions to roll back with a serialization_failure. See Chapter 13 for more information about transaction isolation and concurrency control.
>
> This option is not beneficial for a dump which is intended only for disaster recovery. It could be useful for a dump used to load a copy of the database for reporting or other read-only load sharing

while the original database continues to be updated. Without it the dump may reflect a state which is not consistent with any serial execution of the transactions eventually committed. For example, if batch processing techniques are used, a batch may show as closed in the dump without all of the items which are in the batch appearing.

This option will make no difference if there are no read-write transactions active when pg_dump is started. If read-write transactions are active, the start of the dump may be delayed for an indeterminate length of time. Once running, performance with or without the switch is the same.

`--snapshot=`*snapshotname*

Use the specified synchronized snapshot when making a dump of the database (see Table 9-81 for more details).

This option is useful when needing to synchronize the dump with a logical replication slot (see Chapter 47) or with a concurrent session.

In the case of a parallel dump, the snapshot name defined by this option is used rather than taking a new snapshot.

`--strict-names`

Require that each schema (`-n`/`--schema`) and table (`-t`/`--table`) qualifier match at least one schema/table in the database to be dumped. Note that if none of the schema/table qualifiers find matches, pg_dump will generate an error even without `--strict-names`.

This option has no effect on `-N`/`--exclude-schema`, `-T`/`--exclude-table`, or `--exclude-table-data`. An exclude pattern failing to match any objects is not considered an error.

`--use-set-session-authorization`

Output SQL-standard SET SESSION AUTHORIZATION commands instead of ALTER OWNER commands to determine object ownership. This makes the dump more standards-compatible, but depending on the history of the objects in the dump, might not restore properly. Also, a dump using SET SESSION AUTHORIZATION will certainly require superuser privileges to restore correctly, whereas ALTER OWNER requires lesser privileges.

`-?`
`--help`

Show help about pg_dump command line arguments, and exit.

The following command-line options control the database connection parameters.

`-d` *dbname*
`--dbname=`*dbname*

Specifies the name of the database to connect to. This is equivalent to specifying *dbname* as the first non-option argument on the command line.

If this parameter contains an = sign or starts with a valid URI prefix (`postgresql://` or `postgres://`), it is treated as a `conninfo` string. See Section 32.1 for more information.

`-h` *host*
`--host=`*host*

> Specifies the host name of the machine on which the server is running. If the value begins with a slash, it is used as the directory for the Unix domain socket. The default is taken from the `PGHOST` environment variable, if set, else a Unix domain socket connection is attempted.

`-p` *port*
`--port=`*port*

> Specifies the TCP port or local Unix domain socket file extension on which the server is listening for connections. Defaults to the `PGPORT` environment variable, if set, or a compiled-in default.

`-U` *username*
`--username=`*username*

> User name to connect as.

`-w`
`--no-password`

> Never issue a password prompt. If the server requires password authentication and a password is not available by other means such as a `.pgpass` file, the connection attempt will fail. This option can be useful in batch jobs and scripts where no user is present to enter a password.

`-W`
`--password`

> Force pg_dump to prompt for a password before connecting to a database.
>
> This option is never essential, since pg_dump will automatically prompt for a password if the server demands password authentication. However, pg_dump will waste a connection attempt finding out that the server wants a password. In some cases it is worth typing `-W` to avoid the extra connection attempt.

`--role=`*rolename*

> Specifies a role name to be used to create the dump. This option causes pg_dump to issue a `SET ROLE` *rolename* command after connecting to the database. It is useful when the authenticated user (specified by `-U`) lacks privileges needed by pg_dump, but can switch to a role with the required rights. Some installations have a policy against logging in directly as a superuser, and use of this option allows dumps to be made without violating the policy.

Environment

`PGDATABASE`
`PGHOST`
`PGOPTIONS`
`PGPORT`
`PGUSER`

> Default connection parameters.

This utility, like most other PostgreSQL utilities, also uses the environment variables supported by libpq (see Section 32.14).

Diagnostics

pg_dump internally executes SELECT statements. If you have problems running pg_dump, make sure you are able to select information from the database using, for example, psql. Also, any default connection settings and environment variables used by the libpq front-end library will apply.

The database activity of pg_dump is normally collected by the statistics collector. If this is undesirable, you can set parameter track_counts to false via PGOPTIONS or the ALTER USER command.

Notes

If your database cluster has any local additions to the template1 database, be careful to restore the output of pg_dump into a truly empty database; otherwise you are likely to get errors due to duplicate definitions of the added objects. To make an empty database without any local additions, copy from template0 not template1, for example:

```
CREATE DATABASE foo WITH TEMPLATE template0;
```

When a data-only dump is chosen and the option --disable-triggers is used, pg_dump emits commands to disable triggers on user tables before inserting the data, and then commands to re-enable them after the data has been inserted. If the restore is stopped in the middle, the system catalogs might be left in the wrong state.

The dump file produced by pg_dump does not contain the statistics used by the optimizer to make query planning decisions. Therefore, it is wise to run ANALYZE after restoring from a dump file to ensure optimal performance; see Section 24.1.3 and Section 24.1.6 for more information. The dump file also does not contain any ALTER DATABASE ... SET commands; these settings are dumped by pg_dumpall, along with database users and other installation-wide settings.

Because pg_dump is used to transfer data to newer versions of PostgreSQL, the output of pg_dump can be expected to load into PostgreSQL server versions newer than pg_dump's version. pg_dump can also dump from PostgreSQL servers older than its own version. (Currently, servers back to version 7.0 are supported.) However, pg_dump cannot dump from PostgreSQL servers newer than its own major version; it will refuse to even try, rather than risk making an invalid dump. Also, it is not guaranteed that pg_dump's output can be loaded into a server of an older major version — not even if the dump was taken from a server of that version. Loading a dump file into an older server may require manual editing of the dump file to remove syntax not understood by the older server. Use of the --quote-all-identifiers option is recommended in cross-version cases, as it can prevent problems arising from varying reserved-word lists in different PostgreSQL versions.

Examples

To dump a database called `mydb` into a SQL-script file:

```
$ pg_dump mydb > db.sql
```

To reload such a script into a (freshly created) database named `newdb`:

```
$ psql -d newdb -f db.sql
```

To dump a database into a custom-format archive file:

```
$ pg_dump -Fc mydb > db.dump
```

To dump a database into a directory-format archive:

```
$ pg_dump -Fd mydb -f dumpdir
```

To dump a database into a directory-format archive in parallel with 5 worker jobs:

```
$ pg_dump -Fd mydb -j 5 -f dumpdir
```

To reload an archive file into a (freshly created) database named `newdb`:

```
$ pg_restore -d newdb db.dump
```

To dump a single table named `mytab`:

```
$ pg_dump -t mytab mydb > db.sql
```

To dump all tables whose names start with `emp` in the `detroit` schema, except for the table named `employee_log`:

```
$ pg_dump -t 'detroit.emp*' -T detroit.employee_log mydb > db.sql
```

To dump all schemas whose names start with `east` or `west` and end in `gsm`, excluding any schemas whose names contain the word `test`:

```
$ pg_dump -n 'east*gsm' -n 'west*gsm' -N '*test*' mydb > db.sql
```

The same, using regular expression notation to consolidate the switches:

```
$ pg_dump -n '(east|west)*gsm' -N '*test*' mydb > db.sql
```

To dump all database objects except for tables whose names begin with ts_:

```
$ pg_dump -T 'ts_*' mydb > db.sql
```

To specify an upper-case or mixed-case name in -t and related switches, you need to double-quote the name; else it will be folded to lower case (see *Patterns*). But double quotes are special to the shell, so in turn they must be quoted. Thus, to dump a single table with a mixed-case name, you need something like

```
$ pg_dump -t "\"MixedCaseName\"" mydb > mytab.sql
```

See Also

pg_dumpall, pg_restore, psql

pg_dumpall

Name

pg_dumpall — extract a PostgreSQL database cluster into a script file

Synopsis

pg_dumpall [*connection-option*...] [*option*...]

Description

pg_dumpall is a utility for writing out ("dumping") all PostgreSQL databases of a cluster into one script file. The script file contains SQL commands that can be used as input to psql to restore the databases. It does this by calling pg_dump for each database in a cluster. pg_dumpall also dumps global objects that are common to all databases. (pg_dump does not save these objects.) This currently includes information about database users and groups, tablespaces, and properties such as access permissions that apply to databases as a whole.

Since pg_dumpall reads tables from all databases you will most likely have to connect as a database superuser in order to produce a complete dump. Also you will need superuser privileges to execute the saved script in order to be allowed to add users and groups, and to create databases.

The SQL script will be written to the standard output. Use the [-f|file] option or shell operators to redirect it into a file.

pg_dumpall needs to connect several times to the PostgreSQL server (once per database). If you use password authentication it will ask for a password each time. It is convenient to have a ~/.pgpass file in such cases. See Section 32.15 for more information.

Options

The following command-line options control the content and format of the output.

-a
--data-only

   Dump only the data, not the schema (data definitions).

-c
--clean

   Include SQL commands to clean (drop) databases before recreating them. DROP commands for roles and tablespaces are added as well.

`-f` *filename*

`--file=`*filename*

> Send output to the specified file. If this is omitted, the standard output is used.

`-g`

`--globals-only`

> Dump only global objects (roles and tablespaces), no databases.

`-o`

`--oids`

> Dump object identifiers (OIDs) as part of the data for every table. Use this option if your application references the OID columns in some way (e.g., in a foreign key constraint). Otherwise, this option should not be used.

`-O`

`--no-owner`

> Do not output commands to set ownership of objects to match the original database. By default, pg_dumpall issues ALTER OWNER or SET SESSION AUTHORIZATION statements to set ownership of created schema elements. These statements will fail when the script is run unless it is started by a superuser (or the same user that owns all of the objects in the script). To make a script that can be restored by any user, but will give that user ownership of all the objects, specify `-O`.

`-r`

`--roles-only`

> Dump only roles, no databases or tablespaces.

`-s`

`--schema-only`

> Dump only the object definitions (schema), not data.

`-S` *username*

`--superuser=`*username*

> Specify the superuser user name to use when disabling triggers. This is relevant only if `--disable-triggers` is used. (Usually, it's better to leave this out, and instead start the resulting script as superuser.)

`-t`

`--tablespaces-only`

> Dump only tablespaces, no databases or roles.

`-v`

`--verbose`

> Specifies verbose mode. This will cause pg_dumpall to output start/stop times to the dump file, and progress messages to standard error. It will also enable verbose output in pg_dump.

`-V`

`--version`

> Print the pg_dumpall version and exit.

```
-x
--no-privileges
--no-acl
```

Prevent dumping of access privileges (grant/revoke commands).

```
--binary-upgrade
```

This option is for use by in-place upgrade utilities. Its use for other purposes is not recommended or supported. The behavior of the option may change in future releases without notice.

```
--column-inserts
--attribute-inserts
```

Dump data as INSERT commands with explicit column names (INSERT INTO *table* (*column*, ...) VALUES ...). This will make restoration very slow; it is mainly useful for making dumps that can be loaded into non-PostgreSQL databases.

```
--disable-dollar-quoting
```

This option disables the use of dollar quoting for function bodies, and forces them to be quoted using SQL standard string syntax.

```
--disable-triggers
```

This option is relevant only when creating a data-only dump. It instructs pg_dumpall to include commands to temporarily disable triggers on the target tables while the data is reloaded. Use this if you have referential integrity checks or other triggers on the tables that you do not want to invoke during data reload.

Presently, the commands emitted for --disable-triggers must be done as superuser. So, you should also specify a superuser name with -S, or preferably be careful to start the resulting script as a superuser.

```
--if-exists
```

Use conditional commands (i.e. add an IF EXISTS clause) to clean databases and other objects. This option is not valid unless --clean is also specified.

```
--inserts
```

Dump data as INSERT commands (rather than COPY). This will make restoration very slow; it is mainly useful for making dumps that can be loaded into non-PostgreSQL databases. Note that the restore might fail altogether if you have rearranged column order. The --column-inserts option is safer, though even slower.

```
--lock-wait-timeout=timeout
```

Do not wait forever to acquire shared table locks at the beginning of the dump. Instead, fail if unable to lock a table within the specified *timeout*. The timeout may be specified in any of the formats accepted by SET statement_timeout. Allowed values vary depending on the server version you are dumping from, but an integer number of milliseconds is accepted by all versions since 7.3. This option is ignored when dumping from a pre-7.3 server.

```
--no-security-labels
```

Do not dump security labels.

`--no-tablespaces`

Do not output commands to create tablespaces nor select tablespaces for objects. With this option, all objects will be created in whichever tablespace is the default during restore.

`--no-unlogged-table-data`

Do not dump the contents of unlogged tables. This option has no effect on whether or not the table definitions (schema) are dumped; it only suppresses dumping the table data.

`--quote-all-identifiers`

Force quoting of all identifiers. This option is recommended when dumping a database from a server whose PostgreSQL major version is different from pg_dumpall's, or when the output is intended to be loaded into a server of a different major version. By default, pg_dumpall quotes only identifiers that are reserved words in its own major version. This sometimes results in compatibility issues when dealing with servers of other versions that may have slightly different sets of reserved words. Using `--quote-all-identifiers` prevents such issues, at the price of a harder-to-read dump script.

`--use-set-session-authorization`

Output SQL-standard `SET SESSION AUTHORIZATION` commands instead of `ALTER OWNER` commands to determine object ownership. This makes the dump more standards compatible, but depending on the history of the objects in the dump, might not restore properly.

`-?`

`--help`

Show help about pg_dumpall command line arguments, and exit.

The following command-line options control the database connection parameters.

`-d connstr`

`--dbname=connstr`

Specifies parameters used to connect to the server, as a connection string. See Section 32.1.1 for more information.

The option is called `--dbname` for consistency with other client applications, but because pg_dumpall needs to connect to many databases, database name in the connection string will be ignored. Use `-l` option to specify the name of the database used to dump global objects and to discover what other databases should be dumped.

`-h host`

`--host=host`

Specifies the host name of the machine on which the database server is running. If the value begins with a slash, it is used as the directory for the Unix domain socket. The default is taken from the `PGHOST` environment variable, if set, else a Unix domain socket connection is attempted.

`-l dbname`

`--database=dbname`

Specifies the name of the database to connect to for dumping global objects and discovering what other databases should be dumped. If not specified, the `postgres` database will be used, and if that does not exist, `template1` will be used.

```
-p port
--port=port
```

Specifies the TCP port or local Unix domain socket file extension on which the server is listening for connections. Defaults to the `PGPORT` environment variable, if set, or a compiled-in default.

```
-U username
--username=username
```

User name to connect as.

```
-w
--no-password
```

Never issue a password prompt. If the server requires password authentication and a password is not available by other means such as a `.pgpass` file, the connection attempt will fail. This option can be useful in batch jobs and scripts where no user is present to enter a password.

```
-W
--password
```

Force pg_dumpall to prompt for a password before connecting to a database.

This option is never essential, since pg_dumpall will automatically prompt for a password if the server demands password authentication. However, pg_dumpall will waste a connection attempt finding out that the server wants a password. In some cases it is worth typing `-W` to avoid the extra connection attempt.

Note that the password prompt will occur again for each database to be dumped. Usually, it's better to set up a `~/.pgpass` file than to rely on manual password entry.

```
--role=rolename
```

Specifies a role name to be used to create the dump. This option causes pg_dumpall to issue a `SET ROLE rolename` command after connecting to the database. It is useful when the authenticated user (specified by `-U`) lacks privileges needed by pg_dumpall, but can switch to a role with the required rights. Some installations have a policy against logging in directly as a superuser, and use of this option allows dumps to be made without violating the policy.

Environment

```
PGHOST
PGOPTIONS
PGPORT
PGUSER
```

Default connection parameters

This utility, like most other PostgreSQL utilities, also uses the environment variables supported by libpq (see Section 32.14).

Notes

Since pg_dumpall calls pg_dump internally, some diagnostic messages will refer to pg_dump.

Once restored, it is wise to run ANALYZE on each database so the optimizer has useful statistics. You can also run vacuumdb -a -z to analyze all databases.

pg_dumpall requires all needed tablespace directories to exist before the restore; otherwise, database creation will fail for databases in non-default locations.

Examples

To dump all databases:

```
$ pg_dumpall > db.out
```

To reload database(s) from this file, you can use:

```
$ psql -f db.out postgres
```

(It is not important to which database you connect here since the script file created by pg_dumpall will contain the appropriate commands to create and connect to the saved databases.)

See Also

Check pg_dump for details on possible error conditions.

pg_isready

Name

pg_isready — check the connection status of a PostgreSQL server

Synopsis

pg_isready [connection-option...] [option...]

Description

pg_isready is a utility for checking the connection status of a PostgreSQL database server. The exit status specifies the result of the connection check.

Options

-d dbname
--dbname=dbname

>   Specifies the name of the database to connect to.

>   If this parameter contains an = sign or starts with a valid URI prefix (postgresql:// or postgres://), it is treated as a conninfo string. See Section 32.1.1 for more information.

-h hostname
--host=hostname

>   Specifies the host name of the machine on which the server is running. If the value begins with a slash, it is used as the directory for the Unix-domain socket.

-p port
--port=port

>   Specifies the TCP port or the local Unix-domain socket file extension on which the server is listening for connections. Defaults to the value of the PGPORT environment variable or, if not set, to the port specified at compile time, usually 5432.

-q
--quiet

>   Do not display status message. This is useful when scripting.

-t seconds
--timeout=seconds

>   The maximum number of seconds to wait when attempting connection before returning that the server is not responding. Setting to 0 disables. The default is 3 seconds.

```
-U username
--username=username
```

Connect to the database as the user `username` instead of the default.

```
-V
--version
```

Print the pg_isready version and exit.

```
-?
--help
```

Show help about pg_isready command line arguments, and exit.

Exit Status

pg_isready returns 0 to the shell if the server is accepting connections normally, 1 if the server is rejecting connections (for example during startup), 2 if there was no response to the connection attempt, and 3 if no attempt was made (for example due to invalid parameters).

Environment

`pg_isready`, like most other PostgreSQL utilities, also uses the environment variables supported by libpq (see Section 32.14).

Notes

It is not necessary to supply correct user name, password, or database name values to obtain the server status; however, if incorrect values are provided, the server will log a failed connection attempt.

Examples

Standard Usage:

```
$ pg_isready
/tmp:5432 - accepting connections
$ echo $?
0
```

Running with connection parameters to a PostgreSQL cluster in startup:

```
$ pg_isready -h localhost -p 5433
localhost:5433 - rejecting connections
$ echo $?
1
```

Running with connection parameters to a non-responsive PostgreSQL cluster:

```
$ pg_isready -h someremotehost
someremotehost:5432 - no response
$ echo $?
2
```

pg_receivexlog

Name

`pg_receivexlog` — stream transaction logs from a PostgreSQL server

Synopsis

`pg_receivexlog` [*option*...]

Description

pg_receivexlog is used to stream the transaction log from a running PostgreSQL cluster. The transaction log is streamed using the streaming replication protocol, and is written to a local directory of files. This directory can be used as the archive location for doing a restore using point-in-time recovery (see Section 25.3).

pg_receivexlog streams the transaction log in real time as it's being generated on the server, and does not wait for segments to complete like archive_command does. For this reason, it is not necessary to set archive_timeout when using pg_receivexlog.

Unlike the WAL receiver of a PostgreSQL standby server, pg_receivexlog by default flushes WAL data only when a WAL file is closed. The option `--synchronous` must be specified to flush WAL data in real time.

The transaction log is streamed over a regular PostgreSQL connection and uses the replication protocol. The connection must be made with a superuser or a user having `REPLICATION` permissions (see Section 21.2), and `pg_hba.conf` must permit the replication connection. The server must also be configured with max_wal_senders set high enough to leave at least one session available for the stream.

If the connection is lost, or if it cannot be initially established, with a non-fatal error, pg_receivexlog will retry the connection indefinitely, and reestablish streaming as soon as possible. To avoid this behavior, use the -n parameter.

Options

-D *directory*
--directory=*directory*

    Directory to write the output to.

    This parameter is required.

--if-not-exists

    Do not error out when `--create-slot` is specified and a slot with the specified name already exists.

```
-n
--no-loop
```

Don't loop on connection errors. Instead, exit right away with an error.

```
-s interval
--status-interval=interval
```

Specifies the number of seconds between status packets sent back to the server. This allows for easier monitoring of the progress from server. A value of zero disables the periodic status updates completely, although an update will still be sent when requested by the server, to avoid timeout disconnect. The default value is 10 seconds.

```
-S slotname
--slot=slotname
```

Require pg_receivexlog to use an existing replication slot (see Section 26.2.6). When this option is used, pg_receivexlog will report a flush position to the server, indicating when each segment has been synchronized to disk so that the server can remove that segment if it is not otherwise needed.

When the replication client of pg_receivexlog is configured on the server as a synchronous standby, then using a replication slot will report the flush position to the server, but only when a WAL file is closed. Therefore, that configuration will cause transactions on the primary to wait for a long time and effectively not work satisfactorily. The option --synchronous (see below) must be specified in addition to make this work correctly.

```
--synchronous
```

Flush the WAL data to disk immediately after it has been received. Also send a status packet back to the server immediately after flushing, regardless of --status-interval.

This option should be specified if the replication client of pg_receivexlog is configured on the server as a synchronous standby, to ensure that timely feedback is sent to the server.

```
-v
--verbose
```

Enables verbose mode.

The following command-line options control the database connection parameters.

```
-d connstr
--dbname=connstr
```

Specifies parameters used to connect to the server, as a connection string. See Section 32.1.1 for more information.

The option is called --dbname for consistency with other client applications, but because pg_receivexlog doesn't connect to any particular database in the cluster, database name in the connection string will be ignored.

```
-h host
--host=host
```

Specifies the host name of the machine on which the server is running. If the value begins with a slash, it is used as the directory for the Unix domain socket. The default is taken from the PGHOST environment variable, if set, else a Unix domain socket connection is attempted.

`-p` *port*
`--port=`*port*

>Specifies the TCP port or local Unix domain socket file extension on which the server is listening for connections. Defaults to the `PGPORT` environment variable, if set, or a compiled-in default.

`-U` *username*
`--username=`*username*

>User name to connect as.

`-w`
`--no-password`

>Never issue a password prompt. If the server requires password authentication and a password is not available by other means such as a `.pgpass` file, the connection attempt will fail. This option can be useful in batch jobs and scripts where no user is present to enter a password.

`-W`
`--password`

>Force pg_receivexlog to prompt for a password before connecting to a database.

>This option is never essential, since pg_receivexlog will automatically prompt for a password if the server demands password authentication. However, pg_receivexlog will waste a connection attempt finding out that the server wants a password. In some cases it is worth typing `-W` to avoid the extra connection attempt.

pg_receivexlog can perform one of the two following actions in order to control physical replication slots:

`--create-slot`

>Create a new physical replication slot with the name specified in `--slot`, then exit.

`--drop-slot`

>Drop the replication slot with the name specified in `--slot`, then exit.

Other options are also available:

`-V`
`--version`

>Print the pg_receivexlog version and exit.

`-?`
`--help`

>Show help about pg_receivexlog command line arguments, and exit.

Environment

This utility, like most other PostgreSQL utilities, uses the environment variables supported by libpq (see Section 32.14).

Notes

When using pg_receivexlog instead of archive_command as the main WAL backup method, it is strongly recommended to use replication slots. Otherwise, the server is free to recycle or remove transaction log files before they are backed up, because it does not have any information, either from archive_command or the replication slots, about how far the WAL stream has been archived. Note, however, that a replication slot will fill up the server's disk space if the receiver does not keep up with fetching the WAL data.

Examples

To stream the transaction log from the server at `mydbserver` and store it in the local directory `/usr/local/pgsql/archive`:

```
$ pg_receivexlog -h mydbserver -D /usr/local/pgsql/archive
```

See Also

pg_basebackup

pg_recvlogical

Name

`pg_recvlogical` — control PostgreSQL logical decoding streams

Synopsis

`pg_recvlogical` [*option*...]

Description

`pg_recvlogical` controls logical decoding replication slots and streams data from such replication slots.

It creates a replication-mode connection, so it is subject to the same constraints as pg_receivexlog, plus those for logical replication (see Chapter 47).

Options

At least one of the following options must be specified to select an action:

`--create-slot`

Create a new logical replication slot with the name specified by `--slot`, using the output plugin specified by `--plugin`, for the database specified by `--dbname`.

`--drop-slot`

Drop the replication slot with the name specified by `--slot`, then exit.

`--start`

Begin streaming changes from the logical replication slot specified by `--slot`, continuing until terminated by a signal. If the server side change stream ends with a server shutdown or disconnect, retry in a loop unless `--no-loop` is specified.

The stream format is determined by the output plugin specified when the slot was created.

The connection must be to the same database used to create the slot.

`--create-slot` and `--start` can be specified together. `--drop-slot` cannot be combined with another action.

The following command-line options control the location and format of the output and other replication behavior:

`-f` *filename*
`--file=`*filename*

> Write received and decoded transaction data into this file. Use – for stdout.

`-F` *interval_seconds*
`--fsync-interval=`*interval_seconds*

> Specifies how often pg_recvlogical should issue `fsync()` calls to ensure the output file is safely flushed to disk.

> The server will occasionally request the client to perform a flush and report the flush position to the server. This setting is in addition to that, to perform flushes more frequently.

> Specifying an interval of 0 disables issuing `fsync()` calls altogether, while still reporting progress to the server. In this case, data could be lost in the event of a crash.

`-I` *lsn*
`--startpos=`*lsn*

> In `--start` mode, start replication from the given LSN. For details on the effect of this, see the documentation in Chapter 47 and Section 51.3. Ignored in other modes.

`--if-not-exists`

> Do not error out when `--create-slot` is specified and a slot with the specified name already exists.

`-n`
`--no-loop`

> When the connection to the server is lost, do not retry in a loop, just exit.

`-o` *name*`[=`*value*`]`
`--option=`*name*`[=`*value*`]`

> Pass the option *name* to the output plugin with, if specified, the option value *value*. Which options exist and their effects depends on the used output plugin.

`-P` *plugin*
`--plugin=`*plugin*

> When creating a slot, use the specified logical decoding output plugin. See Chapter 47. This option has no effect if the slot already exists.

`-s` *interval_seconds*
`--status-interval=`*interval_seconds*

> This option has the same effect as the option of the same name in pg_receivexlog. See the description there.

`-S` *slot_name*
`--slot=`*slot_name*

> In `--start` mode, use the existing logical replication slot named *slot_name*. In `--create-slot` mode, create the slot with this name. In `--drop-slot` mode, delete the slot with this name.

`-v`
`--verbose`

> Enables verbose mode.

The following command-line options control the database connection parameters.

`-d` *database*

`--dbname=`*database*

> The database to connect to. See the description of the actions for what this means in detail. This can be a libpq connection string; see Section 32.1.1 for more information. Defaults to user name.

`-h` *hostname-or-ip*

`--host=`*hostname-or-ip*

> Specifies the host name of the machine on which the server is running. If the value begins with a slash, it is used as the directory for the Unix domain socket. The default is taken from the `PGHOST` environment variable, if set, else a Unix domain socket connection is attempted.

`-p` *port*

`--port=`*port*

> Specifies the TCP port or local Unix domain socket file extension on which the server is listening for connections. Defaults to the `PGPORT` environment variable, if set, or a compiled-in default.

`-U` *user*

`--username=`*user*

> User name to connect as. Defaults to current operating system user name.

`-w`

`--no-password`

> Never issue a password prompt. If the server requires password authentication and a password is not available by other means such as a `.pgpass` file, the connection attempt will fail. This option can be useful in batch jobs and scripts where no user is present to enter a password.

`-W`

`--password`

> Force pg_recvlogical to prompt for a password before connecting to a database.
>
> This option is never essential, since pg_recvlogical will automatically prompt for a password if the server demands password authentication. However, pg_recvlogical will waste a connection attempt finding out that the server wants a password. In some cases it is worth typing `-W` to avoid the extra connection attempt.

The following additional options are available:

`-V`

`--version`

> Print the pg_recvlogical version and exit.

`-?`

`--help`

> Show help about pg_recvlogical command line arguments, and exit.

Environment

This utility, like most other PostgreSQL utilities, uses the environment variables supported by libpq (see Section 32.14).

Examples

See Section 47.1 for an example.

See Also

pg_receivexlog

pg_restore

Name

`pg_restore` — restore a PostgreSQL database from an archive file created by pg_dump

Synopsis

`pg_restore` [*connection-option*...] [*option*...] [*filename*]

Description

pg_restore is a utility for restoring a PostgreSQL database from an archive created by pg_dump in one of the non-plain-text formats. It will issue the commands necessary to reconstruct the database to the state it was in at the time it was saved. The archive files also allow pg_restore to be selective about what is restored, or even to reorder the items prior to being restored. The archive files are designed to be portable across architectures.

pg_restore can operate in two modes. If a database name is specified, pg_restore connects to that database and restores archive contents directly into the database. Otherwise, a script containing the SQL commands necessary to rebuild the database is created and written to a file or standard output. This script output is equivalent to the plain text output format of pg_dump. Some of the options controlling the output are therefore analogous to pg_dump options.

Obviously, pg_restore cannot restore information that is not present in the archive file. For instance, if the archive was made using the "dump data as `INSERT` commands" option, pg_restore will not be able to load the data using `COPY` statements.

Options

pg_restore accepts the following command line arguments.

filename

> Specifies the location of the archive file (or directory, for a directory-format archive) to be restored. If not specified, the standard input is used.

`-a`
`--data-only`

> Restore only the data, not the schema (data definitions). Table data, large objects, and sequence values are restored, if present in the archive.

> This option is similar to, but for historical reasons not identical to, specifying `--section=data`.

`-c`

`--clean`

> Clean (drop) database objects before recreating them. (Unless `--if-exists` is used, this might generate some harmless error messages, if any objects were not present in the destination database.)

`-C`

`--create`

> Create the database before restoring into it. If `--clean` is also specified, drop and recreate the target database before connecting to it.

> When this option is used, the database named with `-d` is used only to issue the initial DROP DATABASE and CREATE DATABASE commands. All data is restored into the database name that appears in the archive.

`-d` *dbname*

`--dbname=`*dbname*

> Connect to database *dbname* and restore directly into the database.

`-e`

`--exit-on-error`

> Exit if an error is encountered while sending SQL commands to the database. The default is to continue and to display a count of errors at the end of the restoration.

`-f` *filename*

`--file=`*filename*

> Specify output file for generated script, or for the listing when used with `-l`. Default is the standard output.

`-F` *format*

`--format=`*format*

> Specify format of the archive. It is not necessary to specify the format, since pg_restore will determine the format automatically. If specified, it can be one of the following:

> `c`
>
> `custom`
>
> > The archive is in the custom format of pg_dump.
>
> `d`
>
> `directory`
>
> > The archive is a directory archive.
>
> `t`
>
> `tar`
>
> > The archive is a `tar` archive.

`-I` *index*

`--index=`*index*

> Restore definition of named index only. Multiple indexes may be specified with multiple `-I` switches.

`-j` *number-of-jobs*

`--jobs=`*number-of-jobs*

> Run the most time-consuming parts of pg_restore — those which load data, create indexes, or create constraints — using multiple concurrent jobs. This option can dramatically reduce the time to restore a large database to a server running on a multiprocessor machine.
>
> Each job is one process or one thread, depending on the operating system, and uses a separate connection to the server.
>
> The optimal value for this option depends on the hardware setup of the server, of the client, and of the network. Factors include the number of CPU cores and the disk setup. A good place to start is the number of CPU cores on the server, but values larger than that can also lead to faster restore times in many cases. Of course, values that are too high will lead to decreased performance because of thrashing.
>
> Only the custom and directory archive formats are supported with this option. The input must be a regular file or directory (not, for example, a pipe). This option is ignored when emitting a script rather than connecting directly to a database server. Also, multiple jobs cannot be used together with the option `--single-transaction`.

`-l`

`--list`

> List the contents of the archive. The output of this operation can be used as input to the `-L` option. Note that if filtering switches such as `-n` or `-t` are used with `-l`, they will restrict the items listed.

`-L` *list-file*

`--use-list=`*list-file*

> Restore only those archive elements that are listed in *list-file*, and restore them in the order they appear in the file. Note that if filtering switches such as `-n` or `-t` are used with `-L`, they will further restrict the items restored.
>
> *list-file* is normally created by editing the output of a previous `-l` operation. Lines can be moved or removed, and can also be commented out by placing a semicolon (`;`) at the start of the line. See below for examples.

`-n` *namespace*

`--schema=`*schema*

> Restore only objects that are in the named schema. Multiple schemas may be specified with multiple `-n` switches. This can be combined with the `-t` option to restore just a specific table.

`-O`

`--no-owner`

> Do not output commands to set ownership of objects to match the original database. By default, pg_restore issues ALTER OWNER or SET SESSION AUTHORIZATION statements to set ownership of created schema elements. These statements will fail unless the initial connection to the database is made by a superuser (or the same user that owns all of the objects in the script). With `-O`, any user name can be used for the initial connection, and this user will own all the created objects.

```
-P function-name(argtype [, ...])
--function=function-name(argtype [, ...])
```

> Restore the named function only. Be careful to spell the function name and arguments exactly as they appear in the dump file's table of contents. Multiple functions may be specified with multiple -P switches.

```
-R
--no-reconnect
```

> This option is obsolete but still accepted for backwards compatibility.

```
-s
--schema-only
```

> Restore only the schema (data definitions), not data, to the extent that schema entries are present in the archive.
>
> This option is the inverse of --data-only. It is similar to, but for historical reasons not identical to, specifying --section=pre-data --section=post-data.
>
> (Do not confuse this with the --schema option, which uses the word "schema" in a different meaning.)

```
-S username
--superuser=username
```

> Specify the superuser user name to use when disabling triggers. This is relevant only if --disable-triggers is used.

```
-t table
--table=table
```

> Restore definition and/or data of only the named table. For this purpose, "table" includes views, materialized views, sequences, and foreign tables. Multiple tables can be selected by writing multiple -t switches. This option can be combined with the -n option to specify table(s) in a particular schema.
>
> **Note:** When -t is specified, pg_restore makes no attempt to restore any other database objects that the selected table(s) might depend upon. Therefore, there is no guarantee that a specific-table restore into a clean database will succeed.
>
> **Note:** This flag does not behave identically to the -t flag of pg_dump. There is not currently any provision for wild-card matching in pg_restore, nor can you include a schema name within its -t.
>
> **Note:** In versions prior to PostgreSQL 9.6, this flag matched only tables, not any other type of relation.

```
-T trigger
--trigger=trigger
```

Restore named trigger only. Multiple triggers may be specified with multiple -T switches.

```
-v
--verbose
```

Specifies verbose mode.

```
-V
--version
```

Print the pg_restore version and exit.

```
-x
--no-privileges
--no-acl
```

Prevent restoration of access privileges (grant/revoke commands).

```
-1
--single-transaction
```

Execute the restore as a single transaction (that is, wrap the emitted commands in BEGIN/COMMIT). This ensures that either all the commands complete successfully, or no changes are applied. This option implies --exit-on-error.

```
--disable-triggers
```

This option is relevant only when performing a data-only restore. It instructs pg_restore to execute commands to temporarily disable triggers on the target tables while the data is reloaded. Use this if you have referential integrity checks or other triggers on the tables that you do not want to invoke during data reload.

Presently, the commands emitted for --disable-triggers must be done as superuser. So you should also specify a superuser name with -S or, preferably, run pg_restore as a PostgreSQL superuser.

```
--enable-row-security
```

This option is relevant only when restoring the contents of a table which has row security. By default, pg_restore will set row_security to off, to ensure that all data is restored in to the table. If the user does not have sufficient privileges to bypass row security, then an error is thrown. This parameter instructs pg_restore to set row_security to on instead, allowing the user to attempt to restore the contents of the table with row security enabled. This might still fail if the user does not have the right to insert the rows from the dump into the table.

Note that this option currently also requires the dump be in INSERT format, as COPY TO does not support row security.

```
--if-exists
```

Use conditional commands (i.e. add an IF EXISTS clause) when cleaning database objects. This option is not valid unless --clean is also specified.

`--no-data-for-failed-tables`

By default, table data is restored even if the creation command for the table failed (e.g., because it already exists). With this option, data for such a table is skipped. This behavior is useful if the target database already contains the desired table contents. For example, auxiliary tables for PostgreSQL extensions such as PostGIS might already be loaded in the target database; specifying this option prevents duplicate or obsolete data from being loaded into them.

This option is effective only when restoring directly into a database, not when producing SQL script output.

`--no-security-labels`

Do not output commands to restore security labels, even if the archive contains them.

`--no-tablespaces`

Do not output commands to select tablespaces. With this option, all objects will be created in whichever tablespace is the default during restore.

`--section=sectionname`

Only restore the named section. The section name can be `pre-data`, `data`, or `post-data`. This option can be specified more than once to select multiple sections. The default is to restore all sections.

The data section contains actual table data as well as large-object definitions. Post-data items consist of definitions of indexes, triggers, rules and constraints other than validated check constraints. Pre-data items consist of all other data definition items.

`--strict-names`

Require that each schema (`-n`/`--schema`) and table (`-t`/`--table`) qualifier match at least one schema/table in the backup file.

`--use-set-session-authorization`

Output SQL-standard `SET SESSION AUTHORIZATION` commands instead of `ALTER OWNER` commands to determine object ownership. This makes the dump more standards-compatible, but depending on the history of the objects in the dump, might not restore properly.

`-?`

`--help`

Show help about pg_restore command line arguments, and exit.

pg_restore also accepts the following command line arguments for connection parameters:

`-h host`

`--host=host`

Specifies the host name of the machine on which the server is running. If the value begins with a slash, it is used as the directory for the Unix domain socket. The default is taken from the `PGHOST` environment variable, if set, else a Unix domain socket connection is attempted.

```
-p port
--port=port
```

Specifies the TCP port or local Unix domain socket file extension on which the server is listening for connections. Defaults to the `PGPORT` environment variable, if set, or a compiled-in default.

```
-U username
--username=username
```

User name to connect as.

```
-w
--no-password
```

Never issue a password prompt. If the server requires password authentication and a password is not available by other means such as a `.pgpass` file, the connection attempt will fail. This option can be useful in batch jobs and scripts where no user is present to enter a password.

```
-W
--password
```

Force pg_restore to prompt for a password before connecting to a database.

This option is never essential, since pg_restore will automatically prompt for a password if the server demands password authentication. However, pg_restore will waste a connection attempt finding out that the server wants a password. In some cases it is worth typing `-W` to avoid the extra connection attempt.

```
--role=rolename
```

Specifies a role name to be used to perform the restore. This option causes pg_restore to issue a `SET ROLE rolename` command after connecting to the database. It is useful when the authenticated user (specified by `-U`) lacks privileges needed by pg_restore, but can switch to a role with the required rights. Some installations have a policy against logging in directly as a superuser, and use of this option allows restores to be performed without violating the policy.

Environment

```
PGHOST
PGOPTIONS
PGPORT
PGUSER
```

Default connection parameters

This utility, like most other PostgreSQL utilities, also uses the environment variables supported by libpq (see Section 32.14). However, it does not read `PGDATABASE` when a database name is not supplied.

Diagnostics

When a direct database connection is specified using the -d option, pg_restore internally executes SQL statements. If you have problems running pg_restore, make sure you are able to select information from the database using, for example, psql. Also, any default connection settings and environment variables used by the libpq front-end library will apply.

Notes

If your installation has any local additions to the template1 database, be careful to load the output of pg_restore into a truly empty database; otherwise you are likely to get errors due to duplicate definitions of the added objects. To make an empty database without any local additions, copy from template0 not template1, for example:

CREATE DATABASE foo WITH TEMPLATE template0;

The limitations of pg_restore are detailed below.

- When restoring data to a pre-existing table and the option --disable-triggers is used, pg_restore emits commands to disable triggers on user tables before inserting the data, then emits commands to re-enable them after the data has been inserted. If the restore is stopped in the middle, the system catalogs might be left in the wrong state.

- pg_restore cannot restore large objects selectively; for instance, only those for a specific table. If an archive contains large objects, then all large objects will be restored, or none of them if they are excluded via -L, -t, or other options.

See also the pg_dump documentation for details on limitations of pg_dump.

Once restored, it is wise to run ANALYZE on each restored table so the optimizer has useful statistics; see Section 24.1.3 and Section 24.1.6 for more information.

Examples

Assume we have dumped a database called mydb into a custom-format dump file:

```
$ pg_dump -Fc mydb > db.dump
```

To drop the database and recreate it from the dump:

```
$ dropdb mydb
$ pg_restore -C -d postgres db.dump
```

The database named in the -d switch can be any database existing in the cluster; pg_restore only uses it to issue the CREATE DATABASE command for mydb. With -C, data is always restored into the database name that appears in the dump file.

To reload the dump into a new database called `newdb`:

```
$ createdb -T template0 newdb
$ pg_restore -d newdb db.dump
```

Notice we don't use -C, and instead connect directly to the database to be restored into. Also note that we clone the new database from `template0` not `template1`, to ensure it is initially empty.

To reorder database items, it is first necessary to dump the table of contents of the archive:

```
$ pg_restore -l db.dump > db.list
```

The listing file consists of a header and one line for each item, e.g.:

```
;
; Archive created at Mon Sep 14 13:55:39 2009
;     dbname: DBDEMOS
;     TOC Entries: 81
;     Compression: 9
;     Dump Version: 1.10-0
;     Format: CUSTOM
;     Integer: 4 bytes
;     Offset: 8 bytes
;     Dumped from database version: 8.3.5
;     Dumped by pg_dump version: 8.3.8
;
;
; Selected TOC Entries:
;
3; 2615 2200 SCHEMA - public pasha
1861; 0 0 COMMENT - SCHEMA public pasha
1862; 0 0 ACL - public pasha
317; 1247 17715 TYPE public composite pasha
319; 1247 25899 DOMAIN public domain0 pasha
```

Semicolons start a comment, and the numbers at the start of lines refer to the internal archive ID assigned to each item.

Lines in the file can be commented out, deleted, and reordered. For example:

```
10; 145433 TABLE map_resolutions postgres
;2; 145344 TABLE species postgres
;4; 145359 TABLE nt_header postgres
6; 145402 TABLE species_records postgres
;8; 145416 TABLE ss_old postgres
```

could be used as input to pg_restore and would only restore items 10 and 6, in that order:

```
$ pg_restore -L db.list db.dump
```

See Also

pg_dump, pg_dumpall, psql

psql

Name

psql — PostgreSQL interactive terminal

Synopsis

psql [option...] [dbname [username]]

Description

psql is a terminal-based front-end to PostgreSQL. It enables you to type in queries interactively, issue them to PostgreSQL, and see the query results. Alternatively, input can be from a file or from command line arguments. In addition, psql provides a number of meta-commands and various shell-like features to facilitate writing scripts and automating a wide variety of tasks.

Options

-a
--echo-all

> Print all nonempty input lines to standard output as they are read. (This does not apply to lines read interactively.) This is equivalent to setting the variable ECHO to all.

-A
--no-align

> Switches to unaligned output mode. (The default output mode is otherwise aligned.)

-b
--echo-errors

> Print failed SQL commands to standard error output. This is equivalent to setting the variable ECHO to errors.

-c command
--command=command

> Specifies that psql is to execute the given command string, command. This option can be repeated and combined in any order with the -f option. When either -c or -f is specified, psql does not read commands from standard input; instead it terminates after processing all the -c and -f options in sequence.

> command must be either a command string that is completely parsable by the server (i.e., it contains no psql-specific features), or a single backslash command. Thus you cannot mix SQL and psql meta-commands within a -c option. To achieve that, you could use repeated -c options or pipe the string into psql, for example:

```
psql -c '\x' -c 'SELECT * FROM foo;'
```
or
```
echo '\x \\ SELECT * FROM foo;' | psql
```
(\\ is the separator meta-command.)

Each SQL command string passed to -c is sent to the server as a single query. Because of this, the server executes it as a single transaction even if the string contains multiple SQL commands, unless there are explicit BEGIN/COMMIT commands included in the string to divide it into multiple transactions. Also, psql only prints the result of the last SQL command in the string. This is different from the behavior when the same string is read from a file or fed to psql's standard input, because then psql sends each SQL command separately.

Because of this behavior, putting more than one command in a single -c string often has unexpected results. It's better to use repeated -c commands or feed multiple commands to psql's standard input, either using echo as illustrated above, or via a shell here-document, for example:

```
psql <<EOF
\x
SELECT * FROM foo;
EOF
```

-d *dbname*

--dbname=*dbname*

Specifies the name of the database to connect to. This is equivalent to specifying *dbname* as the first non-option argument on the command line.

If this parameter contains an = sign or starts with a valid URI prefix (postgresql:// or postgres://), it is treated as a conninfo string. See Section 32.1.1 for more information.

-c

--echo-queries

Copy all SQL commands sent to the server to standard output as well. This is equivalent to setting the variable ECHO to queries.

-E

--echo-hidden

Echo the actual queries generated by \d and other backslash commands. You can use this to study psql's internal operations. This is equivalent to setting the variable ECHO_HIDDEN to on.

-f *filename*

--file=*filename*

Read commands from the file *filename*, rather than standard input. This option can be repeated and combined in any order with the -c option. When either -c or -f is specified, psql does not read commands from standard input; instead it terminates after processing all the -c and -f options in sequence. Except for that, this option is largely equivalent to the meta-command \i.

If *filename* is - (hyphen), then standard input is read until an EOF indication or \q meta-command. This can be used to intersperse interactive input with input from files. Note however that Readline is not used in this case (much as if -n had been specified).

Using this option is subtly different from writing psql < *filename*. In general, both will do what you expect, but using -f enables some nice features such as error messages with line numbers. There is also a slight chance that using this option will reduce the start-up overhead. On the other hand, the variant using the shell's input redirection is (in theory) guaranteed to yield exactly the same output you would have received had you entered everything by hand.

`-F` *separator*

`--field-separator=`*separator*

> Use *separator* as the field separator for unaligned output. This is equivalent to `\pset fieldsep` or `\f`.

`-h` *hostname*

`--host=`*hostname*

> Specifies the host name of the machine on which the server is running. If the value begins with a slash, it is used as the directory for the Unix-domain socket.

`-H`

`--html`

> Turn on HTML tabular output. This is equivalent to `\pset format html` or the `\H` command.

`-l`

`--list`

> List all available databases, then exit. Other non-connection options are ignored. This is similar to the meta-command `\list`.

`-L` *filename*

`--log-file=`*filename*

> Write all query output into file *filename*, in addition to the normal output destination.

`-n`

`--no-readline`

> Do not use Readline for line editing and do not use the command history. This can be useful to turn off tab expansion when cutting and pasting.

`-o` *filename*

`--output=`*filename*

> Put all query output into file *filename*. This is equivalent to the command `\o`.

`-p` *port*

`--port=`*port*

> Specifies the TCP port or the local Unix-domain socket file extension on which the server is listening for connections. Defaults to the value of the `PGPORT` environment variable or, if not set, to the port specified at compile time, usually 5432.

`-P` *assignment*

`--pset=`*assignment*

> Specifies printing options, in the style of `\pset`. Note that here you have to separate name and value with an equal sign instead of a space. For example, to set the output format to LaTeX, you could write `-P format=latex`.

`-q`

`--quiet`

> Specifies that psql should do its work quietly. By default, it prints welcome messages and various informational output. If this option is used, none of this happens. This is useful with the `-c` option. This is equivalent to setting the variable QUIET to on.

`-R` *separator*

`--record-separator=`*separator*

> Use *separator* as the record separator for unaligned output. This is equivalent to the `\pset` recordsep command.

`-s`

`--single-step`

> Run in single-step mode. That means the user is prompted before each command is sent to the server, with the option to cancel execution as well. Use this to debug scripts.

`-S`

`--single-line`

> Runs in single-line mode where a newline terminates an SQL command, as a semicolon does.

> > **Note:** This mode is provided for those who insist on it, but you are not necessarily encouraged to use it. In particular, if you mix SQL and meta-commands on a line the order of execution might not always be clear to the inexperienced user.

`-t`

`--tuples-only`

> Turn off printing of column names and result row count footers, etc. This is equivalent to the `\t` command.

`-T` *table_options*

`--table-attr=`*table_options*

> Specifies options to be placed within the HTML `table` tag. See `\pset` for details.

`-U` *username*

`--username=`*username*

> Connect to the database as the user *username* instead of the default. (You must have permission to do so, of course.)

`-v` *assignment*

`--set=`*assignment*

`--variable=`*assignment*

> Perform a variable assignment, like the `\set` meta-command. Note that you must separate name and value, if any, by an equal sign on the command line. To unset a variable, leave off the equal sign. To set a variable with an empty value, use the equal sign but leave off the value. These assignments are done during a very early stage of start-up, so variables reserved for internal purposes might get overwritten later.

```
-V
--version
```

Print the psql version and exit.

```
-w
--no-password
```

Never issue a password prompt. If the server requires password authentication and a password is not available by other means such as a `.pgpass` file, the connection attempt will fail. This option can be useful in batch jobs and scripts where no user is present to enter a password.

Note that this option will remain set for the entire session, and so it affects uses of the meta-command `\connect` as well as the initial connection attempt.

```
-W
--password
```

Force psql to prompt for a password before connecting to a database.

This option is never essential, since psql will automatically prompt for a password if the server demands password authentication. However, psql will waste a connection attempt finding out that the server wants a password. In some cases it is worth typing `-W` to avoid the extra connection attempt.

Note that this option will remain set for the entire session, and so it affects uses of the meta-command `\connect` as well as the initial connection attempt.

```
-x
--expanded
```

Turn on the expanded table formatting mode. This is equivalent to the `\x` command.

```
-X,
--no-psqlrc
```

Do not read the start-up file (neither the system-wide `psqlrc` file nor the user's `~/.psqlrc` file).

```
-z
--field-separator-zero
```

Set the field separator for unaligned output to a zero byte.

```
-0
--record-separator-zero
```

Set the record separator for unaligned output to a zero byte. This is useful for interfacing, for example, with `xargs -0`.

```
-1
--single-transaction
```

This option can only be used in combination with one or more `-c` and/or `-f` options. It causes psql to issue a BEGIN command before the first such option and a COMMIT command after the last one, thereby wrapping all the commands into a single transaction. This ensures that either all the commands complete successfully, or no changes are applied.

If the commands themselves contain BEGIN, COMMIT, or ROLLBACK, this option will not have the desired effects. Also, if an individual command cannot be executed inside a transaction block, specifying this option will cause the whole transaction to fail.

```
-?
--help[=topic]
```

> Show help about psql and exit. The optional `topic` parameter (defaulting to `options`) selects which part of psql is explained: `commands` describes psql's backslash commands; `options` describes the command-line options that can be passed to psql; and `variables` shows help about psql configuration variables.

Exit Status

psql returns 0 to the shell if it finished normally, 1 if a fatal error of its own occurs (e.g. out of memory, file not found), 2 if the connection to the server went bad and the session was not interactive, and 3 if an error occurred in a script and the variable `ON_ERROR_STOP` was set.

Usage

Connecting to a Database

psql is a regular PostgreSQL client application. In order to connect to a database you need to know the name of your target database, the host name and port number of the server, and what user name you want to connect as. psql can be told about those parameters via command line options, namely `-d`, `-h`, `-p`, and `-U` respectively. If an argument is found that does not belong to any option it will be interpreted as the database name (or the user name, if the database name is already given). Not all of these options are required; there are useful defaults. If you omit the host name, psql will connect via a Unix-domain socket to a server on the local host, or via TCP/IP to `localhost` on machines that don't have Unix-domain sockets. The default port number is determined at compile time. Since the database server uses the same default, you will not have to specify the port in most cases. The default user name is your operating-system user name, as is the default database name. Note that you cannot just connect to any database under any user name. Your database administrator should have informed you about your access rights.

When the defaults aren't quite right, you can save yourself some typing by setting the environment variables `PGDATABASE`, `PGHOST`, `PGPORT` and/or `PGUSER` to appropriate values. (For additional environment variables, see Section 32.14.) It is also convenient to have a `~/.pgpass` file to avoid regularly having to type in passwords. See Section 32.15 for more information.

An alternative way to specify connection parameters is in a `conninfo` string or a URI, which is used instead of a database name. This mechanism give you very wide control over the connection. For example:

```
$ psql "service=myservice sslmode=require"
$ psql postgresql://dbmaster:5433/mydb?sslmode=require
```

This way you can also use LDAP for connection parameter lookup as described in Section 32.17. See Section 32.1.2 for more information on all the available connection options.

If the connection could not be made for any reason (e.g., insufficient privileges, server is not running on the targeted host, etc.), psql will return an error and terminate.

If both standard input and standard output are a terminal, then psql sets the client encoding to "auto", which will detect the appropriate client encoding from the locale settings (LC_CTYPE environment variable on Unix systems). If this doesn't work out as expected, the client encoding can be overridden using the environment variable `PGCLIENTENCODING`.

Entering SQL Commands

In normal operation, psql provides a prompt with the name of the database to which psql is currently connected, followed by the string `=>`. For example:

```
$ psql testdb
psql (9.6.0)
Type "help" for help.

testdb=>
```

At the prompt, the user can type in SQL commands. Ordinarily, input lines are sent to the server when a command-terminating semicolon is reached. An end of line does not terminate a command. Thus commands can be spread over several lines for clarity. If the command was sent and executed without error, the results of the command are displayed on the screen.

Whenever a command is executed, psql also polls for asynchronous notification events generated by LISTEN and NOTIFY.

While C-style block comments are passed to the server for processing and removal, SQL-standard comments are removed by psql.

Meta-Commands

Anything you enter in psql that begins with an unquoted backslash is a psql meta-command that is processed by psql itself. These commands make psql more useful for administration or scripting. Meta-commands are often called slash or backslash commands.

The format of a psql command is the backslash, followed immediately by a command verb, then any arguments. The arguments are separated from the command verb and each other by any number of whitespace characters.

To include whitespace in an argument you can quote it with single quotes. To include a single quote in an argument, write two single quotes within single-quoted text. Anything contained in single quotes is furthermore subject to C-like substitutions for `\n` (new line), `\t` (tab), `\b` (backspace), `\r` (carriage return), `\f` (form feed), `\digits` (octal), and `\xdigits` (hexadecimal). A backslash preceding any other character within single-quoted text quotes that single character, whatever it is.

Within an argument, text that is enclosed in backquotes (`) is taken as a command line that is passed to the shell. The output of the command (with any trailing newline removed) replaces the backquoted text.

If an unquoted colon (`:`) followed by a psql variable name appears within an argument, it is replaced by the variable's value, as described in *SQL Interpolation*.

Some commands take an SQL identifier (such as a table name) as argument. These arguments follow the syntax rules of SQL: Unquoted letters are forced to lowercase, while double quotes (") protect letters from case conversion and allow incorporation of whitespace into the identifier. Within double quotes, paired double quotes reduce to a single double quote in the resulting name. For example, FOO"BAR"BAZ is interpreted as fooBARbaz, and "A weird"" name" becomes A weird" name.

Parsing for arguments stops at the end of the line, or when another unquoted backslash is found. An unquoted backslash is taken as the beginning of a new meta-command. The special sequence \\ (two backslashes) marks the end of arguments and continues parsing SQL commands, if any. That way SQL and psql commands can be freely mixed on a line. But in any case, the arguments of a meta-command cannot continue beyond the end of the line.

The following meta-commands are defined:

\a

If the current table output format is unaligned, it is switched to aligned. If it is not unaligned, it is set to unaligned. This command is kept for backwards compatibility. See \pset for a more general solution.

\c or \connect [-reuse-previous=*on*/*off*] [*dbname* [*username*] [*host*] [*port*] | *conninfo*]

Establishes a new connection to a PostgreSQL server. The connection parameters to use can be specified either using a positional syntax, or using *conninfo* connection strings as detailed in Section 32.1.1.

Where the command omits database name, user, host, or port, the new connection can reuse values from the previous connection. By default, values from the previous connection are reused except when processing a *conninfo* string. Passing a first argument of -reuse-previous=on or -reuse-previous=off overrides that default. When the command neither specifies nor reuses a particular parameter, the libpq default is used. Specifying any of *dbname*, *username*, *host* or *port* as - is equivalent to omitting that parameter.

If the new connection is successfully made, the previous connection is closed. If the connection attempt failed (wrong user name, access denied, etc.), the previous connection will only be kept if psql is in interactive mode. When executing a non-interactive script, processing will immediately stop with an error. This distinction was chosen as a user convenience against typos on the one hand, and a safety mechanism that scripts are not accidentally acting on the wrong database on the other hand.

Examples:

```
=> \c mydb myuser host.dom 6432
=> \c service=foo
=> \c "host=localhost port=5432 dbname=mydb connect_timeout=10 sslmode=disable"
=> \c postgresql://tom@localhost/mydb?application_name=myapp
```

\C [*title*]

Sets the title of any tables being printed as the result of a query or unset any such title. This command is equivalent to \pset title *title*. (The name of this command derives from "caption", as it was previously only used to set the caption in an HTML table.)

\cd [*directory*]

Changes the current working directory to *directory*. Without argument, changes to the current user's home directory.

Tip: To print your current working directory, use \! pwd.

\conninfo

Outputs information about the current database connection.

\copy { table [(column_list)] | (query) } { from | to } { 'filename' |
program 'command' | stdin | stdout | pstdin | pstdout } [[with] (option [,
...])]

Performs a frontend (client) copy. This is an operation that runs an SQL COPY command, but instead of the server reading or writing the specified file, psql reads or writes the file and routes the data between the server and the local file system. This means that file accessibility and privileges are those of the local user, not the server, and no SQL superuser privileges are required.

When program is specified, command is executed by psql and the data passed from or to command is routed between the server and the client. Again, the execution privileges are those of the local user, not the server, and no SQL superuser privileges are required.

For \copy ... from stdin, data rows are read from the same source that issued the command, continuing until \. is read or the stream reaches EOF. This option is useful for populating tables in-line within a SQL script file. For \copy ... to stdout, output is sent to the same place as psql command output, and the COPY count command status is not printed (since it might be confused with a data row). To read/write psql's standard input or output regardless of the current command source or \o option, write from pstdin or to pstdout.

The syntax of this command is similar to that of the SQL COPY command. All options other than the data source/destination are as specified for COPY. Because of this, special parsing rules apply to the \copy command. In particular, psql's variable substitution rules and backslash escapes do not apply.

Tip: This operation is not as efficient as the SQL COPY command because all data must pass through the client/server connection. For large amounts of data the SQL command might be preferable.

\copyright

Shows the copyright and distribution terms of PostgreSQL.

\crosstabview [colV [colH [colD [sortcolH]]]]

Executes the current query buffer (like \g) and shows the results in a crosstab grid. The query must return at least three columns. The output column identified by colV becomes a vertical header and the output column identified by colH becomes a horizontal header. colD identifies the output column to display within the grid. sortcolH identifies an optional sort column for the horizontal header.

Each column specification can be a column number (starting at 1) or a column name. The usual SQL case folding and quoting rules apply to column names. If omitted, colV is taken as column 1 and colH as column 2. colH must differ from colV. If colD is not specified, then there must be exactly three columns in the query result, and the column that is neither colV nor colH is taken to be colD.

The vertical header, displayed as the leftmost column, contains the values found in column `colV`, in the same order as in the query results, but with duplicates removed.

The horizontal header, displayed as the first row, contains the values found in column `colH`, with duplicates removed. By default, these appear in the same order as in the query results. But if the optional `sortcolH` argument is given, it identifies a column whose values must be integer numbers, and the values from `colH` will appear in the horizontal header sorted according to the corresponding `sortcolH` values.

Inside the crosstab grid, for each distinct value x of `colH` and each distinct value y of `colV`, the cell located at the intersection (x, y) contains the value of the `colD` column in the query result row for which the value of `colH` is x and the value of `colV` is y. If there is no such row, the cell is empty. If there are multiple such rows, an error is reported.

`\d[S+] [ pattern ]`

For each relation (table, view, index, sequence, or foreign table) or composite type matching the `pattern`, show all columns, their types, the tablespace (if not the default) and any special attributes such as NOT NULL or defaults. Associated indexes, constraints, rules, and triggers are also shown. For foreign tables, the associated foreign server is shown as well. ("Matching the pattern" is defined in *Patterns* below.)

For some types of relation, `\d` shows additional information for each column: column values for sequences, indexed expression for indexes and foreign data wrapper options for foreign tables.

The command form `\d+` is identical, except that more information is displayed: any comments associated with the columns of the table are shown, as is the presence of OIDs in the table, the view definition if the relation is a view, a non-default replica identity setting.

By default, only user-created objects are shown; supply a pattern or the s modifier to include system objects.

> **Note:** If `\d` is used without a `pattern` argument, it is equivalent to `\dtvsE` which will show a list of all visible tables, views, sequences and foreign tables. This is purely a convenience measure.

`\da[S] [ pattern ]`

Lists aggregate functions, together with their return type and the data types they operate on. If `pattern` is specified, only aggregates whose names match the pattern are shown. By default, only user-created objects are shown; supply a pattern or the s modifier to include system objects.

`\dA[+] [ pattern ]`

Lists access methods. If `pattern` is specified, only access methods whose names match the pattern are shown. If + is appended to the command name, each access method is listed with its associated handler function and description.

`\db[+] [ pattern ]`

Lists tablespaces. If `pattern` is specified, only tablespaces whose names match the pattern are shown. If + is appended to the command name, each tablespace is listed with its associated options, on-disk size, permissions and description.

`\dc[S+] [ pattern ]`

Lists conversions between character-set encodings. If `pattern` is specified, only conversions whose names match the pattern are listed. By default, only user-created objects are shown; supply a pattern or the S modifier to include system objects. If + is appended to the command name, each object is listed with its associated description.

`\dC[+] [ pattern ]`

Lists type casts. If `pattern` is specified, only casts whose source or target types match the pattern are listed. If + is appended to the command name, each object is listed with its associated description.

`\dd[S] [ pattern ]`

Shows the descriptions of objects of type `constraint`, `operator class`, `operator family`, `rule`, and `trigger`. All other comments may be viewed by the respective backslash commands for those object types.

`\dd` displays descriptions for objects matching the `pattern`, or of visible objects of the appropriate type if no argument is given. But in either case, only objects that have a description are listed. By default, only user-created objects are shown; supply a pattern or the S modifier to include system objects.

Descriptions for objects can be created with the COMMENT SQL command.

`\ddp [ pattern ]`

Lists default access privilege settings. An entry is shown for each role (and schema, if applicable) for which the default privilege settings have been changed from the built-in defaults. If `pattern` is specified, only entries whose role name or schema name matches the pattern are listed.

The ALTER DEFAULT PRIVILEGES command is used to set default access privileges. The meaning of the privilege display is explained under GRANT.

`\dD[S+] [ pattern ]`

Lists domains. If `pattern` is specified, only domains whose names match the pattern are shown. By default, only user-created objects are shown; supply a pattern or the S modifier to include system objects. If + is appended to the command name, each object is listed with its associated permissions and description.

`\dE[S+] [ pattern ]`
`\di[S+] [ pattern ]`
`\dm[S+] [ pattern ]`
`\ds[S+] [ pattern ]`
`\dt[S+] [ pattern ]`
`\dv[S+] [ pattern ]`

In this group of commands, the letters E, i, m, s, t, and v stand for foreign table, index, materialized view, sequence, table, and view, respectively. You can specify any or all of these letters, in any order, to obtain a listing of objects of these types. For example, `\dit` lists indexes and tables. If + is appended to the command name, each object is listed with its physical size on disk and its associated description, if any. If `pattern` is specified, only objects whose names match the pattern are listed. By default, only user-created objects are shown; supply a pattern or the S modifier to include system objects.

`\des[+]` [*pattern*]

Lists foreign servers (mnemonic: "external servers"). If *pattern* is specified, only those servers whose name matches the pattern are listed. If the form `\des+` is used, a full description of each server is shown, including the server's ACL, type, version, options, and description.

`\det[+]` [*pattern*]

Lists foreign tables (mnemonic: "external tables"). If *pattern* is specified, only entries whose table name or schema name matches the pattern are listed. If the form `\det+` is used, generic options and the foreign table description are also displayed.

`\deu[+]` [*pattern*]

Lists user mappings (mnemonic: "external users"). If *pattern* is specified, only those mappings whose user names match the pattern are listed. If the form `\deu+` is used, additional information about each mapping is shown.

Caution

`\deu+` might also display the user name and password of the remote user, so care should be taken not to disclose them.

`\dew[+]` [*pattern*]

Lists foreign-data wrappers (mnemonic: "external wrappers"). If *pattern* is specified, only those foreign-data wrappers whose name matches the pattern are listed. If the form `\dew+` is used, the ACL, options, and description of the foreign-data wrapper are also shown.

`\df[antwS+]` [*pattern*]

Lists functions, together with their result data types, argument data types, and function types, which are classified as "agg" (aggregate), "normal", "trigger", or "window". To display only functions of specific type(s), add the corresponding letters a, n, t, or w to the command. If *pattern* is specified, only functions whose names match the pattern are shown. By default, only user-created objects are shown; supply a pattern or the S modifier to include system objects. If the form `\df+` is used, additional information about each function is shown, including volatility, parallel safety, owner, security classification, access privileges, language, source code and description.

Tip: To look up functions taking arguments or returning values of a specific data type, use your pager's search capability to scroll through the `\df` output.

`\dF[+]` [*pattern*]

Lists text search configurations. If *pattern* is specified, only configurations whose names match the pattern are shown. If the form `\dF+` is used, a full description of each configuration is shown, including the underlying text search parser and the dictionary list for each parser token type.

`\dFd[+]` [*pattern*]

Lists text search dictionaries. If *pattern* is specified, only dictionaries whose names match the pattern are shown. If the form `\dFd+` is used, additional information is shown about each selected dictionary, including the underlying text search template and the option values.

`\dFp[+]` [*pattern*]

Lists text search parsers. If *pattern* is specified, only parsers whose names match the pattern are shown. If the form `\dFp+` is used, a full description of each parser is shown, including the underlying functions and the list of recognized token types.

`\dFt[+]` [*pattern*]

Lists text search templates. If *pattern* is specified, only templates whose names match the pattern are shown. If the form `\dFt+` is used, additional information is shown about each template, including the underlying function names.

`\dg[S+]` [*pattern*]

Lists database roles. (Since the concepts of "users" and "groups" have been unified into "roles", this command is now equivalent to `\du`.) By default, only user-created roles are shown; supply the S modifier to include system roles. If *pattern* is specified, only those roles whose names match the pattern are listed. If the form `\dg+` is used, additional information is shown about each role; currently this adds the comment for each role.

`\dl`

This is an alias for `\lo_list`, which shows a list of large objects.

`\dL[S+]` [*pattern*]

Lists procedural languages. If *pattern* is specified, only languages whose names match the pattern are listed. By default, only user-created languages are shown; supply the S modifier to include system objects. If + is appended to the command name, each language is listed with its call handler, validator, access privileges, and whether it is a system object.

`\dn[S+]` [*pattern*]

Lists schemas (namespaces). If *pattern* is specified, only schemas whose names match the pattern are listed. By default, only user-created objects are shown; supply a pattern or the S modifier to include system objects. If + is appended to the command name, each object is listed with its associated permissions and description, if any.

`\do[S+]` [*pattern*]

Lists operators with their operand and result types. If *pattern* is specified, only operators whose names match the pattern are listed. By default, only user-created objects are shown; supply a pattern or the S modifier to include system objects. If + is appended to the command name, additional information about each operator is shown, currently just the name of the underlying function.

`\dO[S+]` [*pattern*]

Lists collations. If *pattern* is specified, only collations whose names match the pattern are listed. By default, only user-created objects are shown; supply a pattern or the S modifier to include system objects. If + is appended to the command name, each collation is listed with its associated description, if any. Note that only collations usable with the current database's encoding are shown, so the results may vary in different databases of the same installation.

`\dp` [*pattern*]

Lists tables, views and sequences with their associated access privileges. If *pattern* is specified, only tables, views and sequences whose names match the pattern are listed.

The GRANT and REVOKE commands are used to set access privileges. The meaning of the privilege display is explained under GRANT.

`\drds [ role-pattern [ database-pattern ] ]`

Lists defined configuration settings. These settings can be role-specific, database-specific, or both. `role-pattern` and `database-pattern` are used to select specific roles and databases to list, respectively. If omitted, or if * is specified, all settings are listed, including those not role-specific or database-specific, respectively.

The ALTER ROLE and ALTER DATABASE commands are used to define per-role and per-database configuration settings.

`\dT[S+] [ pattern ]`

Lists data types. If `pattern` is specified, only types whose names match the pattern are listed. If + is appended to the command name, each type is listed with its internal name and size, its allowed values if it is an enum type, and its associated permissions. By default, only user-created objects are shown; supply a pattern or the S modifier to include system objects.

`\du[S+] [ pattern ]`

Lists database roles. (Since the concepts of "users" and "groups" have been unified into "roles", this command is now equivalent to `\dg`.) By default, only user-created roles are shown; supply the S modifier to include system roles. If `pattern` is specified, only those roles whose names match the pattern are listed. If the form `\du+` is used, additional information is shown about each role; currently this adds the comment for each role.

`\dx[+] [ pattern ]`

Lists installed extensions. If `pattern` is specified, only those extensions whose names match the pattern are listed. If the form `\dx+` is used, all the objects belonging to each matching extension are listed.

`\dy[+] [ pattern ]`

Lists event triggers. If `pattern` is specified, only those event triggers whose names match the pattern are listed. If + is appended to the command name, each object is listed with its associated description.

`\e` or `\edit [ filename ] [ line_number ]`

If `filename` is specified, the file is edited; after the editor exits, its content is copied back to the query buffer. If no `filename` is given, the current query buffer is copied to a temporary file which is then edited in the same fashion.

The new query buffer is then re-parsed according to the normal rules of psql, where the whole buffer is treated as a single line. (Thus you cannot make scripts this way. Use `\i` for that.) This means that if the query ends with (or contains) a semicolon, it is immediately executed. Otherwise it will merely wait in the query buffer; type semicolon or `\g` to send it, or `\r` to cancel.

If a line number is specified, psql will position the cursor on the specified line of the file or query buffer. Note that if a single all-digits argument is given, psql assumes it is a line number, not a file name.

Tip: See under *Environment* for how to configure and customize your editor.

\echo *text* [...]

Prints the arguments to the standard output, separated by one space and followed by a newline. This can be useful to intersperse information in the output of scripts. For example:

```
=> \echo `date`
Tue Oct 26 21:40:57 CEST 1999
```

If the first argument is an unquoted -n the trailing newline is not written.

> **Tip:** If you use the \o command to redirect your query output you might wish to use \qecho instead of this command.

\ef [*function_description* [*line_number*]]

This command fetches and edits the definition of the named function, in the form of a CREATE OR REPLACE FUNCTION command. Editing is done in the same way as for \edit. After the editor exits, the updated command waits in the query buffer; type semicolon or \g to send it, or \r to cancel.

The target function can be specified by name alone, or by name and arguments, for example foo(integer, text). The argument types must be given if there is more than one function of the same name.

If no function is specified, a blank CREATE FUNCTION template is presented for editing.

If a line number is specified, psql will position the cursor on the specified line of the function body. (Note that the function body typically does not begin on the first line of the file.)

> **Tip:** See under *Environment* for how to configure and customize your editor.

\encoding [*encoding*]

Sets the client character set encoding. Without an argument, this command shows the current encoding.

\errverbose

Repeats the most recent server error message at maximum verbosity, as though VERBOSITY were set to verbose and SHOW_CONTEXT were set to always.

\ev [*view_name* [*line_number*]]

This command fetches and edits the definition of the named view, in the form of a CREATE OR REPLACE VIEW command. Editing is done in the same way as for \edit. After the editor exits, the updated command waits in the query buffer; type semicolon or \g to send it, or \r to cancel.

If no view is specified, a blank CREATE VIEW template is presented for editing.

If a line number is specified, psql will position the cursor on the specified line of the view definition.

\f [*string*]

Sets the field separator for unaligned query output. The default is the vertical bar (|). See also \pset for a generic way of setting output options.

`\g [ `*`filename`*` ]`
`\g [ `*`|command`*` ]`

> Sends the current query input buffer to the server, and optionally stores the query's output in *filename* or pipes the output to the shell command *command*. The file or command is written to only if the query successfully returns zero or more tuples, not if the query fails or is a non-data-returning SQL command.
>
> A bare \g is essentially equivalent to a semicolon. A \g with argument is a "one-shot" alternative to the \o command.

`\gexec`

> Sends the current query input buffer to the server, then treats each column of each row of the query's output (if any) as a SQL statement to be executed. For example, to create an index on each column of my_table:

```
=> SELECT format('create index on my_table(%I)', attname)
-> FROM pg_attribute
-> WHERE attrelid = 'my_table'::regclass AND attnum > 0
-> ORDER BY attnum
-> \gexec
CREATE INDEX
CREATE INDEX
CREATE INDEX
CREATE INDEX
```

> The generated queries are executed in the order in which the rows are returned, and left-to-right within each row if there is more than one column. NULL fields are ignored. The generated queries are sent literally to the server for processing, so they cannot be psql meta-commands nor contain psql variable references. If any individual query fails, execution of the remaining queries continues unless ON_ERROR_STOP is set. Execution of each query is subject to ECHO processing. (Setting ECHO to all or queries is often advisable when using \gexec.) Query logging, single-step mode, timing, and other query execution features apply to each generated query as well.

`\gset [ `*`prefix`*` ]`

> Sends the current query input buffer to the server and stores the query's output into psql variables (see *Variables*). The query to be executed must return exactly one row. Each column of the row is stored into a separate variable, named the same as the column. For example:

```
=> SELECT 'hello' AS var1, 10 AS var2
-> \gset
=> \echo :var1 :var2
hello 10
```

> If you specify a *prefix*, that string is prepended to the query's column names to create the variable names to use:

```
=> SELECT 'hello' AS var1, 10 AS var2
-> \gset result_
=> \echo :result_var1 :result_var2
hello 10
```

> If a column result is NULL, the corresponding variable is unset rather than being set.
>
> If the query fails or does not return one row, no variables are changed.

\h or \help [*command*]

Gives syntax help on the specified SQL command. If *command* is not specified, then psql will list all the commands for which syntax help is available. If *command* is an asterisk (*), then syntax help on all SQL commands is shown.

> **Note:** To simplify typing, commands that consists of several words do not have to be quoted. Thus it is fine to type **\help alter table**.

\H or \html

Turns on HTML query output format. If the HTML format is already on, it is switched back to the default aligned text format. This command is for compatibility and convenience, but see \pset about setting other output options.

\i or \include *filename*

Reads input from the file *filename* and executes it as though it had been typed on the keyboard.

If *filename* is - (hyphen), then standard input is read until an EOF indication or \q meta-command. This can be used to intersperse interactive input with input from files. Note that Readline behavior will be used only if it is active at the outermost level.

> **Note:** If you want to see the lines on the screen as they are read you must set the variable ECHO to all.

\ir or \include_relative *filename*

The \ir command is similar to \i, but resolves relative file names differently. When executing in interactive mode, the two commands behave identically. However, when invoked from a script, \ir interprets file names relative to the directory in which the script is located, rather than the current working directory.

\l[+] or \list[+] [*pattern*]

List the databases in the server and show their names, owners, character set encodings, and access privileges. If *pattern* is specified, only databases whose names match the pattern are listed. If + is appended to the command name, database sizes, default tablespaces, and descriptions are also displayed. (Size information is only available for databases that the current user can connect to.)

\lo_export *loid filename*

Reads the large object with OID *loid* from the database and writes it to *filename*. Note that this is subtly different from the server function lo_export, which acts with the permissions of the user that the database server runs as and on the server's file system.

> **Tip:** Use \lo_list to find out the large object's OID.

`\lo_import` *filename* `[` *comment* `]`

> Stores the file into a PostgreSQL large object. Optionally, it associates the given comment with the object. Example:

> `foo=>` **`\lo_import '/home/peter/pictures/photo.xcf' 'a picture of me'`**
> `lo_import 152801`
> The response indicates that the large object received object ID 152801, which can be used to access the newly-created large object in the future. For the sake of readability, it is recommended to always associate a human-readable comment with every object. Both OIDs and comments can be viewed with the `\lo_list` command.

> Note that this command is subtly different from the server-side `lo_import` because it acts as the local user on the local file system, rather than the server's user and file system.

`\lo_list`

> Shows a list of all PostgreSQL large objects currently stored in the database, along with any comments provided for them.

`\lo_unlink` *loid*

> Deletes the large object with OID *loid* from the database.

> **Tip:** Use `\lo_list` to find out the large object's OID.

`\o` or `\out` `[` *filename* `]`
`\o` or `\out` `[` `|`*command* `]`

> Arranges to save future query results to the file *filename* or pipe future results to the shell command *command*. If no argument is specified, the query output is reset to the standard output.

> "Query results" includes all tables, command responses, and notices obtained from the database server, as well as output of various backslash commands that query the database (such as `\d`), but not error messages.

> **Tip:** To intersperse text output in between query results, use `\qecho`.

`\p` or `\print`

> Print the current query buffer to the standard output.

`\password` `[` *username* `]`

> Changes the password of the specified user (by default, the current user). This command prompts for the new password, encrypts it, and sends it to the server as an `ALTER ROLE` command. This makes sure that the new password does not appear in cleartext in the command history, the server log, or elsewhere.

`\prompt` `[` *text* `]` *name*

> Prompts the user to supply text, which is assigned to the variable *name*. An optional prompt string, *text*, can be specified. (For multiword prompts, surround the text with single quotes.)

By default, \prompt uses the terminal for input and output. However, if the -f command line switch was used, \prompt uses standard input and standard output.

\pset [*option* [*value*]]

This command sets options affecting the output of query result tables. *option* indicates which option is to be set. The semantics of *value* vary depending on the selected option. For some options, omitting *value* causes the option to be toggled or unset, as described under the particular option. If no such behavior is mentioned, then omitting *value* just results in the current setting being displayed.

\pset without any arguments displays the current status of all printing options.

Adjustable printing options are:

border

> The *value* must be a number. In general, the higher the number the more borders and lines the tables will have, but details depend on the particular format. In HTML format, this will translate directly into the border=... attribute. In most other formats only values 0 (no border), 1 (internal dividing lines), and 2 (table frame) make sense, and values above 2 will be treated the same as border = 2. The latex and latex-longtable formats additionally allow a value of 3 to add dividing lines between data rows.

columns

> Sets the target width for the wrapped format, and also the width limit for determining whether output is wide enough to require the pager or switch to the vertical display in expanded auto mode. Zero (the default) causes the target width to be controlled by the environment variable COLUMNS, or the detected screen width if COLUMNS is not set. In addition, if columns is zero then the wrapped format only affects screen output. If columns is nonzero then file and pipe output is wrapped to that width as well.

expanded (or x)

> If *value* is specified it must be either on or off, which will enable or disable expanded mode, or auto. If *value* is omitted the command toggles between the on and off settings. When expanded mode is enabled, query results are displayed in two columns, with the column name on the left and the data on the right. This mode is useful if the data wouldn't fit on the screen in the normal "horizontal" mode. In the auto setting, the expanded mode is used whenever the query output has more than one column and is wider than the screen; otherwise, the regular mode is used. The auto setting is only effective in the aligned and wrapped formats. In other formats, it always behaves as if the expanded mode is off.

fieldsep

> Specifies the field separator to be used in unaligned output format. That way one can create, for example, tab- or comma-separated output, which other programs might prefer. To set a tab as field separator, type \pset fieldsep '\t'. The default field separator is ' | ' (a vertical bar).

fieldsep_zero

> Sets the field separator to use in unaligned output format to a zero byte.

footer

> If *value* is specified it must be either `on` or `off` which will enable or disable display of the table footer (the `(n rows)` count). If *value* is omitted the command toggles footer display on or off.

format

> Sets the output format to one of `unaligned`, `aligned`, `wrapped`, `html`, `asciidoc`, `latex` (uses `tabular`), `latex-longtable`, or `troff-ms`. Unique abbreviations are allowed. (That would mean one letter is enough.)
>
> `unaligned` format writes all columns of a row on one line, separated by the currently active field separator. This is useful for creating output that might be intended to be read in by other programs (for example, tab-separated or comma-separated format).
>
> `aligned` format is the standard, human-readable, nicely formatted text output; this is the default.
>
> `wrapped` format is like `aligned` but wraps wide data values across lines to make the output fit in the target column width. The target width is determined as described under the `columns` option. Note that psql will not attempt to wrap column header titles; therefore, `wrapped` format behaves the same as `aligned` if the total width needed for column headers exceeds the target.
>
> The `html`, `asciidoc`, `latex`, `latex-longtable`, and `troff-ms` formats put out tables that are intended to be included in documents using the respective mark-up language. They are not complete documents! This might not be necessary in HTML, but in LaTeX you must have a complete document wrapper. `latex-longtable` also requires the LaTeX `longtable` and `booktabs` packages.

linestyle

> Sets the border line drawing style to one of `ascii`, `old-ascii`, or `unicode`. Unique abbreviations are allowed. (That would mean one letter is enough.) The default setting is `ascii`. This option only affects the `aligned` and `wrapped` output formats.
>
> `ascii` style uses plain ASCII characters. Newlines in data are shown using a + symbol in the right-hand margin. When the `wrapped` format wraps data from one line to the next without a newline character, a dot (.) is shown in the right-hand margin of the first line, and again in the left-hand margin of the following line.
>
> `old-ascii` style uses plain ASCII characters, using the formatting style used in PostgreSQL 8.4 and earlier. Newlines in data are shown using a : symbol in place of the left-hand column separator. When the data is wrapped from one line to the next without a newline character, a ; symbol is used in place of the left-hand column separator.
>
> `unicode` style uses Unicode box-drawing characters. Newlines in data are shown using a carriage return symbol in the right-hand margin. When the data is wrapped from one line to the next without a newline character, an ellipsis symbol is shown in the right-hand margin of the first line, and again in the left-hand margin of the following line.
>
> When the `border` setting is greater than zero, the `linestyle` option also determines the characters with which the border lines are drawn. Plain ASCII characters work everywhere, but Unicode characters look nicer on displays that recognize them.

> Sets the string to be printed in place of a null value. The default is to print nothing, which can easily be mistaken for an empty string. For example, one might prefer `\pset null '(null)'`.

numericlocale

> If `value` is specified it must be either `on` or `off` which will enable or disable display of a locale-specific character to separate groups of digits to the left of the decimal marker. If `value` is omitted the command toggles between regular and locale-specific numeric output.

pager

> Controls use of a pager program for query and psql help output. If the environment variable `PAGER` is set, the output is piped to the specified program. Otherwise a platform-dependent default (such as `more`) is used.

> When the `pager` option is `off`, the pager program is not used. When the `pager` option is `on`, the pager is used when appropriate, i.e., when the output is to a terminal and will not fit on the screen. The `pager` option can also be set to `always`, which causes the pager to be used for all terminal output regardless of whether it fits on the screen. `\pset pager` without a `value` toggles pager use on and off.

pager_min_lines

> If `pager_min_lines` is set to a number greater than the page height, the pager program will not be called unless there are at least this many lines of output to show. The default setting is 0.

recordsep

> Specifies the record (line) separator to use in unaligned output format. The default is a newline character.

recordsep_zero

> Sets the record separator to use in unaligned output format to a zero byte.

tableattr (or T)

> In HTML format, this specifies attributes to be placed inside the `table` tag. This could for example be `cellpadding` or `bgcolor`. Note that you probably don't want to specify `border` here, as that is already taken care of by `\pset border`. If no `value` is given, the table attributes are unset.

> In `latex-longtable` format, this controls the proportional width of each column containing a left-aligned data type. It is specified as a whitespace-separated list of values, e.g. `'0.2 0.2 0.6'`. Unspecified output columns use the last specified value.

title (or C)

> Sets the table title for any subsequently printed tables. This can be used to give your output descriptive tags. If no `value` is given, the title is unset.

tuples_only (or t)

> If `value` is specified it must be either `on` or `off` which will enable or disable tuples-only mode. If `value` is omitted the command toggles between regular and tuples-only output. Regular output includes extra information such as column headers, titles, and various footers. In tuples-only mode, only actual table data is shown.

unicode_border_linestyle

Sets the border drawing style for the unicode line style to one of single or double.

unicode_column_linestyle

Sets the column drawing style for the unicode line style to one of single or double.

unicode_header_linestyle

Sets the header drawing style for the unicode line style to one of single or double.

Illustrations of how these different formats look can be seen in the *Examples* section.

Tip: There are various shortcut commands for \pset. See \a, \C, \H, \t, \T, and \x.

\q or \quit

Quits the psql program. In a script file, only execution of that script is terminated.

\qecho *text* [...]

This command is identical to \echo except that the output will be written to the query output channel, as set by \o.

\r or \reset

Resets (clears) the query buffer.

\s [*filename*]

Print psql's command line history to *filename*. If *filename* is omitted, the history is written to the standard output (using the pager if appropriate). This command is not available if psql was built without Readline support.

\set [*name* [*value* [...]]]

Sets the psql variable *name* to *value*, or if more than one value is given, to the concatenation of all of them. If only one argument is given, the variable is set with an empty value. To unset a variable, use the \unset command.

\set without any arguments displays the names and values of all currently-set psql variables.

Valid variable names can contain letters, digits, and underscores. See the section *Variables* below for details. Variable names are case-sensitive.

Although you are welcome to set any variable to anything you want, psql treats several variables as special. They are documented in the section about variables.

Note: This command is unrelated to the SQL command SET.

`\setenv` *name* [*value*]

> Sets the environment variable *name* to *value*, or if the *value* is not supplied, unsets the environment variable. Example:

```
testdb=> \setenv PAGER less
testdb=> \setenv LESS -imx4F
```

`\sf[+]` *function_description*

> This command fetches and shows the definition of the named function, in the form of a CREATE OR REPLACE FUNCTION command. The definition is printed to the current query output channel, as set by `\o`.

> The target function can be specified by name alone, or by name and arguments, for example `foo(integer, text)`. The argument types must be given if there is more than one function of the same name.

> If + is appended to the command name, then the output lines are numbered, with the first line of the function body being line 1.

`\sv[+]` *view_name*

> This command fetches and shows the definition of the named view, in the form of a CREATE OR REPLACE VIEW command. The definition is printed to the current query output channel, as set by `\o`.

> If + is appended to the command name, then the output lines are numbered from 1.

`\t`

> Toggles the display of output column name headings and row count footer. This command is equivalent to `\pset tuples_only` and is provided for convenience.

`\T` *table_options*

> Specifies attributes to be placed within the `table` tag in HTML output format. This command is equivalent to `\pset tableattr` *table_options*.

`\timing` [*on* | *off*]

> Without parameter, toggles a display of how long each SQL statement takes, in milliseconds. With parameter, sets same.

`\unset` *name*

> Unsets (deletes) the psql variable *name*.

`\w` or `\write` *filename*
`\w` or `\write` |*command*

> Outputs the current query buffer to the file *filename* or pipes it to the shell command *command*.

`\watch` [*seconds*]

> Repeatedly execute the current query buffer (as `\g` does) until interrupted or the query fails. Wait the specified number of seconds (default 2) between executions. Each query result is displayed with a header that includes the `\pset title` string (if any), the time as of query start, and the delay interval.

`\x [ on | off | auto ]`

Sets or toggles expanded table formatting mode. As such it is equivalent to `\pset expanded`.

`\z [ pattern ]`

Lists tables, views and sequences with their associated access privileges. If a `pattern` is specified, only tables, views and sequences whose names match the pattern are listed.

This is an alias for `\dp` ("display privileges").

`\! [ command ]`

Escapes to a separate shell or executes the shell command `command`. The arguments are not further interpreted; the shell will see them as-is. In particular, the variable substitution rules and backslash escapes do not apply.

`\? [ topic ]`

Shows help information. The optional `topic` parameter (defaulting to `commands`) selects which part of psql is explained: `commands` describes psql's backslash commands; `options` describes the command-line options that can be passed to psql; and `variables` shows help about psql configuration variables.

Patterns

The various `\d` commands accept a `pattern` parameter to specify the object name(s) to be displayed. In the simplest case, a pattern is just the exact name of the object. The characters within a pattern are normally folded to lower case, just as in SQL names; for example, `\dt FOO` will display the table named `foo`. As in SQL names, placing double quotes around a pattern stops folding to lower case. Should you need to include an actual double quote character in a pattern, write it as a pair of double quotes within a double-quote sequence; again this is in accord with the rules for SQL quoted identifiers. For example, `\dt "FOO""BAR"` will display the table named `FOO"BAR` (not `foo"bar`). Unlike the normal rules for SQL names, you can put double quotes around just part of a pattern, for instance `\dt FOO"FOO"BAR` will display the table named `fooFOObar`.

Whenever the `pattern` parameter is omitted completely, the `\d` commands display all objects that are visible in the current schema search path — this is equivalent to using `*` as the pattern. (An object is said to be *visible* if its containing schema is in the search path and no object of the same kind and name appears earlier in the search path. This is equivalent to the statement that the object can be referenced by name without explicit schema qualification.) To see all objects in the database regardless of visibility, use `*.*` as the pattern.

Within a pattern, `*` matches any sequence of characters (including no characters) and `?` matches any single character. (This notation is comparable to Unix shell file name patterns.) For example, `\dt int*` displays tables whose names begin with `int`. But within double quotes, `*` and `?` lose these special meanings and are just matched literally.

A pattern that contains a dot (`.`) is interpreted as a schema name pattern followed by an object name pattern. For example, `\dt foo*.*bar*` displays all tables whose table name includes `bar` that are in schemas whose schema name starts with `foo`. When no dot appears, then the pattern matches only objects that are visible in the current schema search path. Again, a dot within double quotes loses its special meaning and is matched literally.

Advanced users can use regular-expression notations such as character classes, for example `[0-9]` to match any digit. All regular expression special characters work as specified in Section 9.7.3, except for `.` which is taken as a separator as mentioned above, `*` which is translated to the regular-expression notation `.*`, `?` which is translated to `.`, and `$` which is matched literally. You can emulate these pattern characters at need by writing `?` for `.`, `(R+|)` for `R*`, or `(R|)` for `R?`. `$` is not needed as a regular-expression character since the pattern must match the whole name, unlike the usual interpretation of regular expressions (in other words, `$` is automatically appended to your pattern). Write `*` at the beginning and/or end if you don't wish the pattern to be anchored. Note that within double quotes, all regular expression special characters lose their special meanings and are matched literally. Also, the regular expression special characters are matched literally in operator name patterns (i.e., the argument of `\do`).

Advanced Features

Variables

psql provides variable substitution features similar to common Unix command shells. Variables are simply name/value pairs, where the value can be any string of any length. The name must consist of letters (including non-Latin letters), digits, and underscores.

To set a variable, use the psql meta-command `\set`. For example,

```
testdb=> \set foo bar
```

sets the variable `foo` to the value `bar`. To retrieve the content of the variable, precede the name with a colon, for example:

```
testdb=> \echo :foo
bar
```

This works in both regular SQL commands and meta-commands; there is more detail in *SQL Interpolation*, below.

If you call `\set` without a second argument, the variable is set, with an empty string as value. To unset (i.e., delete) a variable, use the command `\unset`. To show the values of all variables, call `\set` without any argument.

> **Note:** The arguments of `\set` are subject to the same substitution rules as with other commands. Thus you can construct interesting references such as `\set :foo 'something'` and get "soft links" or "variable variables" of Perl or PHP fame, respectively. Unfortunately (or fortunately?), there is no way to do anything useful with these constructs. On the other hand, `\set bar :foo` is a perfectly valid way to copy a variable.

A number of these variables are treated specially by psql. They represent certain option settings that can be changed at run time by altering the value of the variable, or in some cases represent changeable state of psql. Although you can use these variables for other purposes, this is not recommended, as the program behavior might grow really strange really quickly. By convention, all specially treated variables' names consist of all upper-case ASCII letters (and possibly digits and underscores). To ensure maximum compatibility in the future, avoid using such variable names for your own purposes. A list of all specially treated variables follows.

AUTOCOMMIT

> When on (the default), each SQL command is automatically committed upon successful completion. To postpone commit in this mode, you must enter a BEGIN or START TRANSACTION SQL command. When off or unset, SQL commands are not committed until you explicitly issue COMMIT or END. The autocommit-off mode works by issuing an implicit BEGIN for you, just before any command that is not already in a transaction block and is not itself a BEGIN or other transaction-control command, nor a command that cannot be executed inside a transaction block (such as VACUUM).

> > **Note:** In autocommit-off mode, you must explicitly abandon any failed transaction by entering ABORT or ROLLBACK. Also keep in mind that if you exit the session without committing, your work will be lost.

> > **Note:** The autocommit-on mode is PostgreSQL's traditional behavior, but autocommit-off is closer to the SQL spec. If you prefer autocommit-off, you might wish to set it in the system-wide psqlrc file or your ~/.psqlrc file.

COMP_KEYWORD_CASE

> Determines which letter case to use when completing an SQL key word. If set to lower or upper, the completed word will be in lower or upper case, respectively. If set to preserve-lower or preserve-upper (the default), the completed word will be in the case of the word already entered, but words being completed without anything entered will be in lower or upper case, respectively.

DBNAME

> The name of the database you are currently connected to. This is set every time you connect to a database (including program start-up), but can be unset.

ECHO

> If set to all, all nonempty input lines are printed to standard output as they are read. (This does not apply to lines read interactively.) To select this behavior on program start-up, use the switch -a. If set to queries, psql prints each query to standard output as it is sent to the server. The switch for this is -e. If set to errors, then only failed queries are displayed on standard error output. The switch for this is -b. If unset, or if set to none (or any other value than those above) then no queries are displayed.

ECHO_HIDDEN

> When this variable is set to on and a backslash command queries the database, the query is first shown. This feature helps you to study PostgreSQL internals and provide similar functionality in your own programs. (To select this behavior on program start-up, use the switch -E.) If you set the variable to the value noexec, the queries are just shown but are not actually sent to the server and executed.

ENCODING

> The current client character set encoding.

FETCH_COUNT

If this variable is set to an integer value > 0, the results of SELECT queries are fetched and displayed in groups of that many rows, rather than the default behavior of collecting the entire result set before display. Therefore only a limited amount of memory is used, regardless of the size of the result set. Settings of 100 to 1000 are commonly used when enabling this feature. Keep in mind that when using this feature, a query might fail after having already displayed some rows.

> **Tip:** Although you can use any output format with this feature, the default aligned format tends to look bad because each group of FETCH_COUNT rows will be formatted separately, leading to varying column widths across the row groups. The other output formats work better.

HISTCONTROL

If this variable is set to ignorespace, lines which begin with a space are not entered into the history list. If set to a value of ignoredups, lines matching the previous history line are not entered. A value of ignoreboth combines the two options. If unset, or if set to none (or any other value than those above), all lines read in interactive mode are saved on the history list.

> **Note:** This feature was shamelessly plagiarized from Bash.

HISTFILE

The file name that will be used to store the history list. The default value is ~/.psql_history. For example, putting:

```
\set HISTFILE ~/.psql_history- :DBNAME
```
in ~/.psqlrc will cause psql to maintain a separate history for each database.

> **Note:** This feature was shamelessly plagiarized from Bash.

HISTSIZE

The number of commands to store in the command history. The default value is 500.

> **Note:** This feature was shamelessly plagiarized from Bash.

HOST

The database server host you are currently connected to. This is set every time you connect to a database (including program start-up), but can be unset.

IGNOREEOF

If unset, sending an EOF character (usually **Control+D**) to an interactive session of psql will terminate the application. If set to a numeric value, that many EOF characters are ignored before the application terminates. If the variable is set but has no numeric value, the default is 10.

Note: This feature was shamelessly plagiarized from Bash.

LASTOID

> The value of the last affected OID, as returned from an INSERT or \lo_import command. This variable is only guaranteed to be valid until after the result of the next SQL command has been displayed.

ON_ERROR_ROLLBACK

> When set to on, if a statement in a transaction block generates an error, the error is ignored and the transaction continues. When set to interactive, such errors are only ignored in interactive sessions, and not when reading script files. When unset or set to off, a statement in a transaction block that generates an error aborts the entire transaction. The error rollback mode works by issuing an implicit SAVEPOINT for you, just before each command that is in a transaction block, and then rolling back to the savepoint if the command fails.

ON_ERROR_STOP

> By default, command processing continues after an error. When this variable is set to on, processing will instead stop immediately. In interactive mode, psql will return to the command prompt; other-wise, psql will exit, returning error code 3 to distinguish this case from fatal error conditions, which are reported using error code 1. In either case, any currently running scripts (the top-level script, if any, and any other scripts which it may have in invoked) will be terminated immediately. If the top-level command string contained multiple SQL commands, processing will stop with the current command.

PORT

> The database server port to which you are currently connected. This is set every time you connect to a database (including program start-up), but can be unset.

PROMPT1
PROMPT2
PROMPT3

> These specify what the prompts psql issues should look like. See *Prompting* below.

QUIET

> Setting this variable to on is equivalent to the command line option -q. It is probably not too useful in interactive mode.

SHOW_CONTEXT

> This variable can be set to the values never, errors, or always to control whether CONTEXT fields are displayed in messages from the server. The default is errors (meaning that context will be shown in error messages, but not in notice or warning messages). This setting has no effect when VERBOSITY is set to terse. (See also \errverbose, for use when you want a verbose version of the error you just got.)

SINGLELINE

> Setting this variable to on is equivalent to the command line option -s.

SINGLESTEP

> Setting this variable to `on` is equivalent to the command line option `-s`.

USER

> The database user you are currently connected as. This is set every time you connect to a database (including program start-up), but can be unset.

VERBOSITY

> This variable can be set to the values `default`, `verbose`, or `terse` to control the verbosity of error reports. (See also `\errverbose`, for use when you want a verbose version of the error you just got.)

SQL Interpolation

A key feature of psql variables is that you can substitute ("interpolate") them into regular SQL statements, as well as the arguments of meta-commands. Furthermore, psql provides facilities for ensuring that variable values used as SQL literals and identifiers are properly quoted. The syntax for interpolating a value without any quoting is to prepend the variable name with a colon (`:`). For example,

```
testdb=> \set foo 'my_table'
testdb=> SELECT * FROM :foo;
```

would query the table `my_table`. Note that this may be unsafe: the value of the variable is copied literally, so it can contain unbalanced quotes, or even backslash commands. You must make sure that it makes sense where you put it.

When a value is to be used as an SQL literal or identifier, it is safest to arrange for it to be quoted. To quote the value of a variable as an SQL literal, write a colon followed by the variable name in single quotes. To quote the value as an SQL identifier, write a colon followed by the variable name in double quotes. These constructs deal correctly with quotes and other special characters embedded within the variable value. The previous example would be more safely written this way:

```
testdb=> \set foo 'my_table'
testdb=> SELECT * FROM :"foo";
```

Variable interpolation will not be performed within quoted SQL literals and identifiers. Therefore, a construction such as `':foo'` doesn't work to produce a quoted literal from a variable's value (and it would be unsafe if it did work, since it wouldn't correctly handle quotes embedded in the value).

One example use of this mechanism is to copy the contents of a file into a table column. First load the file into a variable and then interpolate the variable's value as a quoted string:

```
testdb=> \set content `cat my_file.txt`
testdb=> INSERT INTO my_table VALUES (:'content');
```

(Note that this still won't work if `my_file.txt` contains NUL bytes. psql does not support embedded NUL bytes in variable values.)

Since colons can legally appear in SQL commands, an apparent attempt at interpolation (that is, `:name`, `:'name'`, or `:"name"`) is not replaced unless the named variable is currently set. In any case, you can escape a colon with a backslash to protect it from substitution.

The colon syntax for variables is standard SQL for embedded query languages, such as ECPG. The colon syntaxes for array slices and type casts are PostgreSQL extensions, which can sometimes conflict with the standard usage. The colon-quote syntax for escaping a variable's value as an SQL literal or identifier is a psql extension.

Prompting

The prompts psql issues can be customized to your preference. The three variables PROMPT1, PROMPT2, and PROMPT3 contain strings and special escape sequences that describe the appearance of the prompt. Prompt 1 is the normal prompt that is issued when psql requests a new command. Prompt 2 is issued when more input is expected during command entry, for example because the command was not terminated with a semicolon or a quote was not closed. Prompt 3 is issued when you are running an SQL COPY FROM STDIN command and you need to type in a row value on the terminal.

The value of the selected prompt variable is printed literally, except where a percent sign (%) is encountered. Depending on the next character, certain other text is substituted instead. Defined substitutions are:

%M

The full host name (with domain name) of the database server, or [local] if the connection is over a Unix domain socket, or [local:/dir/name], if the Unix domain socket is not at the compiled in default location.

%m

The host name of the database server, truncated at the first dot, or [local] if the connection is over a Unix domain socket.

%>

The port number at which the database server is listening.

%n

The database session user name. (The expansion of this value might change during a database session as the result of the command SET SESSION AUTHORIZATION.)

%/

The name of the current database.

%~

Like %/, but the output is ~ (tilde) if the database is your default database.

%#

If the session user is a database superuser, then a #, otherwise a >. (The expansion of this value might change during a database session as the result of the command SET SESSION AUTHORIZATION.)

%p

The process ID of the backend currently connected to.

%R

In prompt 1 normally =, but ^ if in single-line mode, or ! if the session is disconnected from the database (which can happen if \connect fails). In prompt 2 %R is replaced by a character that depends on why psql expects more input: - if the command simply wasn't terminated yet, but * if there is an unfinished /* ... */ comment, a single quote if there is an unfinished quoted string, a double quote if there is an unfinished quoted identifier, a dollar sign if there is an unfinished dollar-quoted string, or (if there is an unmatched left parenthesis. In prompt 3 %R doesn't produce anything.

%x

Transaction status: an empty string when not in a transaction block, or * when in a transaction block, or ! when in a failed transaction block, or ? when the transaction state is indeterminate (for example, because there is no connection).

%l

The line number inside the current statement, starting from 1.

%*digits*

The character with the indicated octal code is substituted.

%:*name*:

The value of the psql variable *name*. See the section *Variables* for details.

%`*command*`

The output of *command*, similar to ordinary "back-tick" substitution.

%[... %]

Prompts can contain terminal control characters which, for example, change the color, background, or style of the prompt text, or change the title of the terminal window. In order for the line editing features of Readline to work properly, these non-printing control characters must be designated as invisible by surrounding them with %[and %]. Multiple pairs of these can occur within the prompt. For example:

```
testdb=> \set PROMPT1 '%[%033[1;33;40m%]%n@%/%R%[%033[0m%]%# '
```
results in a boldfaced (1;) yellow-on-black (33;40) prompt on VT100-compatible, color-capable terminals.

To insert a percent sign into your prompt, write %%. The default prompts are '%/%R%# ' for prompts 1 and 2, and '>> ' for prompt 3.

Note: This feature was shamelessly plagiarized from tcsh.

Command-Line Editing

psql supports the Readline library for convenient line editing and retrieval. The command history is automatically saved when psql exits and is reloaded when psql starts up. Tab-completion is also supported, although the completion logic makes no claim to be an SQL parser. The queries generated by tab-completion can also interfere with other SQL commands, e.g. SET TRANSACTION ISOLATION LEVEL. If for some reason you do not like the tab completion, you can turn it off by putting this in a file named .inputrc in your home directory:

```
$if psql
set disable-completion on
$endif
```

(This is not a psql but a Readline feature. Read its documentation for further details.)

Environment

COLUMNS

If `\pset columns` is zero, controls the width for the `wrapped` format and width for determining if wide output requires the pager or should be switched to the vertical format in expanded auto mode.

PAGER

If the query results do not fit on the screen, they are piped through this command. Typical values are `more` or `less`. The default is platform-dependent. The use of the pager can be disabled by using the `\pset` command.

PGDATABASE
PGHOST
PGPORT
PGUSER

Default connection parameters (see Section 32.14).

PSQL_EDITOR
EDITOR
VISUAL

Editor used by the `\e`, `\ef`, and `\ev` commands. These variables are examined in the order listed; the first that is set is used.

The built-in default editors are `vi` on Unix systems and `notepad.exe` on Windows systems.

PSQL_EDITOR_LINENUMBER_ARG

When `\e`, `\ef`, or `\ev` is used with a line number argument, this variable specifies the command-line argument used to pass the starting line number to the user's editor. For editors such as Emacs or vi, this is a plus sign. Include a trailing space in the value of the variable if there needs to be space between the option name and the line number. Examples:

```
PSQL_EDITOR_LINENUMBER_ARG='+'
PSQL_EDITOR_LINENUMBER_ARG='--line '
```

The default is + on Unix systems (corresponding to the default editor `vi`, and useful for many other common editors); but there is no default on Windows systems.

PSQL_HISTORY

Alternative location for the command history file. Tilde (~) expansion is performed.

PSQLRC

Alternative location of the user's `.psqlrc` file. Tilde (~) expansion is performed.

SHELL

Command executed by the `\!` command.

TMPDIR

> Directory for storing temporary files. The default is /tmp.

This utility, like most other PostgreSQL utilities, also uses the environment variables supported by libpq (see Section 32.14).

Files

psqlrc and ~/.psqlrc

> Unless it is passed an -X option, psql attempts to read and execute commands from the system-wide startup file (psqlrc) and then the user's personal startup file (~/.psqlrc), after connecting to the database but before accepting normal commands. These files can be used to set up the client and/or the server to taste, typically with \set and SET commands.

> The system-wide startup file is named psqlrc and is sought in the installation's "system configuration" directory, which is most reliably identified by running pg_config --sysconfdir. By default this directory will be ../etc/ relative to the directory containing the PostgreSQL executables. The name of this directory can be set explicitly via the PGSYSCONFDIR environment variable.

> The user's personal startup file is named .psqlrc and is sought in the invoking user's home directory. On Windows, which lacks such a concept, the personal startup file is named %APPDATA%\postgresql\psqlrc.conf. The location of the user's startup file can be set explicitly via the PSQLRC environment variable.

> Both the system-wide startup file and the user's personal startup file can be made psql-version-specific by appending a dash and the PostgreSQL major or minor release number to the file name, for example ~/.psqlrc-9.2 or ~/.psqlrc-9.2.5. The most specific version-matching file will be read in preference to a non-version-specific file.

.psql_history

> The command-line history is stored in the file ~/.psql_history, or %APPDATA%\postgresql\psql_history on Windows.

> The location of the history file can be set explicitly via the PSQL_HISTORY environment variable.

Notes

- psql works best with servers of the same or an older major version. Backslash commands are particularly likely to fail if the server is of a newer version than psql itself. However, backslash commands of the \d family should work with servers of versions back to 7.4, though not necessarily with servers newer than psql itself. The general functionality of running SQL commands and displaying query results should also work with servers of a newer major version, but this cannot be guaranteed in all cases.

- If you want to use psql to connect to several servers of different major versions, it is recommended that you use the newest version of psql. Alternatively, you can keep around a copy of psql from each major version and be sure to use the version that matches the respective server. But in practice, this additional complication should not be necessary.

- Before PostgreSQL 9.6, the -c option implied -X (--no-psqlrc); this is no longer the case.

- Before PostgreSQL 8.4, psql allowed the first argument of a single-letter backslash command to start directly after the command, without intervening whitespace. Now, some whitespace is required.

Notes for Windows Users

psql is built as a "console application". Since the Windows console windows use a different encoding than the rest of the system, you must take special care when using 8-bit characters within psql. If psql detects a problematic console code page, it will warn you at startup. To change the console code page, two things are necessary:

- Set the code page by entering **cmd.exe /c chcp 1252**. (1252 is a code page that is appropriate for German; replace it with your value.) If you are using Cygwin, you can put this command in /etc/profile.

- Set the console font to Lucida Console, because the raster font does not work with the ANSI code page.

Examples

The first example shows how to spread a command over several lines of input. Notice the changing prompt:

```
testdb=> CREATE TABLE my_table (
testdb(>  first integer not null default 0,
testdb(>  second text)
testdb-> ;
CREATE TABLE
```

Now look at the table definition again:

```
testdb=> \d my_table
            Table "my_table"
 Attribute |  Type   |       Modifier
-----------+---------+--------------------
 first     | integer | not null default 0
 second    | text    |
```

Now we change the prompt to something more interesting:

```
testdb=> \set PROMPT1 '%n@%m %~%R%# '
peter@localhost testdb=>
```

Let's assume you have filled the table with data and want to take a look at it:

```
peter@localhost testdb=> SELECT * FROM my_table;
 first | second
-------+--------
```

```
   1 | one
   2 | two
   3 | three
   4 | four
(4 rows)
```

You can display tables in different ways by using the \pset command:

```
peter@localhost testdb=> \pset border 2
Border style is 2.
peter@localhost testdb=> SELECT * FROM my_table;
+-------+--------+
| first | second |
+-------+--------+
|     1 | one    |
|     2 | two    |
|     3 | three  |
|     4 | four   |
+-------+--------+
(4 rows)

peter@localhost testdb=> \pset border 0
Border style is 0.
peter@localhost testdb=> SELECT * FROM my_table;
first second
----- ------
    1 one
    2 two
    3 three
    4 four
(4 rows)

peter@localhost testdb=> \pset border 1
Border style is 1.
peter@localhost testdb=> \pset format unaligned
Output format is unaligned.
peter@localhost testdb=> \pset fieldsep ","
Field separator is ",".
peter@localhost testdb=> \pset tuples_only
Showing only tuples.
peter@localhost testdb=> SELECT second, first FROM my_table;
one,1
two,2
three,3
four,4
```

Alternatively, use the short commands:

```
peter@localhost testdb=> \a \t \x
Output format is aligned.
Tuples only is off.
Expanded display is on.
peter@localhost testdb=> SELECT * FROM my_table;
```

```
-[ RECORD 1 ]-
first  | 1
second | one
-[ RECORD 2 ]-
first  | 2
second | two
-[ RECORD 3 ]-
first  | 3
second | three
-[ RECORD 4 ]-
first  | 4
second | four
```

When suitable, query results can be shown in a crosstab representation with the \crosstabview command:

```
testdb=> SELECT first, second, first > 2 AS gt2 FROM my_table;
 first | second | ge2
-------+--------+-----
     1 | one    | f
     2 | two    | f
     3 | three  | t
     4 | four   | t
(4 rows)

testdb=> \crosstabview first second
 first | one | two | three | four
       |-----+-----+-------+------
     1 | f   |     |       |
     2 |     | f   |       |
     3 |     |     | t     |
     4 |     |     |       | t
(4 rows)
```

This second example shows a multiplication table with rows sorted in reverse numerical order and columns with an independent, ascending numerical order.

```
testdb=> SELECT t1.first as "A", t2.first+100 AS "B", t1.first*(t2.first+100) as "AxB",
testdb(> row_number() over(order by t2.first) AS ord
testdb(> FROM my_table t1 CROSS JOIN my_table t2 ORDER BY 1 DESC
testdb(> \crosstabview "A" "B" "AxB" ord
 A | 101 | 102 | 103 | 104
---+-----+-----+-----+-----
 4 | 404 | 408 | 412 | 416
 3 | 303 | 306 | 309 | 312
 2 | 202 | 204 | 206 | 208
 1 | 101 | 102 | 103 | 104
(4 rows)
```

reindexdb

Name

reindexdb — reindex a PostgreSQL database

Synopsis

reindexdb [*connection-option*...] [*option*...] [--schema | -S *schema*] ... [--table | -t *table*] ... [--index | -i *index*] ... [*dbname*]

reindexdb [*connection-option*...] [*option*...] --all | -a

reindexdb [*connection-option*...] [*option*...] --system | -s [*dbname*]

Description

reindexdb is a utility for rebuilding indexes in a PostgreSQL database.

reindexdb is a wrapper around the SQL command REINDEX. There is no effective difference between reindexing databases via this utility and via other methods for accessing the server.

Options

reindexdb accepts the following command-line arguments:

-a
--all

    Reindex all databases.

[-d] *dbname*
[--dbname=]*dbname*

    Specifies the name of the database to be reindexed. If this is not specified and -a (or --all) is not used, the database name is read from the environment variable PGDATABASE. If that is not set, the user name specified for the connection is used.

-e
--echo

    Echo the commands that reindexdb generates and sends to the server.

-i *index*
--index=*index*

    Recreate *index* only. Multiple indexes can be recreated by writing multiple -i switches.

`-q`

`--quiet`

>   Do not display progress messages.

`-s`

`--system`

>   Reindex database's system catalogs.

`-S` *schema*

`--schema=`*schema*

>   Reindex *schema* only. Multiple schemas can be reindexed by writing multiple `-S` switches.

`-t` *table*

`--table=`*table*

>   Reindex *table* only. Multiple tables can be reindexed by writing multiple `-t` switches.

`-v`

`--verbose`

>   Print detailed information during processing.

`-V`

`--version`

>   Print the reindexdb version and exit.

`-?`

`--help`

>   Show help about reindexdb command line arguments, and exit.

reindexdb also accepts the following command-line arguments for connection parameters:

`-h` *host*

`--host=`*host*

>   Specifies the host name of the machine on which the server is running. If the value begins with a slash, it is used as the directory for the Unix domain socket.

`-p` *port*

`--port=`*port*

>   Specifies the TCP port or local Unix domain socket file extension on which the server is listening for connections.

`-U` *username*

`--username=`*username*

>   User name to connect as.

`-w`

`--no-password`

>   Never issue a password prompt. If the server requires password authentication and a password is not available by other means such as a `.pgpass` file, the connection attempt will fail. This option can be useful in batch jobs and scripts where no user is present to enter a password.

```
-W
--password
```

Force reindexdb to prompt for a password before connecting to a database.

This option is never essential, since reindexdb will automatically prompt for a password if the server demands password authentication. However, reindexdb will waste a connection attempt finding out that the server wants a password. In some cases it is worth typing `-W` to avoid the extra connection attempt.

```
--maintenance-db=dbname
```

Specifies the name of the database to connect to discover what other databases should be reindexed. If not specified, the `postgres` database will be used, and if that does not exist, `template1` will be used.

Environment

```
PGDATABASE
PGHOST
PGPORT
PGUSER
```

Default connection parameters

This utility, like most other PostgreSQL utilities, also uses the environment variables supported by libpq (see Section 32.14).

Diagnostics

In case of difficulty, see REINDEX and psql for discussions of potential problems and error messages. The database server must be running at the targeted host. Also, any default connection settings and environment variables used by the libpq front-end library will apply.

Notes

reindexdb might need to connect several times to the PostgreSQL server, asking for a password each time. It is convenient to have a `~/.pgpass` file in such cases. See Section 32.15 for more information.

Examples

To reindex the database `test`:

```
$ reindexdb test
```

To reindex the table `foo` and the index `bar` in a database named `abcd`:

```
$ reindexdb --table foo --index bar abcd
```

See Also

REINDEX

vacuumdb

Name

`vacuumdb` — garbage-collect and analyze a PostgreSQL database

Synopsis

vacuumdb [*connection-option*...] [*option*...] [--table | -t *table* [(*column* [,...])]] ...
[*dbname*]

vacuumdb [*connection-option*...] [*option*...] --all | -a

Description

vacuumdb is a utility for cleaning a PostgreSQL database. vacuumdb will also generate internal statistics used by the PostgreSQL query optimizer.

vacuumdb is a wrapper around the SQL command VACUUM. There is no effective difference between vacuuming and analyzing databases via this utility and via other methods for accessing the server.

Options

vacuumdb accepts the following command-line arguments:

-a
--all

> Vacuum all databases.

[-d] *dbname*
[--dbname=]*dbname*

> Specifies the name of the database to be cleaned or analyzed. If this is not specified and -a (or --all) is not used, the database name is read from the environment variable PGDATABASE. If that is not set, the user name specified for the connection is used.

-e
--echo

> Echo the commands that vacuumdb generates and sends to the server.

-f
--full

> Perform "full" vacuuming.

```
-F
--freeze
```

Aggressively "freeze" tuples.

```
-j njobs
--jobs=njobs
```

Execute the vacuum or analyze commands in parallel by running *njobs* commands simultaneously. This option reduces the time of the processing but it also increases the load on the database server.

vacuumdb will open *njobs* connections to the database, so make sure your max_connections setting is high enough to accommodate all connections.

Note that using this mode together with the -f (FULL) option might cause deadlock failures if certain system catalogs are processed in parallel.

```
-q
--quiet
```

Do not display progress messages.

```
-t table [ (column [,...]) ]
--table=table [ (column [,...]) ]
```

Clean or analyze *table* only. Column names can be specified only in conjunction with the --analyze or --analyze-only options. Multiple tables can be vacuumed by writing multiple -t switches.

> **Tip:** If you specify columns, you probably have to escape the parentheses from the shell. (See examples below.)

```
-v
--verbose
```

Print detailed information during processing.

```
-V
--version
```

Print the vacuumdb version and exit.

```
-z
--analyze
```

Also calculate statistics for use by the optimizer.

```
-Z
--analyze-only
```

Only calculate statistics for use by the optimizer (no vacuum).

```
--analyze-in-stages
```

Only calculate statistics for use by the optimizer (no vacuum), like --analyze-only. Run several (currently three) stages of analyze with different configuration settings, to produce usable statistics faster.

This option is useful to analyze a database that was newly populated from a restored dump or by `pg_upgrade`. This option will try to create some statistics as fast as possible, to make the database usable, and then produce full statistics in the subsequent stages.

`-?`

`--help`

> Show help about vacuumdb command line arguments, and exit.

vacuumdb also accepts the following command-line arguments for connection parameters:

`-h` *host*

`--host=`*host*

> Specifies the host name of the machine on which the server is running. If the value begins with a slash, it is used as the directory for the Unix domain socket.

`-p` *port*

`--port=`*port*

> Specifies the TCP port or local Unix domain socket file extension on which the server is listening for connections.

`-U` *username*

`--username=`*username*

> User name to connect as.

`-w`

`--no-password`

> Never issue a password prompt. If the server requires password authentication and a password is not available by other means such as a `.pgpass` file, the connection attempt will fail. This option can be useful in batch jobs and scripts where no user is present to enter a password.

`-W`

`--password`

> Force vacuumdb to prompt for a password before connecting to a database.
>
> This option is never essential, since vacuumdb will automatically prompt for a password if the server demands password authentication. However, vacuumdb will waste a connection attempt finding out that the server wants a password. In some cases it is worth typing `-W` to avoid the extra connection attempt.

`--maintenance-db=`*dbname*

> Specifies the name of the database to connect to discover what other databases should be vacuumed. If not specified, the `postgres` database will be used, and if that does not exist, `template1` will be used.

Environment

```
PGDATABASE
PGHOST
PGPORT
PGUSER
```

> Default connection parameters

This utility, like most other PostgreSQL utilities, also uses the environment variables supported by libpq (see Section 32.14).

Diagnostics

In case of difficulty, see VACUUM and psql for discussions of potential problems and error messages. The database server must be running at the targeted host. Also, any default connection settings and environment variables used by the libpq front-end library will apply.

Notes

vacuumdb might need to connect several times to the PostgreSQL server, asking for a password each time. It is convenient to have a ~/.pgpass file in such cases. See Section 32.15 for more information.

Examples

To clean the database test:

```
$ vacuumdb test
```

To clean and analyze for the optimizer a database named bigdb:

```
$ vacuumdb --analyze bigdb
```

To clean a single table foo in a database named xyzzy, and analyze a single column bar of the table for the optimizer:

```
$ vacuumdb --analyze --verbose --table 'foo(bar)' xyzzy
```

See Also

VACUUM

III. PostgreSQL Server Applications

This part contains reference information for PostgreSQL server applications and support utilities. These commands can only be run usefully on the host where the database server resides. Other utility programs are listed in Reference II, *PostgreSQL Client Applications*.

initdb

Name

initdb — create a new PostgreSQL database cluster

Synopsis

initdb [option...] [--pgdata | -D] directory

Description

initdb creates a new PostgreSQL database cluster. A database cluster is a collection of databases that are managed by a single server instance.

Creating a database cluster consists of creating the directories in which the database data will live, generating the shared catalog tables (tables that belong to the whole cluster rather than to any particular database), and creating the template1 and postgres databases. When you later create a new database, everything in the template1 database is copied. (Therefore, anything installed in template1 is automatically copied into each database created later.) The postgres database is a default database meant for use by users, utilities and third party applications.

Although initdb will attempt to create the specified data directory, it might not have permission if the parent directory of the desired data directory is root-owned. To initialize in such a setup, create an empty data directory as root, then use chown to assign ownership of that directory to the database user account, then su to become the database user to run initdb.

initdb must be run as the user that will own the server process, because the server needs to have access to the files and directories that initdb creates. Since the server cannot be run as root, you must not run initdb as root either. (It will in fact refuse to do so.)

initdb initializes the database cluster's default locale and character set encoding. The character set encoding, collation order (LC_COLLATE) and character set classes (LC_CTYPE, e.g. upper, lower, digit) can be set separately for a database when it is created. initdb determines those settings for the template1 database, which will serve as the default for all other databases.

To alter the default collation order or character set classes, use the --lc-collate and --lc-ctype options. Collation orders other than C or POSIX also have a performance penalty. For these reasons it is important to choose the right locale when running initdb.

The remaining locale categories can be changed later when the server is started. You can also use --locale to set the default for all locale categories, including collation order and character set classes. All server locale values (lc_*) can be displayed via SHOW ALL. More details can be found in Section 23.1.

To alter the default encoding, use the --encoding. More details can be found in Section 23.3.

Options

-A *authmethod*

--auth=*authmethod*

> This option specifies the authentication method for local users used in pg_hba.conf (host and local lines). Do not use trust unless you trust all local users on your system. trust is the default for ease of installation.

--auth-host=*authmethod*

> This option specifies the authentication method for local users via TCP/IP connections used in pg_hba.conf (host lines).

--auth-local=*authmethod*

> This option specifies the authentication method for local users via Unix-domain socket connections used in pg_hba.conf (local lines).

-D *directory*

--pgdata=*directory*

> This option specifies the directory where the database cluster should be stored. This is the only information required by initdb, but you can avoid writing it by setting the PGDATA environment variable, which can be convenient since the database server (postgres) can find the database directory later by the same variable.

-E *encoding*

--encoding=*encoding*

> Selects the encoding of the template database. This will also be the default encoding of any database you create later, unless you override it there. The default is derived from the locale, or SQL_ASCII if that does not work. The character sets supported by the PostgreSQL server are described in Section 23.3.1.

-k

--data-checksums

> Use checksums on data pages to help detect corruption by the I/O system that would otherwise be silent. Enabling checksums may incur a noticeable performance penalty. This option can only be set during initialization, and cannot be changed later. If set, checksums are calculated for all objects, in all databases.

--locale=*locale*

> Sets the default locale for the database cluster. If this option is not specified, the locale is inherited from the environment that initdb runs in. Locale support is described in Section 23.1.

--lc-collate=*locale*

--lc-ctype=*locale*

--lc-messages=*locale*

--lc-monetary=*locale*

--lc-numeric=*locale*

--lc-time=*locale*

> Like --locale, but only sets the locale in the specified category.

`--no-locale`

> Equivalent to `--locale=C`.

`-N`

`--nosync`

> By default, `initdb` will wait for all files to be written safely to disk. This option causes `initdb` to return without waiting, which is faster, but means that a subsequent operating system crash can leave the data directory corrupt. Generally, this option is useful for testing, but should not be used when creating a production installation.

`--pwfile=`*filename*

> Makes `initdb` read the database superuser's password from a file. The first line of the file is taken as the password.

`-S`

`--sync-only`

> Safely write all database files to disk and exit. This does not perform any of the normal initdb operations.

`-T` *CFG*

`--text-search-config=`*CFG*

> Sets the default text search configuration. See default_text_search_config for further information.

`-U` *username*

`--username=`*username*

> Selects the user name of the database superuser. This defaults to the name of the effective user running `initdb`. It is really not important what the superuser's name is, but one might choose to keep the customary name postgres, even if the operating system user's name is different.

`-W`

`--pwprompt`

> Makes `initdb` prompt for a password to give the database superuser. If you don't plan on using password authentication, this is not important. Otherwise you won't be able to use password authentication until you have a password set up.

`-X` *directory*

`--xlogdir=`*directory*

> This option specifies the directory where the transaction log should be stored.

Other, less commonly used, options are also available:

`-d`

`--debug`

> Print debugging output from the bootstrap backend and a few other messages of lesser interest for the general public. The bootstrap backend is the program `initdb` uses to create the catalog tables. This option generates a tremendous amount of extremely boring output.

-L *directory*

> Specifies where initdb should find its input files to initialize the database cluster. This is normally not necessary. You will be told if you need to specify their location explicitly.

-n

--noclean

> By default, when initdb determines that an error prevented it from completely creating the database cluster, it removes any files it might have created before discovering that it cannot finish the job. This option inhibits tidying-up and is thus useful for debugging.

Other options:

-V

--version

> Print the initdb version and exit.

-?

--help

> Show help about initdb command line arguments, and exit.

Environment

PGDATA

> Specifies the directory where the database cluster is to be stored; can be overridden using the -D option.

TZ

> Specifies the default time zone of the created database cluster. The value should be a full time zone name (see Section 8.5.3).

This utility, like most other PostgreSQL utilities, also uses the environment variables supported by libpq (see Section 32.14).

Notes

initdb can also be invoked via pg_ctl initdb.

See Also

pg_ctl, postgres

pg_archivecleanup

Name

pg_archivecleanup — clean up PostgreSQL WAL archive files

Synopsis

pg_archivecleanup [*option*...] *archivelocation oldestkeptwalfile*

Description

pg_archivecleanup is designed to be used as an `archive_cleanup_command` to clean up WAL file archives when running as a standby server (see Section 26.2). pg_archivecleanup can also be used as a standalone program to clean WAL file archives.

To configure a standby server to use pg_archivecleanup, put this into its `recovery.conf` configuration file:

```
archive_cleanup_command = 'pg_archivecleanup archivelocation %r'
```

where `archivelocation` is the directory from which WAL segment files should be removed.

When used within archive_cleanup_command, all WAL files logically preceding the value of the `%r` argument will be removed from `archivelocation`. This minimizes the number of files that need to be retained, while preserving crash-restart capability. Use of this parameter is appropriate if the `archivelocation` is a transient staging area for this particular standby server, but *not* when the `archivelocation` is intended as a long-term WAL archive area, or when multiple standby servers are recovering from the same archive location.

When used as a standalone program all WAL files logically preceding the `oldestkeptwalfile` will be removed from `archivelocation`. In this mode, if you specify a `.partial` or `.backup` file name, then only the file prefix will be used as the `oldestkeptwalfile`. This treatment of `.backup` file name allows you to remove all WAL files archived prior to a specific base backup without error. For example, the following example will remove all files older than WAL file name 000000010000003700000010:

```
pg_archivecleanup -d archive 000000010000003700000010.00000020.backup

pg_archivecleanup:  keep WAL file "archive/000000010000003700000010" and later
pg_archivecleanup:  removing file "archive/00000001000000370000000F"
pg_archivecleanup:  removing file "archive/00000001000000370000000E"
```

pg_archivecleanup assumes that `archivelocation` is a directory readable and writable by the server-owning user.

Options

pg_archivecleanup accepts the following command-line arguments:

`-d`

> Print lots of debug logging output on `stderr`.

`-n`

> Print the names of the files that would have been removed on `stdout` (performs a dry run).

`-V`
`--version`

> Print the pg_archivecleanup version and exit.

`-x extension`

> Provide an extension that will be stripped from all file names before deciding if they should be deleted. This is typically useful for cleaning up archives that have been compressed during storage, and therefore have had an extension added by the compression program. For example: `-x .gz`.

`-?`
`--help`

> Show help about pg_archivecleanup command line arguments, and exit.

Notes

pg_archivecleanup is designed to work with PostgreSQL 8.0 and later when used as a standalone utility, or with PostgreSQL 9.0 and later when used as an archive cleanup command.

pg_archivecleanup is written in C and has an easy-to-modify source code, with specifically designated sections to modify for your own needs

Examples

On Linux or Unix systems, you might use:

```
archive_cleanup_command = 'pg_archivecleanup -d /mnt/standby/archive %r 2>>cleanup.l
```

where the archive directory is physically located on the standby server, so that the `archive_command` is accessing it across NFS, but the files are local to the standby. This will:

• produce debugging output in `cleanup.log`

• remove no-longer-needed files from the archive directory

See Also

pg_standby

pg_controldata

Name

pg_controldata — display control information of a PostgreSQL database cluster

Synopsis

pg_controldata [*option*] [[-D] *datadir*]

Description

pg_controldata prints information initialized during initdb, such as the catalog version. It also shows information about write-ahead logging and checkpoint processing. This information is cluster-wide, and not specific to any one database.

This utility can only be run by the user who initialized the cluster because it requires read access to the data directory. You can specify the data directory on the command line, or use the environment variable PGDATA. This utility supports the options -V and --version, which print the pg_controldata version and exit. It also supports options -? and --help, which output the supported arguments.

Environment

PGDATA

    Default data directory location

pg_ctl

Name

pg_ctl — initialize, start, stop, or control a PostgreSQL server

Synopsis

pg_ctl init[db] [-s] [-D *datadir*] [-o *initdb-options*]

pg_ctl start [-w] [-t *seconds*] [-s] [-D *datadir*] [-l *filename*] [-o *options*] [-p *path*] [-c]

pg_ctl stop [-W] [-t *seconds*] [-s] [-D *datadir*] [-m s[mart] | f[ast] | i[mmediate]]

pg_ctl restart [-w] [-t *seconds*] [-s] [-D *datadir*] [-c] [-m s[mart] | f[ast] | i[mmediate]] [-o *options*]

pg_ctl reload [-s] [-D *datadir*]

pg_ctl status [-D *datadir*]

pg_ctl promote [-s] [-D *datadir*]

pg_ctl kill *signal_name process_id*

pg_ctl register [-N *servicename*] [-U *username*] [-P *password*] [-D *datadir*] [-S a[uto] | d[emand]] [-w] [-t *seconds*] [-s] [-o *options*]

pg_ctl unregister [-N *servicename*]

Description

pg_ctl is a utility for initializing a PostgreSQL database cluster, starting, stopping, or restarting the PostgreSQL database server (postgres), or displaying the status of a running server. Although the server can be started manually, pg_ctl encapsulates tasks such as redirecting log output and properly detaching from the terminal and process group. It also provides convenient options for controlled shutdown.

The init or initdb mode creates a new PostgreSQL database cluster. A database cluster is a collection of databases that are managed by a single server instance. This mode invokes the initdb command. See initdb for details.

In `start` mode, a new server is launched. The server is started in the background, and its standard input is attached to `/dev/null` (or `nul` on Windows). On Unix-like systems, by default, the server's standard output and standard error are sent to pg_ctl's standard output (not standard error). The standard output of pg_ctl should then be redirected to a file or piped to another process such as a log rotating program like rotatelogs; otherwise `postgres` will write its output to the controlling terminal (from the background) and will not leave the shell's process group. On Windows, by default the server's standard output and standard error are sent to the terminal. These default behaviors can be changed by using `-l` to append the server's output to a log file. Use of either `-l` or output redirection is recommended.

In `stop` mode, the server that is running in the specified data directory is shut down. Three different shutdown methods can be selected with the `-m` option. "Smart" mode waits for all active clients to disconnect and any online backup to finish. If the server is in hot standby, recovery and streaming replication will be terminated once all clients have disconnected. "Fast" mode (the default) does not wait for clients to disconnect and will terminate an online backup in progress. All active transactions are rolled back and clients are forcibly disconnected, then the server is shut down. "Immediate" mode will abort all server processes immediately, without a clean shutdown. This will lead to a crash-recovery run on the next restart.

`restart` mode effectively executes a stop followed by a start. This allows changing the `postgres` command-line options. `restart` might fail if relative paths specified were specified on the command-line during server start.

`reload` mode simply sends the `postgres` process a SIGHUP signal, causing it to reread its configuration files (`postgresql.conf`, `pg_hba.conf`, etc.). This allows changing of configuration-file options that do not require a complete restart to take effect.

`status` mode checks whether a server is running in the specified data directory. If it is, the PID and the command line options that were used to invoke it are displayed. If the server is not running, the process returns an exit status of 3. If an accessible data directory is not specified, the process returns an exit status of 4.

In `promote` mode, the standby server that is running in the specified data directory is commanded to exit recovery and begin read-write operations.

`kill` mode allows you to send a signal to a specified process. This is particularly valuable for Microsoft Windows which does not have a kill command. Use `--help` to see a list of supported signal names.

`register` mode allows you to register a system service on Microsoft Windows. The `-S` option allows selection of service start type, either "auto" (start service automatically on system startup) or "demand" (start service on demand).

`unregister` mode allows you to unregister a system service on Microsoft Windows. This undoes the effects of the `register` command.

Options

`-c`
`--core-file`

> Attempt to allow server crashes to produce core files, on platforms where this is possible, by lifting any soft resource limit placed on core files. This is useful in debugging or diagnosing problems by allowing a stack trace to be obtained from a failed server process.

`-D` *datadir*

`--pgdata` *datadir*

> Specifies the file system location of the database configuration files. If this is omitted, the environment variable `PGDATA` is used.

`-l` *filename*

`--log` *filename*

> Append the server log output to *filename*. If the file does not exist, it is created. The umask is set to 077, so access to the log file is disallowed to other users by default.

`-m` *mode*

`--mode` *mode*

> Specifies the shutdown mode. *mode* can be `smart`, `fast`, or `immediate`, or the first letter of one of these three. If this is omitted, `fast` is used.

`-o` *options*

> Specifies options to be passed directly to the `postgres` command; multiple option invocations are appended.

> The options should usually be surrounded by single or double quotes to ensure that they are passed through as a group.

`-o` *initdb-options*

> Specifies options to be passed directly to the `initdb` command.

> The options should usually be surrounded by single or double quotes to ensure that they are passed through as a group.

`-p` *path*

> Specifies the location of the `postgres` executable. By default the `postgres` executable is taken from the same directory as `pg_ctl`, or failing that, the hard-wired installation directory. It is not necessary to use this option unless you are doing something unusual and get errors that the `postgres` executable was not found.

> In `init` mode, this option analogously specifies the location of the `initdb` executable.

`-s`

`--silent`

> Print only errors, no informational messages.

`-t`

`--timeout`

> The maximum number of seconds to wait when waiting for startup or shutdown to complete. Defaults to the value of the `PGCTLTIMEOUT` environment variable or, if not set, to 60 seconds.

`-V`

`--version`

> Print the pg_ctl version and exit.

-w

Wait for the startup or shutdown to complete. Waiting is the default option for shutdowns, but not startups. When waiting for startup, `pg_ctl` repeatedly attempts to connect to the server. When waiting for shutdown, `pg_ctl` waits for the server to remove its PID file. This option allows the entry of an SSL passphrase on startup. `pg_ctl` returns an exit code based on the success of the startup or shutdown.

-W

Do not wait for startup or shutdown to complete. This is the default for start and restart modes.

-?
--help

Show help about pg_ctl command line arguments, and exit.

Options for Windows

-e *source*

Name of the event source for pg_ctl to use for logging to the event log when running as a Windows service. The default is `PostgreSQL`. Note that this only controls the logging from pg_ctl itself; once started, the server will use the event source specified by event_source. Should the server fail during early startup, it might also log using the default event source `PostgreSQL`.

-N *servicename*

Name of the system service to register. The name will be used as both the service name and the display name.

-P *password*

Password for the user to start the service.

-S *start-type*

Start type of the system service to register. start-type can be `auto`, or `demand`, or the first letter of one of these two. If this is omitted, `auto` is used.

-U *username*

User name for the user to start the service. For domain users, use the format `DOMAIN\username`.

Environment

PGCTLTIMEOUT

Default limit on the number of seconds to wait when waiting for startup or shutdown to complete. If not set, the default is 60 seconds.

PGDATA

Default data directory location.

pg_ctl, like most other PostgreSQL utilities, also uses the environment variables supported by libpq (see Section 32.14). For additional server variables, see postgres.

Files

postmaster.pid

> The existence of this file in the data directory is used to help pg_ctl determine if the server is currently running.

postmaster.opts

> If this file exists in the data directory, pg_ctl (in restart mode) will pass the contents of the file as options to postgres, unless overridden by the -o option. The contents of this file are also displayed in status mode.

Examples

Starting the Server

To start the server:

```
$ pg_ctl start
```

To start the server, waiting until the server is accepting connections:

```
$ pg_ctl -w start
```

To start the server using port 5433, and running without fsync, use:

```
$ pg_ctl -o "-F -p 5433" start
```

Stopping the Server

To stop the server, use:

```
$ pg_ctl stop
```

The -m option allows control over *how* the server shuts down:

```
$ pg_ctl stop -m fast
```

Restarting the Server

Restarting the server is almost equivalent to stopping the server and starting it again, except that `pg_ctl` saves and reuses the command line options that were passed to the previously running instance. To restart the server in the simplest form, use:

```
$ pg_ctl restart
```

To restart the server, waiting for it to shut down and restart:

```
$ pg_ctl -w restart
```

To restart using port 5433, disabling `fsync` upon restart:

```
$ pg_ctl -o "-F -p 5433" restart
```

Showing the Server Status

Here is sample status output from pg_ctl:

```
$ pg_ctl status
pg_ctl: server is running (PID: 13718)
/usr/local/pgsql/bin/postgres "-D" "/usr/local/pgsql/data" "-p" "5433" "-B" "128"
```

This is the command line that would be invoked in restart mode.

See Also

initdb, postgres

pg_resetxlog

Name

`pg_resetxlog` — reset the write-ahead log and other control information of a PostgreSQL database cluster

Synopsis

`pg_resetxlog` [-f] [-n] [*option*...] {[-D] *datadir*}

Description

`pg_resetxlog` clears the write-ahead log (WAL) and optionally resets some other control information stored in the `pg_control` file. This function is sometimes needed if these files have become corrupted. It should be used only as a last resort, when the server will not start due to such corruption.

After running this command, it should be possible to start the server, but bear in mind that the database might contain inconsistent data due to partially-committed transactions. You should immediately dump your data, run `initdb`, and reload. After reload, check for inconsistencies and repair as needed.

This utility can only be run by the user who installed the server, because it requires read/write access to the data directory. For safety reasons, you must specify the data directory on the command line. `pg_resetxlog` does not use the environment variable `PGDATA`.

If `pg_resetxlog` complains that it cannot determine valid data for `pg_control`, you can force it to proceed anyway by specifying the -f (force) option. In this case plausible values will be substituted for the missing data. Most of the fields can be expected to match, but manual assistance might be needed for the next OID, next transaction ID and epoch, next multitransaction ID and offset, and WAL starting address fields. These fields can be set using the options discussed below. If you are not able to determine correct values for all these fields, -f can still be used, but the recovered database must be treated with even more suspicion than usual: an immediate dump and reload is imperative. *Do not* execute any data-modifying operations in the database before you dump, as any such action is likely to make the corruption worse.

Options

-f

Force `pg_resetxlog` to proceed even if it cannot determine valid data for `pg_control`, as explained above.

-n

The -n (no operation) option instructs `pg_resetxlog` to print the values reconstructed from `pg_control` and values about to be changed, and then exit without modifying anything. This is mainly a debugging tool, but can be useful as a sanity check before allowing `pg_resetxlog` to proceed for real.

`-V`

`--version`

Display version information, then exit.

`-?`

`--help`

Show help, then exit.

The following options are only needed when `pg_resetxlog` is unable to determine appropriate values by reading `pg_control`. Safe values can be determined as described below. For values that take numeric arguments, hexadecimal values can be specified by using the prefix `0x`.

`-c xid,xid`

Manually set the oldest and newest transaction IDs for which the commit time can be retrieved.

A safe value for the oldest transaction ID for which the commit time can be retrieved (first part) can be determined by looking for the numerically smallest file name in the directory `pg_commit_ts` under the data directory. Conversely, a safe value for the newest transaction ID for which the commit time can be retrieved (second part) can be determined by looking for the numerically greatest file name in the same directory. The file names are in hexadecimal.

`-e xid_epoch`

Manually set the next transaction ID's epoch.

The transaction ID epoch is not actually stored anywhere in the database except in the field that is set by `pg_resetxlog`, so any value will work so far as the database itself is concerned. You might need to adjust this value to ensure that replication systems such as Slony-I and Skytools work correctly — if so, an appropriate value should be obtainable from the state of the downstream replicated database.

`-l xlogfile`

Manually set the WAL starting address.

The WAL starting address should be larger than any WAL segment file name currently existing in the directory `pg_xlog` under the data directory. These names are also in hexadecimal and have three parts. The first part is the "timeline ID" and should usually be kept the same. For example, if `00000001000000320000004A` is the largest entry in `pg_xlog`, use `-l 00000001000000320000004B` or higher.

> **Note:** `pg_resetxlog` itself looks at the files in `pg_xlog` and chooses a default `-l` setting beyond the last existing file name. Therefore, manual adjustment of `-l` should only be needed if you are aware of WAL segment files that are not currently present in `pg_xlog`, such as entries in an offline archive; or if the contents of `pg_xlog` have been lost entirely.

`-m mxid,mxid`

Manually set the next and oldest multitransaction ID.

A safe value for the next multitransaction ID (first part) can be determined by looking for the numerically largest file name in the directory `pg_multixact/offsets` under the data directory, adding one, and then multiplying by 65536 (0x10000). Conversely, a safe value for the oldest multitransaction ID (second part of -m) can be determined by looking for the numerically smallest file name in the same directory and multiplying by 65536. The file names are in hexadecimal, so the easiest way to do this is to specify the option value in hexadecimal and append four zeroes.

`-o oid`

Manually set the next OID.

There is no comparably easy way to determine a next OID that's beyond the largest one in the database, but fortunately it is not critical to get the next-OID setting right.

`-O mxoff`

Manually set the next multitransaction offset.

A safe value can be determined by looking for the numerically largest file name in the directory `pg_multixact/members` under the data directory, adding one, and then multiplying by 52352 (0xCC80). The file names are in hexadecimal. There is no simple recipe such as the ones for other options of appending zeroes.

`-x xid`

Manually set the next transaction ID.

A safe value can be determined by looking for the numerically largest file name in the directory `pg_clog` under the data directory, adding one, and then multiplying by 1048576 (0x100000). Note that the file names are in hexadecimal. It is usually easiest to specify the option value in hexadecimal too. For example, if `0011` is the largest entry in `pg_clog`, `-x 0x1200000` will work (five trailing zeroes provide the proper multiplier).

Notes

This command must not be used when the server is running. `pg_resetxlog` will refuse to start up if it finds a server lock file in the data directory. If the server crashed then a lock file might have been left behind; in that case you can remove the lock file to allow `pg_resetxlog` to run. But before you do so, make doubly certain that there is no server process still alive.

See Also

pg_controldata

pg_rewind

Name

pg_rewind — synchronize a PostgreSQL data directory with another data directory that was forked from it

Synopsis

pg_rewind [*option*...] {-D | --target-pgdata} *directory* {--source-pgdata=*directory* | --source-server=*connstr*}

Description

pg_rewind is a tool for synchronizing a PostgreSQL cluster with another copy of the same cluster, after the clusters' timelines have diverged. A typical scenario is to bring an old master server back online after failover as a standby that follows the new master.

The result is equivalent to replacing the target data directory with the source one. Only changed blocks from relation files are copied; all other files are copied in full, including configuration files. The advantage of pg_rewind over taking a new base backup, or tools like rsync, is that pg_rewind does not require reading through unchanged blocks in the cluster. This makes it a lot faster when the database is large and only a small fraction of blocks differ between the clusters.

pg_rewind examines the timeline histories of the source and target clusters to determine the point where they diverged, and expects to find WAL in the target cluster's pg_xlog directory reaching all the way back to the point of divergence. The point of divergence can be found either on the target timeline, the source timeline, or their common ancestor. In the typical failover scenario where the target cluster was shut down soon after the divergence, this is not a problem, but if the target cluster ran for a long time after the divergence, the old WAL files might no longer be present. In that case, they can be manually copied from the WAL archive to the pg_xlog directory, or fetched on startup by configuring recovery.conf. The use of pg_rewind is not limited to failover, e.g. a standby server can be promoted, run some write transactions, and then rewinded to become a standby again.

When the target server is started for the first time after running pg_rewind, it will go into recovery mode and replay all WAL generated in the source server after the point of divergence. If some of the WAL was no longer available in the source server when pg_rewind was run, and therefore could not be copied by the pg_rewind session, it must be made available when the target server is started. This can be done by creating a recovery.conf file in the target data directory with a suitable restore_command.

pg_rewind requires that the target server either has the wal_log_hints option enabled in postgresql.conf or data checksums enabled when the cluster was initialized with initdb. Neither of these are currently on by default. full_page_writes must also be set to on, but is enabled by default.

Options

pg_rewind accepts the following command-line arguments:

`-D directory`
`--target-pgdata=directory`

> This option specifies the target data directory that is synchronized with the source. The target server must be shut down cleanly before running pg_rewind

`--source-pgdata=directory`

> Specifies the file system path to the data directory of the source server to synchronize the target with. This option requires the source server to be cleanly shut down.

`--source-server=connstr`

> Specifies a libpq connection string to connect to the source PostgreSQL server to synchronize the target with. The connection must be a normal (non-replication) connection with superuser access. This option requires the source server to be running and not in recovery mode.

`-n`
`--dry-run`

> Do everything except actually modifying the target directory.

`-P`
`--progress`

> Enables progress reporting. Turning this on will deliver an approximate progress report while copying data from the source cluster.

`--debug`

> Print verbose debugging output that is mostly useful for developers debugging pg_rewind.

`-V`
`--version`

> Display version information, then exit.

`-?`
`--help`

> Show help, then exit.

Environment

When `--source-server` option is used, pg_rewind also uses the environment variables supported by libpq (see Section 32.14).

Notes

How it works

The basic idea is to copy all file system-level changes from the source cluster to the target cluster:

1.   Scan the WAL log of the target cluster, starting from the last checkpoint before the point where the source cluster's timeline history forked off from the target cluster. For each WAL record, record each data block that was touched. This yields a list of all the data blocks that were changed in the target cluster, after the source cluster forked off.

2.   Copy all those changed blocks from the source cluster to the target cluster, either using direct file system access (`--source-pgdata`) or SQL (`--source-server`).

3.   Copy all other files such as `pg_clog` and configuration files from the source cluster to the target cluster (everything except the relation files).

4.   Apply the WAL from the source cluster, starting from the checkpoint created at failover. (Strictly speaking, pg_rewind doesn't apply the WAL, it just creates a backup label file that makes PostgreSQL start by replaying all WAL from that checkpoint forward.)

pg_test_fsync

Name

`pg_test_fsync` — determine fastest `wal_sync_method` for PostgreSQL

Synopsis

`pg_test_fsync` [*option*...]

Description

pg_test_fsync is intended to give you a reasonable idea of what the fastest wal_sync_method is on your specific system, as well as supplying diagnostic information in the event of an identified I/O problem. However, differences shown by pg_test_fsync might not make any significant difference in real database throughput, especially since many database servers are not speed-limited by their transaction logs. pg_test_fsync reports average file sync operation time in microseconds for each `wal_sync_method`, which can also be used to inform efforts to optimize the value of commit_delay.

Options

pg_test_fsync accepts the following command-line options:

`-f`
`--filename`

> Specifies the file name to write test data in. This file should be in the same file system that the `pg_xlog` directory is or will be placed in. (`pg_xlog` contains the WAL files.) The default is `pg_test_fsync.out` in the current directory.

`-s`
`--secs-per-test`

> Specifies the number of seconds for each test. The more time per test, the greater the test's accuracy, but the longer it takes to run. The default is 5 seconds, which allows the program to complete in under 2 minutes.

`-V`
`--version`

> Print the pg_test_fsync version and exit.

`-?`
`--help`

> Show help about pg_test_fsync command line arguments, and exit.

See Also

postgres

pg_test_timing

Name

pg_test_timing — measure timing overhead

Synopsis

pg_test_timing [option...]

Description

pg_test_timing is a tool to measure the timing overhead on your system and confirm that the system time never moves backwards. Systems that are slow to collect timing data can give less accurate EXPLAIN ANALYZE results.

Options

pg_test_timing accepts the following command-line options:

-d duration
--duration-duration

> Specifies the test duration, in seconds. Longer durations give slightly better accuracy, and are more likely to discover problems with the system clock moving backwards. The default test duration is 3 seconds.

-V
--version

> Print the pg_test_timing version and exit.

-?
--help

> Show help about pg_test_timing command line arguments, and exit.

Usage

Interpreting results

Good results will show most (>90%) individual timing calls take less than one microsecond. Average per loop overhead will be even lower, below 100 nanoseconds. This example from an Intel i7-860 system using a TSC clock source shows excellent performance:

```
Testing timing overhead for 3 seconds.
Per loop time including overhead: 35.96 nsec
Histogram of timing durations:
< usec    % of total      count
     1     96.40465     80435604
     2      3.59518      2999652
     4      0.00015          126
     8      0.00002           13
    16      0.00000            2
```

Note that different units are used for the per loop time than the histogram. The loop can have resolution within a few nanoseconds (nsec), while the individual timing calls can only resolve down to one microsecond (usec).

Measuring executor timing overhead

When the query executor is running a statement using EXPLAIN ANALYZE, individual operations are timed as well as showing a summary. The overhead of your system can be checked by counting rows with the psql program:

```
CREATE TABLE t AS SELECT * FROM generate_series(1,100000);
\timing
SELECT COUNT(*) FROM t;
EXPLAIN ANALYZE SELECT COUNT(*) FROM t;
```

The i7-860 system measured runs the count query in 9.8 ms while the EXPLAIN ANALYZE version takes 16.6 ms, each processing just over 100,000 rows. That 6.8 ms difference means the timing overhead per row is 68 ns, about twice what pg_test_timing estimated it would be. Even that relatively small amount of overhead is making the fully timed count statement take almost 70% longer. On more substantial queries, the timing overhead would be less problematic.

Changing time sources

On some newer Linux systems, it's possible to change the clock source used to collect timing data at any time. A second example shows the slowdown possible from switching to the slower acpi_pm time source, on the same system used for the fast results above:

```
# cat /sys/devices/system/clocksource/clocksource0/available_clocksource
tsc hpet acpi_pm
# echo acpi_pm > /sys/devices/system/clocksource/clocksource0/current_clocksource
# pg_test_timing
Per loop time including overhead: 722.92 nsec
Histogram of timing durations:
< usec    % of total      count
     1     27.84870      1155682
```

```
      2     72.05956    2990371
      4      0.07810       3241
      8      0.01357        563
     16      0.00007          3
```

In this configuration, the sample EXPLAIN ANALYZE above takes 115.9 ms. That's 1061 nsec of timing overhead, again a small multiple of what's measured directly by this utility. That much timing overhead means the actual query itself is only taking a tiny fraction of the accounted for time, most of it is being consumed in overhead instead. In this configuration, any EXPLAIN ANALYZE totals involving many timed operations would be inflated significantly by timing overhead.

FreeBSD also allows changing the time source on the fly, and it logs information about the timer selected during boot:

```
# dmesg | grep "Timecounter"
Timecounter "ACPI-fast" frequency 3579545 Hz quality 900
Timecounter "i8254" frequency 1193182 Hz quality 0
Timecounters tick every 10.000 msec
Timecounter "TSC" frequency 2531787134 Hz quality 800
# sysctl kern.timecounter.hardware=TSC
kern.timecounter.hardware: ACPI-fast -> TSC
```

Other systems may only allow setting the time source on boot. On older Linux systems the "clock" kernel setting is the only way to make this sort of change. And even on some more recent ones, the only option you'll see for a clock source is "jiffies". Jiffies are the older Linux software clock implementation, which can have good resolution when it's backed by fast enough timing hardware, as in this example:

```
$ cat /sys/devices/system/clocksource/clocksource0/available_clocksource
jiffies
$ dmesg | grep time.c
time.c: Using 3.579545 MHz WALL PM GTOD PIT/TSC timer.
time.c: Detected 2400.153 MHz processor.
$ pg_test_timing
Testing timing overhead for 3 seconds.
Per timing duration including loop overhead: 97.75 ns
Histogram of timing durations:
< usec    % of total       count
      1     90.23734    27694571
      2      9.75277     2993204
      4      0.00981        3010
      8      0.00007          22
     16      0.00000           1
     32      0.00000           1
```

Clock hardware and timing accuracy

Collecting accurate timing information is normally done on computers using hardware clocks with various levels of accuracy. With some hardware the operating systems can pass the system clock time almost directly to programs. A system clock can also be derived from a chip that simply provides timing interrupts, periodic ticks at some known time interval. In either case, operating system kernels provide a clock source that hides these details. But the accuracy of that clock source and how quickly it can return results varies based on the underlying hardware.

Inaccurate time keeping can result in system instability. Test any change to the clock source very carefully. Operating system defaults are sometimes made to favor reliability over best accuracy. And if you are using a virtual machine, look into the recommended time sources compatible with it. Virtual hardware faces additional difficulties when emulating timers, and there are often per operating system settings suggested by vendors.

The Time Stamp Counter (TSC) clock source is the most accurate one available on current generation CPUs. It's the preferred way to track the system time when it's supported by the operating system and the TSC clock is reliable. There are several ways that TSC can fail to provide an accurate timing source, making it unreliable. Older systems can have a TSC clock that varies based on the CPU temperature, making it unusable for timing. Trying to use TSC on some older multicore CPUs can give a reported time that's inconsistent among multiple cores. This can result in the time going backwards, a problem this program checks for. And even the newest systems can fail to provide accurate TSC timing with very aggressive power saving configurations.

Newer operating systems may check for the known TSC problems and switch to a slower, more stable clock source when they are seen. If your system supports TSC time but doesn't default to that, it may be disabled for a good reason. And some operating systems may not detect all the possible problems correctly, or will allow using TSC even in situations where it's known to be inaccurate.

The High Precision Event Timer (HPET) is the preferred timer on systems where it's available and TSC is not accurate. The timer chip itself is programmable to allow up to 100 nanosecond resolution, but you may not see that much accuracy in your system clock.

Advanced Configuration and Power Interface (ACPI) provides a Power Management (PM) Timer, which Linux refers to as the acpi_pm. The clock derived from acpi_pm will at best provide 300 nanosecond resolution.

Timers used on older PC hardware include the 8254 Programmable Interval Timer (PIT), the real-time clock (RTC), the Advanced Programmable Interrupt Controller (APIC) timer, and the Cyclone timer. These timers aim for millisecond resolution.

See Also

EXPLAIN

pg_upgrade

Name

`pg_upgrade` — upgrade a PostgreSQL server instance

Synopsis

`pg_upgrade -b` *oldbindir* `-B` *newbindir* `-d` *olddatadir* `-D` *newdatadir* [*option*...]

Description

pg_upgrade (formerly called pg_migrator) allows data stored in PostgreSQL data files to be upgraded to a later PostgreSQL major version without the data dump/reload typically required for major version upgrades, e.g. from 8.4.7 to the current major release of PostgreSQL. It is not required for minor version upgrades, e.g. from 9.0.1 to 9.0.4.

Major PostgreSQL releases regularly add new features that often change the layout of the system tables, but the internal data storage format rarely changes. pg_upgrade uses this fact to perform rapid upgrades by creating new system tables and simply reusing the old user data files. If a future major release ever changes the data storage format in a way that makes the old data format unreadable, pg_upgrade will not be usable for such upgrades. (The community will attempt to avoid such situations.)

pg_upgrade does its best to make sure the old and new clusters are binary compatible, e.g. by checking for compatible compile-time settings, including 32/64-bit binaries. It is important that any external modules are also binary compatible, though this cannot be checked by pg_upgrade.

pg_upgrade supports upgrades from 8.4.X and later to the current major release of PostgreSQL, including snapshot and alpha releases.

Options

pg_upgrade accepts the following command-line arguments:

`-b` *bindir*
`--old-bindir=`*bindir*

    the old PostgreSQL executable directory; environment variable `PGBINOLD`

`-B` *bindir*
`--new-bindir=`*bindir*

    the new PostgreSQL executable directory; environment variable `PGBINNEW`

`-c`
`--check`

    check clusters only, don't change any data

`-d` *datadir*

`--old-datadir=`*datadir*

> the old cluster data directory; environment variable `PGDATAOLD`

`-D` *datadir*

`--new-datadir=`*datadir*

> the new cluster data directory; environment variable `PGDATANEW`

`-j`

`--jobs`

> number of simultaneous processes or threads to use

`-k`

`--link`

> use hard links instead of copying files to the new cluster (use junction points on Windows)

`-o` *options*

`--old-options` *options*

> options to be passed directly to the old `postgres` command; multiple option invocations are appended

`-O` *options*

`--new-options` *options*

> options to be passed directly to the new `postgres` command; multiple option invocations are appended

`-p` *port*

`--old-port=`*port*

> the old cluster port number; environment variable `PGPORTOLD`

`-P` *port*

`--new-port=`*port*

> the new cluster port number; environment variable `PGPORTNEW`

`-r`

`--retain`

> retain SQL and log files even after successful completion

`-U` *username*

`--username=`*username*

> cluster's install user name; environment variable `PGUSER`

`-v`

`--verbose`

> enable verbose internal logging

`-V`

`--version`

> display version information, then exit

```
-?
--help
```
show help, then exit

Usage

These are the steps to perform an upgrade with pg_upgrade:

1. Optionally move the old cluster

   If you are using a version-specific installation directory, e.g. `/opt/PostgreSQL/9.1`, you do not need to move the old cluster. The graphical installers all use version-specific installation directories.

   If your installation directory is not version-specific, e.g. `/usr/local/pgsql`, it is necessary to move the current PostgreSQL install directory so it does not interfere with the new PostgreSQL installation. Once the current PostgreSQL server is shut down, it is safe to rename the PostgreSQL installation directory; assuming the old directory is `/usr/local/pgsql`, you can do:

   `mv /usr/local/pgsql /usr/local/pgsql.old`
   to rename the directory.

2. For source installs, build the new version

   Build the new PostgreSQL source with `configure` flags that are compatible with the old cluster. pg_upgrade will check `pg_controldata` to make sure all settings are compatible before starting the upgrade.

3. Install the new PostgreSQL binaries

   Install the new server's binaries and support files. pg_upgrade is included in a default installation.

   For source installs, if you wish to install the new server in a custom location, use the `prefix` variable:

   `make prefix=/usr/local/pgsql.new install`

4. Initialize the new PostgreSQL cluster

   Initialize the new cluster using `initdb`. Again, use compatible `initdb` flags that match the old cluster. Many prebuilt installers do this step automatically. There is no need to start the new cluster.

5. Install custom shared object files

   Install any custom shared object files (or DLLs) used by the old cluster into the new cluster, e.g. `pgcrypto.so`, whether they are from `contrib` or some other source. Do not install the schema definitions, e.g. `pgcrypto.sql`, because these will be upgraded from the old cluster. Also, any custom full text search files (dictionary, synonym, thesaurus, stop words) must also be copied to the new cluster.

6. Adjust authentication

   `pg_upgrade` will connect to the old and new servers several times, so you might want to set authentication to `peer` in `pg_hba.conf` or use a `~/.pgpass` file (see Section 32.15).

7. Stop both servers

Make sure both database servers are stopped using, on Unix, e.g.:

```
pg_ctl -D /opt/PostgreSQL/8.4 stop
pg_ctl -D /opt/PostgreSQL/9.0 stop
```

or on Windows, using the proper service names:

```
NET STOP postgresql-8.4
NET STOP postgresql-9.0
```

Streaming replication and log-shipping standby servers can remain running until a later step.

8. Verify standby servers

   If you are upgrading Streaming Replication and Log-Shipping standby servers, verify that the old standby servers are caught up by running pg_controldata against the old primary and standby clusters. Verify that the "Latest checkpoint location" values match in all clusters. (There will be a mismatch if old standby servers were shut down before the old primary.)

9. Run pg_upgrade

   Always run the pg_upgrade binary of the new server, not the old one. pg_upgrade requires the specification of the old and new cluster's data and executable (`bin`) directories. You can also specify user and port values, and whether you want the data linked instead of copied (the default).

   If you use link mode, the upgrade will be much faster (no file copying) and use less disk space, but you will not be able to access your old cluster once you start the new cluster after the upgrade. Link mode also requires that the old and new cluster data directories be in the same file system. (Tablespaces and `pg_xlog` can be on different file systems.) See `pg_upgrade --help` for a full list of options.

   The `--jobs` option allows multiple CPU cores to be used for copying/linking of files and to dump and reload database schemas in parallel; a good place to start is the maximum of the number of CPU cores and tablespaces. This option can dramatically reduce the time to upgrade a multi-database server running on a multiprocessor machine.

   For Windows users, you must be logged into an administrative account, and then start a shell as the `postgres` user and set the proper path:

```
RUNAS /USER:postgres "CMD.EXE"
SET PATH=%PATH%;C:\Program Files\PostgreSQL\9.0\bin;
```

   and then run pg_upgrade with quoted directories, e.g.:

```
pg_upgrade.exe
        --old-datadir "C:/Program Files/PostgreSQL/8.4/data"
        --new-datadir "C:/Program Files/PostgreSQL/9.0/data"
        --old-bindir "C:/Program Files/PostgreSQL/8.4/bin"
        --new-bindir "C:/Program Files/PostgreSQL/9.0/bin"
```

   Once started, `pg_upgrade` will verify the two clusters are compatible and then do the upgrade. You can use `pg_upgrade --check` to perform only the checks, even if the old server is still running. `pg_upgrade --check` will also outline any manual adjustments you will need to make after the upgrade. If you are going to be using link mode, you should use the `--link` option with `--check` to enable link-mode-specific checks. `pg_upgrade` requires write permission in the current directory.

   Obviously, no one should be accessing the clusters during the upgrade. pg_upgrade defaults to running servers on port 50432 to avoid unintended client connections. You can use the same port number for both clusters when doing an upgrade because the old and new clusters will not be running at the same time. However, when checking an old running server, the old and new port numbers must be different.

If an error occurs while restoring the database schema, `pg_upgrade` will exit and you will have to revert to the old cluster as outlined in step 16 below. To try `pg_upgrade` again, you will need to modify the old cluster so the pg_upgrade schema restore succeeds. If the problem is a `contrib` module, you might need to uninstall the `contrib` module from the old cluster and install it in the new cluster after the upgrade, assuming the module is not being used to store user data.

10. Upgrade Streaming Replication and Log-Shipping standby servers

    If you have Streaming Replication (see Section 26.2.5) or Log-Shipping (see Section 26.2) standby servers, follow these steps to upgrade them. You will not be running pg_upgrade on the standby servers, but rather rsync. Do not start any servers yet.

    a. Install the new PostgreSQL binaries on standby servers

       Make sure the new binaries and support files are installed on all standby servers.

    b. Make sure the new standby data directories do *not* exist

       Make sure the new standby data directories do *not* exist or are empty. If initdb was run, delete the standby server data directories.

    c. Install custom shared object files

       Install the same custom shared object files on the new standbys that you installed in the new master cluster.

    d. Stop standby servers

       If the standby servers are still running, stop them now using the above instructions.

    e. Save configuration files

       Save any configuration files from the standbys you need to keep, e.g. `postgresql.conf`, `recovery.conf`, as these will be overwritten or removed in the next step.

    f. Start and stop the new master cluster

       In the new master cluster, change `wal_level` to `replica` in the `postgresql.conf` file and then start and stop the cluster.

    g. Run rsync

       From a directory that is above the old and new database cluster directories, run this for each slave:

       ```
       rsync --archive --delete --hard-links --size-only old_pgdata new_pgdata re
       ```
       where `old_pgdata` and `new_pgdata` are relative to the current directory, and `remote_dir` is *above* the old and new cluster directories on the standby server. The old and new relative cluster paths must match on the master and standby server. Consult the rsync manual page for details on specifying the remote directory, e.g. `standbyhost:/opt/PostgreSQL/`. rsync will be fast when pg_upgrade's `--link` mode is used because it will create hard links on the remote server rather than transferring user data. Unfortunately, rsync needlessly copies the files associated with temporary and unlogged tables.

       If you have tablespaces, you will need to run a similar rsync command for each tablespace directory. If you have relocated `pg_xlog` outside the data directories, rsync must be run on those directories too.

h. Configure streaming replication and log-shipping standby servers

Configure the servers for log shipping. (You do not need to run `pg_start_backup()` and `pg_stop_backup()` or take a file system backup as the slaves are still synchronized with the master.)

11. Restore `pg_hba.conf`

If you modified `pg_hba.conf`, restore its original settings. It might also be necessary to adjust other configuration files in the new cluster to match the old cluster, e.g. `postgresql.conf`.

12. Start the new server

The new server can now be safely started, and then any rsync'ed standby servers.

13. Post-Upgrade processing

If any post-upgrade processing is required, pg_upgrade will issue warnings as it completes. It will also generate script files that must be run by the administrator. The script files will connect to each database that needs post-upgrade processing. Each script should be run using:

`psql --username postgres --file script.sql postgres`
The scripts can be run in any order and can be deleted once they have been run.

> ## Caution
>
> In general it is unsafe to access tables referenced in rebuild scripts until the rebuild scripts have run to completion; doing so could yield incorrect results or poor performance. Tables not referenced in rebuild scripts can be accessed immediately.

14. Statistics

Because optimizer statistics are not transferred by `pg_upgrade`, you will be instructed to run a command to regenerate that information at the end of the upgrade. You might need to set connection parameters to match your new cluster.

15. Delete old cluster

Once you are satisfied with the upgrade, you can delete the old cluster's data directories by running the script mentioned when `pg_upgrade` completes. (Automatic deletion is not possible if you have user-defined tablespaces inside the old data directory.) You can also delete the old installation directories (e.g. `bin`, `share`).

16. Reverting to old cluster

If, after running `pg_upgrade`, you wish to revert to the old cluster, there are several options:

• If you ran `pg_upgrade` with `--check`, no modifications were made to the old cluster and you can re-use it anytime.

• If you ran `pg_upgrade` with `--link`, the data files are shared between the old and new cluster. If you started the new cluster, the new server has written to those shared files and it is unsafe to use the old cluster.

• If you ran `pg_upgrade` *without* `--link` or did not start the new server, the old cluster was not modified except that, if linking started, a `.old` suffix was appended to

$PGDATA/global/pg_control. To reuse the old cluster, possibly remove the .old suffix from $PGDATA/global/pg_control; you can then restart the old cluster.

Notes

pg_upgrade does not support upgrading of databases containing these reg* OID-referencing system data types: regproc, regprocedure, regoper, regoperator, regconfig, and regdictionary. (regtype can be upgraded.)

All failure, rebuild, and reindex cases will be reported by pg_upgrade if they affect your installation; post-upgrade scripts to rebuild tables and indexes will be generated automatically. If you are trying to automate the upgrade of many clusters, you should find that clusters with identical database schemas require the same post-upgrade steps for all cluster upgrades; this is because the post-upgrade steps are based on the database schemas, and not user data.

For deployment testing, create a schema-only copy of the old cluster, insert dummy data, and upgrade that.

If you are upgrading a pre-PostgreSQL 9.2 cluster that uses a configuration-file-only directory, you must pass the real data directory location to pg_upgrade, and pass the configuration directory location to the server, e.g. -d /real-data-directory -o '-D /configuration-directory'.

If using a pre-9.1 old server that is using a non-default Unix-domain socket directory or a default that differs from the default of the new cluster, set PGHOST to point to the old server's socket location. (This is not relevant on Windows.)

If you want to use link mode and you do not want your old cluster to be modified when the new cluster is started, make a copy of the old cluster and upgrade that in link mode. To make a valid copy of the old cluster, use rsync to create a dirty copy of the old cluster while the server is running, then shut down the old server and run rsync --checksum again to update the copy with any changes to make it consistent. (--checksum is necessary because rsync only has file modification-time granularity of one second.) You might want to exclude some files, e.g. postmaster.pid, as documented in Section 25.3.3. If your file system supports file system snapshots or copy-on-write file copies, you can use that to make a backup of the old cluster and tablespaces, though the snapshot and copies must be created simultaneously or while the database server is down.

See Also

initdb, pg_ctl, pg_dump, postgres

pg_xlogdump

Name

pg_xlogdump — display a human-readable rendering of the write-ahead log of a PostgreSQL database cluster

Synopsis

pg_xlogdump [option...] [startseg [endseg]]

Description

pg_xlogdump displays the write-ahead log (WAL) and is mainly useful for debugging or educational purposes.

This utility can only be run by the user who installed the server, because it requires read-only access to the data directory.

Options

The following command-line options control the location and format of the output:

startseg

> Start reading at the specified log segment file. This implicitly determines the path in which files will be searched for, and the timeline to use.

endseg

> Stop after reading the specified log segment file.

-b
--bkp-details

> Output detailed information about backup blocks.

-e end
--end=end

> Stop reading at the specified log position, instead of reading to the end of the log stream.

-f
--follow

> After reaching the end of valid WAL, keep polling once per second for new WAL to appear.

-n limit
--limit=limit

> Display the specified number of records, then stop.

`-p` *path*
`--path=`*path*

>   Directory in which to find log segment files. The default is to search for them in the `pg_xlog` subdirectory of the current directory.

`-r` *rmgr*
`--rmgr=`*rmgr*

>   Only display records generated by the specified resource manager. If `list` is passed as name, print a list of valid resource manager names, and exit.

`-s` *start*
`--start=`*start*

>   Log position at which to start reading. The default is to start reading the first valid log record found in the earliest file found.

`-t` *timeline*
`--timeline=`*timeline*

>   Timeline from which to read log records. The default is to use the value in *startseg*, if that is specified; otherwise, the default is 1.

`-V`
`--version`

>   Print the pg_xlogdump version and exit.

`-x` *xid*
`--xid=`*xid*

>   Only display records marked with the given transaction ID.

`-z`
`--stats[=record]`

>   Display summary statistics (number and size of records and full-page images) instead of individual records. Optionally generate statistics per-record instead of per-rmgr.

`-?`
`--help`

>   Show help about pg_xlogdump command line arguments, and exit.

Notes

Can give wrong results when the server is running.

Only the specified timeline is displayed (or the default, if none is specified). Records in other timelines are ignored.

pg_xlogdump cannot read WAL files with suffix `.partial`. If those files need to be read, `.partial` suffix needs to be removed from the file name.

See Also

Section 30.5

postgres

Name

postgres — PostgreSQL database server

Synopsis

postgres [*option*...]

Description

postgres is the PostgreSQL database server. In order for a client application to access a database it connects (over a network or locally) to a running postgres instance. The postgres instance then starts a separate server process to handle the connection.

One postgres instance always manages the data of exactly one database cluster. A database cluster is a collection of databases that is stored at a common file system location (the "data area"). More than one postgres instance can run on a system at one time, so long as they use different data areas and different communication ports (see below). When postgres starts it needs to know the location of the data area. The location must be specified by the -D option or the PGDATA environment variable; there is no default. Typically, -D or PGDATA points directly to the data area directory created by initdb. Other possible file layouts are discussed in Section 19.2.

By default postgres starts in the foreground and prints log messages to the standard error stream. In practical applications postgres should be started as a background process, perhaps at boot time.

The postgres command can also be called in single-user mode. The primary use for this mode is during bootstrapping by initdb. Sometimes it is used for debugging or disaster recovery; note that running a single-user server is not truly suitable for debugging the server, since no realistic interprocess communication and locking will happen. When invoked in single-user mode from the shell, the user can enter queries and the results will be printed to the screen, but in a form that is more useful for developers than end users. In the single-user mode, the session user will be set to the user with ID 1, and implicit superuser powers are granted to this user. This user does not actually have to exist, so the single-user mode can be used to manually recover from certain kinds of accidental damage to the system catalogs.

Options

postgres accepts the following command-line arguments. For a detailed discussion of the options consult Chapter 19. You can save typing most of these options by setting up a configuration file. Some (safe) options can also be set from the connecting client in an application-dependent way to apply only for that session. For example, if the environment variable PGOPTIONS is set, then libpq-based clients will pass that string to the server, which will interpret it as postgres command-line options.

General Purpose

-B *nbuffers*

Sets the number of shared buffers for use by the server processes. The default value of this parameter is chosen automatically by initdb. Specifying this option is equivalent to setting the shared_buffers configuration parameter.

-c *name=value*

Sets a named run-time parameter. The configuration parameters supported by PostgreSQL are described in Chapter 19. Most of the other command line options are in fact short forms of such a parameter assignment. -c can appear multiple times to set multiple parameters.

-C *name*

Prints the value of the named run-time parameter, and exits. (See the -c option above for details.) This can be used on a running server, and returns values from postgresql.conf, modified by any parameters supplied in this invocation. It does not reflect parameters supplied when the cluster was started.

This option is meant for other programs that interact with a server instance, such as pg_ctl, to query configuration parameter values. User-facing applications should instead use SHOW or the pg_settings view.

-d *debug-level*

Sets the debug level. The higher this value is set, the more debugging output is written to the server log. Values are from 1 to 5. It is also possible to pass -d 0 for a specific session, which will prevent the server log level of the parent postgres process from being propagated to this session.

-D *datadir*

Specifies the file system location of the database configuration files. See Section 19.2 for details.

-e

Sets the default date style to "European", that is DMY ordering of input date fields. This also causes the day to be printed before the month in certain date output formats. See Section 8.5 for more information.

-F

Disables fsync calls for improved performance, at the risk of data corruption in the event of a system crash. Specifying this option is equivalent to disabling the fsync configuration parameter. Read the detailed documentation before using this!

-h *hostname*

Specifies the IP host name or address on which postgres is to listen for TCP/IP connections from client applications. The value can also be a comma-separated list of addresses, or * to specify listening on all available interfaces. An empty value specifies not listening on any IP addresses, in which case only Unix-domain sockets can be used to connect to the server. Defaults to listening only on localhost. Specifying this option is equivalent to setting the listen_addresses configuration parameter.

-i

Allows remote clients to connect via TCP/IP (Internet domain) connections. Without this option, only local connections are accepted. This option is equivalent to setting listen_addresses to * in postgresql.conf or via -h.

This option is deprecated since it does not allow access to the full functionality of listen_addresses. It's usually better to set listen_addresses directly.

-k *directory*

Specifies the directory of the Unix-domain socket on which postgres is to listen for connections from client applications. The value can also be a comma-separated list of directories. An empty value specifies not listening on any Unix-domain sockets, in which case only TCP/IP sockets can be used to connect to the server. The default value is normally /tmp, but that can be changed at build time. Specifying this option is equivalent to setting the unix_socket_directories configuration parameter.

-l

Enables secure connections using SSL. PostgreSQL must have been compiled with support for SSL for this option to be available. For more information on using SSL, refer to Section 18.9.

-N *max-connections*

Sets the maximum number of client connections that this server will accept. The default value of this parameter is chosen automatically by initdb. Specifying this option is equivalent to setting the max_connections configuration parameter.

-o *extra-options*

The command-line-style arguments specified in *extra-options* are passed to all server processes started by this postgres process.

Spaces within *extra-options* are considered to separate arguments, unless escaped with a backslash (\); write \\ to represent a literal backslash. Multiple arguments can also be specified via multiple uses of -o.

The use of this option is obsolete; all command-line options for server processes can be specified directly on the postgres command line.

-p *port*

Specifies the TCP/IP port or local Unix domain socket file extension on which postgres is to listen for connections from client applications. Defaults to the value of the PGPORT environment variable, or if PGPORT is not set, then defaults to the value established during compilation (normally 5432). If you specify a port other than the default port, then all client applications must specify the same port using either command-line options or PGPORT.

-s

Print time information and other statistics at the end of each command. This is useful for benchmarking or for use in tuning the number of buffers.

-S *work-mem*

Specifies the amount of memory to be used by internal sorts and hashes before resorting to temporary disk files. See the description of the work_mem configuration parameter in Section 19.4.1.

-V

--version

Print the postgres version and exit.